From Children to Citizens

Mark Harrison Moore

From Children to Citizens

Volume I

The Mandate for Juvenile Justice

With Thomas Bearrows Jeffrey Bleich Francis X. Hartmann
George L. Kelling Michael Oshima Saul Weingart

With 14 Illustrations

Springer-Verlag
New York Berlin Heidelberg
London Paris Tokyo

Mark Harrison Moore
Program in Criminal Justice Policy
and Management
John F. Kennedy School of Government
Harvard University
Cambridge, MA 02138
USA

Library of Congress Cataloging-in-Publication Data
From children to citizens.
Includes indexes.
Contents: v. I. The mandate for juvenile justice.
1. Juvenile justice, Administration of—United States.
I. Moore, Mark Harrison
KF9779.F76 1987 345.73'08 87-9976
ISBN 0-387-96474-6 (v. I) 347.3058

Softcover reprint of the hardcover 1st edition 1987

Typeset by TCSystems, Shippensburg, Pennsylvania.

9 8 7 6 5 4 3 2 1
ISBN-13: 978-1-4613-8709-1 e-ISBN-13: 978-1-4613-8707-7
DOI: 10.1007/978-1-4613-8707-7

To Jean McFeely Moore
and
Martha Church Moore

Preface

History has dealt the juvenile court (and more broadly the juvenile justice system) a cruel blow. What began as a promising social experiment has disappointed nearly everyone. Those who hoped that the system might fashion an effective, nonpunitive response to children who committed crimes or who were neglected and abused now see the court as a grotesque, overreaching state institution that abuses those who come before it and overpunishes in the name of treatment. Those who hoped that the court might instill respect for the law and community values among undisciplined children are now indignant about the court's willingness to excuse criminal conduct and to dispose of cases in ways that not only fail to instill respect for the law among youthful offenders, but leave the community vulnerable to their continued depredations.

Inevitably, disillusionment has weakened the mandate of the juvenile justice system. Conflicts in philosophy, once held at bay by general enthusiasm for the enterprise, have now surfaced with great urgency. What, in fact, is the purpose of the juvenile justice system? Is it to protect the community from youth crime, or to help children grow up? Is it primarily a court dominated by a concern for justice? Or is it more fundamentally a social agency concerned with providing services to children? Is the court an independent institution that stands apart from the community and administers justice in a fair and impartial way? Or is it an agent of the community in the sense that it establishes norms of conduct and draws both public and private agencies to the task of socializing children? Should the court be more concerned with administering the law simply and equitably? Or should it use its discretion to tune its decisions to the particulars of individual cases? Are the appropriate objectives of youth corrections programs to provide services that children lacked in their home, to hold children in a therapeutic regime that promises to rehabilitate, to prevent children from committing additional crimes while under state supervision, to remind children of their responsibilities to the broader society and to frighten them about the consequences of future offending through explicit punishment, or to deter other children (and satisfy the community that its laws are being taken seriously) by punishing fairly for past crimes?

On occasion, these philosophical conflicts have ripened into public debates yielding new legislative foundations for the juvenile court and the juvenile justice system. Such actions do not permanently resolve the basic contradictions of the system, of course. At best they rebalance the conflicting values and ideologies in a way that more accurately reflects the current temper. More often, however, the underlying conflicts flare up in news stories or legislative hearings and then quickly die away, leaving nothing more than confusion and lowered morale in their wake.

The weakening of the juvenile justice mandate has important operational consequences for the system. It means that every operational decision becomes a battleground on which the broadest philosophical issues are contested. In deciding the number and distribution of programs within the youth corrections system, the society weighs the virtues of building more community-based facilities against worries that the "net" will be widened and more children taken into state custody. And, in deciding how children should be represented in the juvenile court, the society balances interests in recognizing the rights and emerging autonomy of the children against the interests in drawing the children into a more intimate relationship with their parents and the state.

Operational decisions about the portfolio of rehabilitation programs available to children and the style of juvenile court proceedings clearly do have philosophical significance. Moreover, the accumulation of such decisions does determine the overall character of the juvenile justice system. The point, then, is not that operational decisions should be seen independently of their broader implications. It is simply that when every decision occasions a major philosophical battle, it is very difficult for the system to operate in a coherent way. It becomes fragmented—even unaccountable—because it operates with no guiding concept.

The lack of a coherent, durable mandate for juvenile justice also makes difficult long-term investments and sustained experimentation in the system. If everything is up for grabs, if what was desperately required today is discarded tomorrow, there is little incentive for anyone to make investments in the system because there is a reasonable chance that the effort will be wasted.

This observation leads to the third and most debilitating operational consequence of a weakened mandate: loss of morale, initiative, self-confidence, and responsibility among the people who run the institutions—the judges who hear the cases and make the dispositions, the probation officers who manage the cases that are informally adjusted, the corrections administrators who distribute a heterogeneous youth population across a limited number and variety of programs, and so on. Without a sense of mission and purpose that dignifies the enterprise and gives it some direction, it is hard for the institutions of the system to attract talented and committed people, or to use their talents well once they are attracted.

To deal with the problem of a weakened, confused mandate for juvenile justice, the Office of Juvenile Justice and Delinquency Prevention of the United States Department of Justice and the Program in Criminal Justice Policy and Management at Harvard's Kennedy School of Government convened an Executive Session on the Future of Juvenile Justice. Members of this session were 30 individuals who led important agencies within the juvenile justice system or shaped public opinion about juvenile justice by offering commentaries and reviews from academic positions. The members of the Executive Session were the following:

Richard W. Barnum, Director of the Juvenile Court Clinic of Boston's Municipal Court
James W. Brown, Director of the Community Research Center at the University of Illinois at Champaign-Urbana
Robbie Callaway, Director of Government Relations, Boys Club of America
Philip J. Cook, Professor of Public Policy at Duke University, Durham, NC
Sidney Dwoskin, Chairman, Board of Directors of the American Probation and Parole Association
Janet Fink, Assistant Attorney-in-Charge for Legal Affairs, New York City Legal Aid Society, Juvenile Rights Division
Barbara Flicker, Director, Institute of Judicial Administration, New York University Law School
Honorable William E. Gladstone, Juvenile Division of Florida's 11th Judicial Circuit
Peter W. Greenwood, The Rand Corporation, Santa Monica, CA
Donna M. Hamparian, Co-Director, Ohio Serious Juvenile Offender Project
Francis X. Hartmann, Kennedy School of Government, Cambridge, MA
George L. Kelling, Kennedy School of Government, Cambridge, MA
Orlando L. Martinez, Director, Division of Youth Services, State of Colorado
Representative Don McCorkell, Jr., Oklahoma House of Representatives
Honorable John Milligan, Court of Appeals, State of Ohio
Mark H. Moore, Kennedy School of Government, Cambridge, MA
Edward M. Murphy, Commissioner, Massachusetts Department of Youth Services
Lloyd Ohlin, Harvard Law School, Cambridge, MA
Honorable Luke Quinn, Juvenile Division, Probate Court, State of Michigan
Alfred P. Regnery, Office of Juvenile Justice and Delinquency Prevention, U.S. Department of Justice
James Rowland, Director, California Department of Youth Authority
Catherine M. Ryan, Assistant State's Attorney, Juvenile Division, State of Illinois

Ellen Schall, Commissioner of the New York City Department of Juvenile Justice
Mark Sidran, Assistant Chief Prosecuting Attorney, King County, State of Washington
Michael Smith, Director, Vera Institute of Justice, New York, NY
Pamela Swain, Office of Juvenile Justice and Delinquency Prevention, U.S. Department of Justice
James Weissman, Chief Deputy, Juvenile Division of the Office of the District Attorney, State of Colorado
Honorable William Sylvester White, Illinois Appellate Court
Hubert Williams, Director of the Newark Police Department
James Wootton, Office of Juvenile Justice and Delinquency Prevention, U.S. Department of Justice

This group met five times over the course of 2½ years. It met as individuals who felt responsible for stewarding the enterprise of juvenile justice and the institutions that comprise the system: the juvenile court, the youth corrections agencies, the probation departments, the prosecuting and defense attorneys who specialize in juvenile cases, the volunteer community agencies that take much of the responsibility for handling less serious cases, and the police who encounter the problems for which the juvenile justice system is the intended solution. The aim was to see if the group could reach agreement on a philosophical framework to guide operations and investments in juvenile justice. The assumption was that if this group could agree on a philosophical framework, the society would be well on its way toward establishing a new, stronger mandate for juvenile justice. Failing that ambitious goal, the group might at least develop some alternative ideas about how the court and system might develop, and the society might therefore see its choices more clearly.

In seeking a firmer, more coherent mandate for juvenile justice, the Executive Session accepted some basic assumptions and orientations. First, we acknowledged that the responsibilities of stewardship did not suggest that the institutions of the juvenile justice system should remain unchanged. To our mind, all institutions must adapt. When community values change, when new technologies or administrative procedures become available, or when the nature of the society's problem changes, social institutions must be prepared to keep in step. Otherwise they become outmoded. At the same time, we understood that institutions survive because, over time, they have developed some distinctive competences—some things that they do better than any other institution. Moreover, we understand that even when institutions are under severe pressure, as the juvenile justice system is, they nonetheless change only slowly and incrementally. Thus, in thinking through the future of juvenile justice, we did not imagine wiping the slate clean and starting over. Like an executor presiding over a bankruptcy, our task was to slough off what had become a costly liability and to protect what would be valuable in the future.

Second, in positioning the institutions for the future, the Executive Session tried not only to maintain continuity but also to create an accord between the goals and purposes of the juvenile justice system, and the sources from which it draws legitimacy and support, and its operational capabilities. It would do little good to imagine an attractive purpose that could command support and claim legitimacy if the institutions of the juvenile justice system could not achieve the goal. The recent history of juvenile justice has surely taught us not to claim too much for the enterprise.

It would be equally foolish to establish a goal well suited to the current capabilities of the juvenile justice system if there were little support or legitimacy behind it. For example, the system is now capable of incapacitating unruly juveniles, and there is arguably some value in producing this result. But if that were the sole purpose of the system, it seems likely that there would be little political support or legitimacy for the enterprise, because the society seems to demand more from its juvenile justice system.

The point is simply that a durable concept of juvenile justice must establish some consistency among its substantive goals; its ability to attract support from the legislators, courts, and interest groups that oversee its operations; and its own operational capacities to deliver on its promised objectives.

Third, in acting as stewards the Executive Session realized that it had only a frail instrument to wield—the suggestive power of ideas. We had few illusions about the power of ideas to shape the character and operations of a vast, institutionalized enterprise such as the juvenile justice system. Given the sharp ideological conflicts surrounding juvenile justice, it is possible that the only ideas that can command wide and enthusiastic support are so abstract that they fail to provide any operational guidance to the system. On the other hand, any idea specific and concrete enough to guide future operations might fail to attract sufficient support to make it compelling. Thus, concepts might well lack power to shape the system.

On the other hand, we noted that some ideas become conventional wisdom. When they do, they have great power to organize and legitimate social enterprises. For example, the idea of alcoholism has played a very important role in justifying and shaping the society's response to the problems associated with drinking. It has focused attention on drinkers rather than on alcohol itself, and has isolated a small segment of the drinking population to receive special attention. Similarly, in the foreign policy area, the principle of containment and the image of falling dominoes have played a central role in shaping our foreign policy toward less developed countries. We also noted that many companies in the private sector have been successful precisely because they adopted and stuck with a basic strategic conception of their enterprise.

Much closer to the subject at hand, we noted that the juvenile court itself was once nothing more than an idea. Yet it gave rise to an institution that has lasted for nearly a century and probably could not be abolished despite its current troubles.

We also noted that powerful forces were converging to produce a particular new idea of juvenile justice. If left to the natural course of events, the juvenile justice system would come to reflect, on the one hand, the political left's concern for limited jurisdiction and due process protections of defendants, and on the other hand, the political right's concern for doing justice and achieving effective crime control through deterrence and incapacitation. A "constitutionalized" and "criminalized" juvenile justice system responds appropriately to the most powerful criticisms that have been made of the current system and is consistent with some older and more important ideas about how the state should structure its relations with its citizens. Nonetheless, it has important weaknesses as well. The point of mentioning this at this stage is not to discuss the merits of this emerging new idea, but to illustrate that we might all be more in the grip of ideas and ideologies than we now think. In short, ideas may have substantial power to organize social action.

In any case, it is hard to imagine what other instrument the Executive Session could use to influence the vast, complicated, and fragmented elements of the juvenile justice system. The system stands on legislative foundations erected in 50 different states, and its operations span judicial and executive branches in each of those states. Moreover, its administrative structure typically leaves a great deal of discretion to the individual officials who deal with cases—the police on the street, the probation officer, the judge, and the manager of the youth corrections facility. To say that the system is decentralized would be a wild understatement. As in all decentralized systems, then, the primary control comes more from shared ideas and culture than from administrative procedures and control. That simple fact alone elevates the importance of concepts, philosophies, and the spirit of the enterprise over its mechanics.

What the Executive Session on the Future of Juvenile Justice was uniquely equipped to do—its distinctive competences and authorization—was to develop broad ideas that could guide the future development of the juvenile court and the juvenile justice system. That is what we did.

I wish I could report that we reached agreement, and that the ideas presented in this volume are a consensus view of the distinguished practitioners and academics who assembled. Unfortunately, I do not believe they have that standing.

This volume was written principally by me with the assistance of my colleagues in the Program in Criminal Justice Policy and Management at the Kennedy School of Government. It profoundly reflects what we learned from our discussions with the Executive Session. In fact, the volume is written to them as an audience whose views we care deeply about. In my mind, their voices commented on each line—not always favorably, and never unanimously. It will be obvious that this volume draws shamelessly on papers the members of the Executive Session prepared for our deliberations and that are published in Volumes II and III of this series. In the end, however, I cannot claim the Executive Session as a coauthor.

I can (and must) claim my colleagues in the Program in Criminal Justice Policy and Management as coauthors. In fact, the argument of this volume most accurately reflects the conclusions of internal discussions in which we tried to come to grips with the various paradoxes and dilemmas of juvenile justice in a liberal state. It is this group whose voice speaks through this volume.

In any sustained collaborative enterprise, it becomes difficult to say who was responsible for what particular insight or idea. It even becomes difficult to remember who wrote what first. Nonetheless, I have tried to record the individual contributions to this volume by indicating who shared with me the responsibility for writing each of the various chapters. I am enormously indebted to my colleagues who helped me with this book: Thomas Bearrows, whose interest and enthusiasm for our discussions kept us going even when we felt confused; Jeffrey Bleich, whose careful work on state legislation, the inherent powers of the court, and the difficult issue of dangerous juvenile offenders established some of the basic pillars supporting the argument of this book; Francis Hartmann, whose steady administrative hand, exquisite editorial judgment, and deep sensitivity to the issues kept us on course; George Kelling, whose nose for what happens at the street levels of criminal justice organizations first drew our attention to the curious fact that parents seem to be largely ignored by the juvenile court, and whose love of history drew us back into colonial America and made us wonder how the world had changed since then; Michael Oshima, whose patient and scholarly legal inquiries taught us about the "offices" of parents and children in our society; and Saul Weingart, whose early work on the future problems confronting the system focused our attention on the "civil" side of the court, and who returned later to provide invaluable assistance and encouragement in getting the book out the door.

I should also acknowledge the enormous contribution made by my own family to this enterprise. My mother, Jean McFeely Moore, and my wife, Martha Church Moore, have shown me how much work goes into the enterprise of rearing children. I admire them for their effort and skill more than I can say. My sister, Gaylen Moore, was an exacting, but consistently encouraging, editor. Her efforts to keep our family together after my mother died last year provided yet another example of the crucial importance of family work willingly shouldered by resourceful women. My other sister, Trina Moore, had the foresight to befriend an artist, Jeffrey Arfer, who helped me to produce pictures that captured my ideas more accurately than words could. My secretary, Diana Murray, not only coped with the endless revisions of the book, but also took responsibility for our children when my wife and I desperately needed a vacation. So not only is this book about families, it is by my family.

I owe a great deal to my colleagues and my family. I do not owe them my errors, however. I wish there were fewer so that I could honor them more.

What I ave produced with their assistance is an extended essay that seeks to come honestly to grips with a problem that resists simple solutions. It makes an argument for a version of the juvenile court and the juvenile justice system that helps families to do the work of transforming dependent children into resourceful citizens. It resists narrowing the focus of the court to criminal offenses committed by children, though there are many attractive reasons to do so. It also resists viewing moral exhortation and coercive authority as inevitably destructive and inconsistent with assistance. Instead, it views rules and obligations (along with assistance of various kinds) as important devices for mobilizing private, individual efforts to aid public purposes. The essay also refuses to draw a sharp line between private informal arrangements and public interventions, since they are inevitably linked together in complicated interactions in which the existence of one kind of institution conditions the actions of the others. Perhaps most important, the essay insists on the public importance of the task of raising children well, and seeks to establish an institution that can not only stand for this but also help to carry it out.

So the essay is meant to be challenging to current conceptions of juvenile justice. I am keenly aware that the easiest way to be challenging is to be deeply wrong. I freely admit this possibility. But I wonder how our society can have gone on for so long without noticing how important is the task of raising children, how disastrous the public consequences of failure, and how inevitably both public obligation and assistance are involved in the effort. I learned a great deal about our society by reasoning through this problem in excellent company. I hope that readers will enjoy the same experience and challenge.

Cambridge, MA
November 1986

Mark Harrison Moore

Contents

1
The Problem

Sometimes children become social problems. It happens when they commit crimes, or frighten other citizens. Or, it happens when they are exposed to dangers from which the society would like to shield them. The following cases, drawn from the dockets of a municipal juvenile court,[1] illustrate these possibilities.

Kevin: A Young Robber

Kevin is a 16-year-old boy charged with robbery. He knocked a middle-aged businessman to the ground, kicked him twice in the stomach, and took his watch and wallet.

Kevin is well known to the juvenile court. When he was 13, his mother filed a Child-in-Need-of-Supervision (CHINS) petition asking the court to keep him from running away and staying out late at night. Before that petition could be heard, Kevin was brought before the court on a delinquency petition for breaking and entering. Both petitions were dismissed. At age 14, Kevin ran away for a week, and his mother filed another CHINS petition. That petition, too, was dismissed. At age 15, Kevin was adjudicated delinquent for breaking and entering and was placed on probation. When he was 16, new burglary offenses were filed against him and Kevin was committed to the Youth Authority and placed in a private residential facility. He ran away. Now Kevin has been arrested for unarmed robbery and for a murder committed in a different jurisdiction.

Kevin's background includes physical abuse by his father. He admits he has difficulty controlling his temper, but talks often about the injustice of the world and his determination to fight back to get what he is owed.

A juvenile court judge is trying to decide whether Kevin should be transferred to the adult court for trial on the robbery charge.

Julie: An Angry Young Woman

Julie, a 15-year-old girl, has been arrested for attempted murder. Her boyfriend was shot when a gun held by Julie either was fired or went off accidentally. He is now in a coma and unable to testify as to the circumstances of the crime.

Though Julie has had minor discipline problems in school, she has never before been in serious trouble. Julie's mother divorced Julie's father eight years ago because he was alcoholic. The mother then lived with another man who acted as a father to Julie, and the family seemed to do well. Recently, however, Julie's mother left this second man for a third. Julie claims that the most recent man has abused her physically and sexually. As a result she has spent more time with her own boyfriend, often staying away from home for several days at a time. Her mother denies that Julie has been abused.

The prosecutor is trying to decide what charge to file and whether to proceed in the juvenile or adult court.

Paul: A Teenaged Drunk Driver

Paul, a 16-year-old boy, has been arrested for vehicular homicide. He admits that he was driving his father's car home late at night after dropping his girl friend at her house. He also admits having taken advantage of his parents' absence to organize a party for his friends, and that he bought a keg of beer for the occasion. He further admits drinking a nightcap at his girl friend's house. On the way home, Paul accelerated through an intersection as the light was turning red. He hit an oncoming car as it turned left in front of him and killed the person on the passenger side.

The relatives of the victims are not vengeful; in their words, they are not "eager to throw Paul's life down the drain, too." Paul has previously been caught drinking twice at school. Paul's parents express great concern and promise to supervise him much more closely in the future. A juvenile court judge must decide what disposition to make.

Angelique: A Battered Child

Three-year-old Angelique was brought to the hospital by her mother. X-ray films showed a fractured skull. Angelique's mother explained that she hit Angelique's head against the wall in a momentary rage, just after she herself was beaten by her boyfriend. The boyfriend then left the house and was not expected to return.

There is no previous record of either abuse or neglect, and Angelique's medical and day-care records indicate that she is developing normally. The hospital has petitioned the juvenile court to place Angelique in foster care. Angelique's mother is adamantly opposed. The judge must decide what to do.

Royce: A Brash Delinquent

Royce, a 15-year-old boy, has just been arrested and charged with auto theft for the fourth time in three years. After his second offense, Royce was adjudicated delinquent and placed in an open residential program for multidrug abusers. During this period he continued to live at home with his aunt but spent a great deal of time in the program.

He seems intelligent and is able to relate well to others. He is proud of his criminal career, and brags that he has "only four busts for hundreds of thefts." He has a steady girl friend whom he says he would like to marry. He also says that he understands the penalties of crime will increase when he becomes an adult in the eyes of the law, and that he will then probably give up stealing cars. He justifies his current crimes by the simple statement that they "improve his life-style."

Chris: An Angry Son

Chris, a strapping 16-year-old, recently punched his father in the face and his father is now threatening to press charges for assault. Chris and his father have often argued about Chris's future, and this is not the first time the arguments have led to violence. Chris has also repeatedly run away from home. He usually returns within a short time when he runs out of money, but sometimes he has stayed away for several weeks. A year ago, Chris's father filed a CHINS petition asking the court to help him keep Chris at home. Chris's school record is good, but he has been held back because of frequent absences. The case is currently in the hands of the police who responded to the father's call.

Tina: A Malnourished Adolescent

Tina, a 12-year-old girl, has been referred to the Department of Public Health by her teacher, who believes that Tina is malnourished because she is always hungry, cold, and tired in class. The Health Department has found that Tina lives in a sparsely furnished apartment which, at the time of the investigation, contained little food. Moreover, two younger siblings seem to have nutrition-related health problems as well. Tina's mother, a single parent, works full-time to support her seven children. She also receives aid to families with dependent children (AFDC). She resents the school's interference and claims that she does her best to provide for her children. The public health officials are deciding whether to file an abuse and neglect petition with the juvenile court.

Tom: A Late-Night Loiterer

Tom is a 15-year-old boy who stays out late. The police recently picked him up for the fourth time loitering on the street at 2:00 a.m.—a violation of the city's curfew. His late-night companions are older men whom the police suspect of crimes. Tom has no criminal record. His older brother is in prison for heroin possession. His father is dead. Tom's mother seems surprised each time he is brought home by the police. The police must decide what to do with Tom.

Alphonse: A Runaway

Fifteen-year-old Alphonse has run away from home. The police found him sleeping in an abandoned car. Alphonse's mother works part-time but spends much of her time and effort caring for Alphonse's younger sister who is developmentally disabled. She explains to the police that Alphonse's wayward tendencies are the least of her worries. In addition to running away from home, Alphonse has often been truant from school. The police wonder what they should do.

Public Nomination

The children just described are social problems in two different senses. As a practical matter, they are social problems because someone has put their cases before the public. This is noteworthy because ordinarily the conduct of children and the arrangements made for their care, protection, and supervision escape public scrutiny. As a matter of both justice and prudence, the society leaves the task of raising children to parents (or other legal guardians), granting them wide autonomy in meeting the responsibility.[2] Yet in the cases cited, inhibitions about interfering with families have been overcome. Something about the children's conduct or condition has stimulated someone, usually an "outsider," to raise an alarm and focus public attention on the children and their situation.

This is hardly surprising in the cases of Kevin, the robber; Julie, the angry girl friend; Paul, the drunk driver; and Royce, the car thief. They have all committed deeds that would be treated as crimes if the doers were adults. The outsiders who have raised the alarm are the victims or relatives of the victims. They want their losses acknowledged, and they want assurances that the offenders will be sufficiently disciplined and supervised in the future so that they and others can be safe.

In the case of Chris, the angry son, the person nominating the case for public attention is also the victim of a crime. But this time he is a parent, who has asked for public assistance in managing his child.

In the cases of Angelique, the battered child; Tina, the malnourished adolescent; and Alphonse, the runaway, the outsiders who have nominated the cases for public attention are public officials in a hospital, a school, and the police department who have become concerned about the conditions under which the children seem to be living. In focusing public attention on these children, they seem to want a guarantee that the children will receive minimum levels of supervision and care.

To a degree, one can view these nominations as formally authorized or mandated by the society. There is a body of law—both common and statutory, civil and criminal—that prescribes the duties of children and parents to one another and also *to the broader society*.[3] Children are not supposed to commit criminal offenses.[4] They are usually obliged to be at home at night.[5] They are not allowed to drink.[6] They are supposed to remain responsive to parental supervision.[7] Parents are prohibited from attacking their children.[8] Parents are obligated to provide food and shelter.[9] And so on. Since these duties are owed not only between children and parents but also to the broader society, it is the legal right (and sometimes even the duty) of citizens to bring violations of these duties to light.

As a practical matter, however, interventions are probably animated more by custom and commonly shared notions of just and proper conduct than by any formal authorization.[10] The nominators in the cases act because they judge the situation to be dangerous, not because there is a formal authorization.

Public Risks

This is the second sense in which the children described are social problems. Someone has made the judgment that the situation in each case contains material threats to social welfare, now or in the future. The nature of the threats differs across the cases, however.

Generally speaking, paramount in the public mind is the immediate threat of criminal victimization. In some cases the child is the offender and the society the victim. The cases involving Kevin, the robber; Julie, the angry girl friend; Paul, the drunk driver; and Royce, the car thief, most obviously represent threats of this type. In other cases the threat is *to* the child: society is the offender and the child is the victim. The case involving Angelique, the battered child, is the most obvious example.

The cases of Tom, the loiterer; and Alphonse, the runaway, are different, for in these there seems to be no immediate or certain threat to life or property. With Tom, the salient threat is that Tom seems headed (with some probability) toward a life of crime.[11] The threat is neither certain nor imminent, but may nonetheless be real. With Alphonse, too, the worry is about the future, but in this case the threat is more to Alphonse than to the society. The worry is more that Alphonse will be victimized and will end up a social dependent than that he will become a criminal offender.

Figure 1.1 highlights the differences in these cases by arraying them two-dimensionally. The horizontal dimension shows the risk the *child presents to the society* relative to the risk *the society presents to the child.* This dimension measures whether the child is relatively more threatening or more threatened (taking into consideration that each case contains elements of both): the farther to the right, the greater the relative risk to the society; the farther to the left, the more salient the risk to the child.

The vertical dimension shows the absolute magnitude and imminence of the risk to the society and to the child of each case. The higher up the

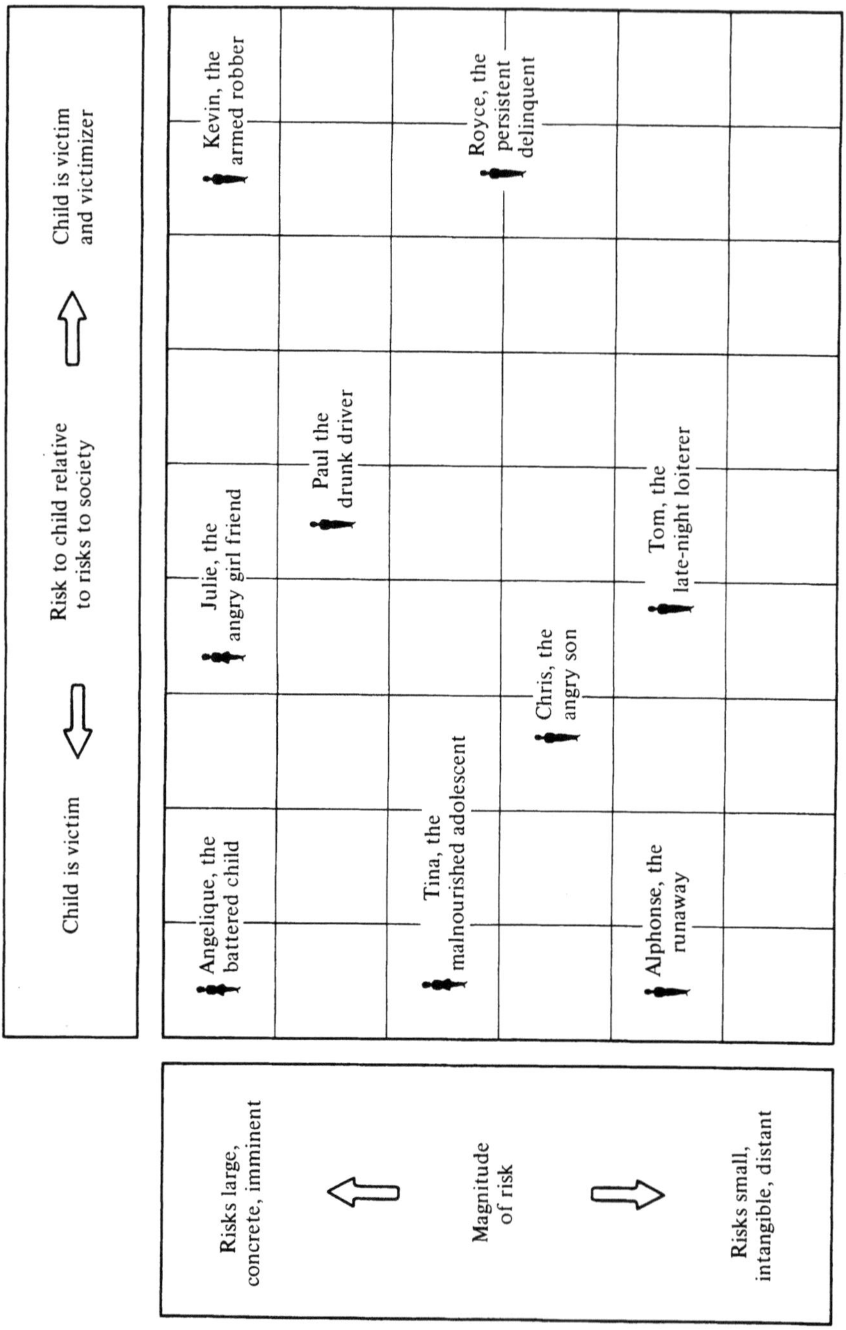

FIGURE 1.1. The domain of problems for juvenile justice.

scale the case appears, the more serious the risk appears. Cases toward the top of the scale involve large, imminent threats to life and property. Cases toward the bottom involve less tangible, less imminent, and less certain threats.[12]

Public Intervention

The effect of intervention in these cases—of raising public alarm about the conduct of the children or the conditions under which they are being raised—is to create a crisis in the existing arrangements for raising the children. The issue before the community is not only the current conduct of the children, but also the adequacy of the existing private arrangements to achieve the society's interests in supervising, protecting, and guiding the children.

Sometimes these issues will be dealt with quite formally. The cases of Kevin, Angelique, Julie, and Paul, for example, will probably be handled in a formal court adjudication because the risks involved seem to be more certain and imminent than those involved in the other cases. The case of Chris might also be handled formally if his father insists on pressing charges or if he petitions the court to help him supervise his son, but a great deal of effort will probably be expended to keep this case out of the court itself.

In the other cases, public agencies such as welfare and police departments will be involved in the discussion but the cases will not come directly before the court. The welfare department is already involved in the case of Tina, the malnourished teenager. The conversation will include people from a network of social work agencies; the issues will be whether Tina's mother is eligible for additional aid or could benefit from nutrition counseling. The conversation about Tom, the late-night loiterer, will be initiated by the police. They are likely to impress on Tom's mother the importance of more effective supervision of Tom and to threaten (or promise) their continuing efforts to keep him off the streets late at night.

These discussions can lead to a more or less radical restructuring of the existing arrangements for supervising the children. In a few cases, the primary responsibility for the child might be shifted from private institutions to public custody to ensure that the community's interests in protecting itself from violent children (or protecting children from violent parents) are met. Thus, Kevin may be placed in a secure facility or even in an adult prison. Angelique may be placed in a foster home where the threat of attack is judged to be less than in her own home.

In other cases, new obligations may be formally imposed on the parents or children or both. Royce might be obligated to make restitution to those whose cars he "borrowed." Paul and his parents may have to report regularly to a probation officer about the parents' supervision of his drinking. Chris might be obligated by the court to not run away, under threat of legal punishment.

In still other cases, the conversation might result in additional resources, such as financial assistance or psychological counseling, being used to buttress the existing private arrangement. A review of Tina's situation might lead to her mother receiving additional AFDC benefits, or being provided with food stamps and nutrition counseling. Alphonse's mother might be referred to services for her disabled daughter so that she can have more time and energy for Alphonse.

A significant price must be paid for public interventions. To the extent that private arrangements for supervising and caring for children have been subjected to public scrutiny, an important principle has been breached. The state, or the community, has intruded into an area where it should not go. The breaching of this principle may be regarded as a price in itself. But it also has behavioral effects. Those previously responsible for the supervision, care, and guidance of the child may become demoralized and reduce their own level of effort.[13] Alternatively, they may become hostile to the public or private agencies that are trying to help. In either case, their overall capacity to care for the child will be reduced and the society's objectives thwarted.

Intervention also engages public resources. To the extent that families are supplied with assistance and that this assistance is financed with tax dollars, the society pays a direct financial price for intervention. To the extent that the formal authority of the state is invoked to impose new obligations on parents or children, a different kind of resource is engaged—namely, the coercive power of the state. In a society that loves privacy and freedom as much as ours does, that resource is always in short supply and must be husbanded.

Juvenile Justice

In an ideal society, the two different senses in which these cases are social problems would be closely related. Cases involving the conduct and condition of children would be nominated for public attention only when the intervention was formally authorized, the problems were serious enough to warrant the attention, and the situations could be improved by the resulting intervention.[14] Cases that were considered beyond the authorization of the society to act, or that were less serious or less amenable to public intervention would be left alone in the interest of minimizing intrusion and economizing on public resources. In this ideal society, the costs of public intervention would always be balanced by the benefits associated with reducing the short- or long-term public risks that motivated the intervention.

It is no easy task to produce this happy result. Yet precisely this result is the goal of the juvenile court and the juvenile justice system. This book aims to develop a perspective on the juvenile court and the juvenile justice system in which the philosophical foundations and the concrete operations will be closer to this goal.

It is useful at the outset to cast doubt on a familiar principle that is tacitly accepted as the philosophical foundation for juvenile justice and to set out a less familiar but potentially more accurate and useful principle. The familiar principle is that the state's primary (perhaps exclusive) justification for intruding into the private affairs of family and children is to control conduct that threatens the lives or property of citizens.[15] In this conception, the juvenile justice system is viewed as an adjunct to the adult criminal justice system that is designed to deal with the special problems of crimes committed by (and perhaps against) children. Its powers derive from the society's general police powers.

The principle proposed in contrast is that the state's motivations and justifications derive less from concern about crimes than from concern about superintending the relationships between parents and children and interest in maintaining minimally satisfactory conditions for the care, supervision, and guidance of children.[16] In this conception, the juvenile justice system is perceived as drawing on civil powers held by the state to oversee public institutions to ensure that they meet their public responsibilities. Just as the state (through the courts) now oversees businesses to make sure they meet their contractual obligations to lenders and creditors fairly when they go bankrupt,[17] oversees landlords to guarantee that they meet their obligations to tenants,[18] and oversees government agencies to ensure that their decision-making procedures meet standards of representation and rationality,[19] the state might have an interest in overseeing families to ensure that they meet minimal obligations to the society with respect to raising children. Such supervisory civil powers are exceedingly loose, and are triggered only by major problems. Nonetheless, the state has the power to regulate family relationships.

To clarify the subtle but important differences between these two principles, it is useful to look once again at society's stakes in the cases presented previously and at the particular ways in which the juvenile justice system intervenes. My contention is that while one can make one's institutions about the proper way to respond to these cases fit the police powers model, one must make a great many exceptions to do so. Moreover, once one has looked at the group of exceptions, one can formulate a different conception of the court that easily accommodates the anomalies. That different conception is the one that emphasizes civil powers over families and the conditions of child rearing rather than police powers over the conduct of children and parents.

Police Powers and Civil Powers

The cases that are most consistent with the notion that the juvenile justice system is an adjunct to the adult criminal justice system are those involving Kevin and Royce. In these, the court draws on its police powers. These boys have committed real crimes, and have done so repeatedly. They seem determined to continue offending. In fact, the question with respect to these cases is, why should they not be handled within the *adult* criminal court?

The answer generally given to this question is that, from a legal point of view, children are different from adults. Children are less mature and autonomous and therefore somewhat less responsible.[20] They are more easily moved by outside influences (such as the encouragement of peers or the provocation of victims) and more vulnerable to transient impulses that do not reflect their basic character and values. For these reasons parents (or legal guardians) have special responsibilities for supervision and guidance of children.

When a child commits an act that would be a crime if committed by an adult, then, we do not immediately assume it is a crime. We consider it just and reasonable to look behind the offense.[21] We examine the immediate context of the offense in an effort to determine whether the youthful offender was the prime mover or the relatively innocent dupe of other influences, such as the encouragement of peers, the manipulations of an adult criminal, or the provocative behavior of the victim. We explore the history of the offender to determine whether the offense was characteristic of him or her or was an odd and presumably transient impulse. And we assess the family background of the offender and his or her social circumstances to determine what part of the current conduct might be attributed to failure of private and public caretakers to live up to their obligations to provide care and guidance, rather than to the child's reluctance to learn or to accept obligations.

The society makes such examinations partly out of a concern for justice. If the offense seems out of character or explicable in terms of the failures of others to discharge their responsibilities to the child, the child's conduct would seem less culpable. This is what it means to view the offending child as a victim rather than as a victimizer.

The examination is also motivated by practical concerns. Analysis of the context of the offense may help in deciding the best response to the child's current conduct and condition. If the child seems to be basically sound but temporarily under the influence of bad associates (as in the case of Tom), the best response might be to impose conditions on the child that strengthen his or her contacts with family, school, and other healthy elements of the community. If the child seems to have deep personal problems that, whatever their cause, exist independently of the conduct of the parents (as in the cases of Julie and Alphonse), the appropriate response may be sustained, individually based psychotherapy. And so on. The point is that the response should be tailored to the individual characteristics and social background of the child.

Such niceties may cut little ice in the cases of Kevin and Royce. There is little in their personal background or in the level of parental supervision to mitigate or excuse their offenses. For this reason their cases are simultaneously the purest objects of the state's police powers and the most obvious to be considered for handling in the adult court.

Considerations of individual characteristics and social background seem more relevant in the cases of Julie and Paul. There is no doubt in these cases that someone has been injured. What is in question is whether Julie and Paul *intended* to harm, and therefore whether they should be held criminally responsible.[22] Julie is clearly guilty of reckless conduct in handling the gun, but she might not have intended to shoot. The gun could have gone off by accident, or she might have fired in self-defense. The thought is also present that if her parents had dealt with her more sensitively and supervised her more effectively, the offense might not have occurred. None of these rationalizations excuse the deed, but they mitigate guilt and might lead to a different disposition than would be made in the adult criminal court.

In the case of Paul, one can argue that Paul is an incipient alcoholic, not a murderer. That is, it is increasingly characteristic of him to drink but not to kill. His drunk driving can and should be responded to as a crime.[23] But just as Julie's moral (and legal) guilt for shooting her boyfriend might be mitigated by the lack of intention, so might Paul's for the death of the passenger in the other car. As with Julie, Paul's parents are implicated to some degree in the crime and might therefore be included in the disposition. Their neglect was a contributing cause.

These concerns can be understood as just and useful qualifications of the state's ordinary police powers. Indeed, the quality of justice meted out in the adult courts might well be improved by the kind of probing investigation characteristic of the juvenile court.[24] But it is also possible that this concern for the background of the offense signals a different kind of state interest than the just and efficacious handling of crimes committed by juveniles. The concern about the character of the child and the capacity of parents to supervise him or her may be the *center* of the state's interest, rather than a side issue.

The case of Angelique presents a different kind of problem. It is similar to the cases of Kevin, Royce, Julie, and Paul in that there is physical injury. Hence, the state's response falls clearly within its police powers. Angelique, however, is the victim, rather than the offender. This circumstance does not answer the question of why Angelique's case should be handled in the juvenile court rather than the adult criminal court. Two features differentiate it from an ordinary assault case.

One is that an attack by a parent (or legal guardian) on a child seems more serious than other physical assaults. It is not just that the attacker is so much more powerful than the victim. It is also that the society believes that parents have special moral and social responsibilities to their children. For the most part, this belief does not have to be acknowledged in law because it is so widely understood. But precisely for this reason the community is particularly offended when a parent breaks this code. The parent violates not only a general responsibility of citizenship, but a special responsibility that attaches to the "office" of parent in the society.[25]

A second difference is that if the parent is convicted of assault (or for the special offense of child abuse), the society must face the question of what to do with the child. In deciding whether to jail the parent or place him or her on probation, the court has to balance the general interests of the community in having its laws against child abuse strictly enforced and in ensuring that children are adequately protected from parental assault against the interests of parents and those of children and the society in salvaging the natural family.

What makes this situation different from an ordinary crime, then, is the prominence of the community's interest in family relationships. It is the sense that parents possess especially important responsibilities to their children that makes the offense of child abuse so repugnant and so deserving of community indignation and punishment. It is the society's interest in keeping the family together and functioning, however, that tempts the state not to punish a clear criminal offense with tough criminal sanctions. And the prospect that family functioning might be restored with counseling backed by the authority of the court motivates a shift from a punitive to a therapeutic style of social intervention.[26]

The interest in salvaging family relationships in cases of child abuse can be seen as an expression of a broad state interest in preserving families as the basic institution responsible for the development and socialization of children. It can also be seen as an indication of an even broader interest of the community (with the state and the juvenile justice system as its representatives) in overseeing the conditions under which children are raised. Indeed, these interests are implicit in the power of the state to maintain or fragment the family by shifting the custody of children when there is trouble within the family.

This set of interests seems quite different from the society's general interest in avoiding criminal attacks. Of course, interest in intervening in situations of child abuse may be linked to concern about criminal attack by arguing that the abused child is likely to become a criminal or an abusing parent in the future and therefore intervention is justified as a preventive effort.[27] But this is a long way around the barn. It seems much simpler to assert that the community has an obvious interest in the circumstances under which children are raised because it has an interest in the quality of citizenship they offer when they become adults. This may be linked to a prudential interest in preventing future criminal conduct by or dependence of its citizens. Or it might simply be linked to the notion that a just society requires that all children receive that minimal level of care, investment, and guidance that gives them a fighting chance to become resourceful citizens.

The case of Chris raises a similar kind of issue. At first glance it seems that Chris's case belongs in the same category as those of Kevin and Royce, rather than that of Angelique. After all, it is Chris who is the attacker. The attack is physical. It has happened before. It seems likely to happen again.

What makes Chris's case different from Kevin's and Royce's and similar to Angelique's is the fact that Chris's victim is not a stranger: It is his father. This means that the *relationship* between Chris and his father is a casualty of the offense as well as the father. That plausibly is a social problem because the society is depending on the relationship between Chris and his father to accomplish some important objectives, for example, protection of Chris from threats, supervision so that Chris does not victimize others, and guidance of Chris toward responsible citizenship. If the relationship has fallen apart or become one in which violence occurs, the society's goals are thwarted.

The idea that the court is interested in the quality of family relationships and the future development of children helps to make sense of the society's response to the cases of Tom and Alphonse. From the perspective of police powers, the response makes little sense. No one's life or property has been attacked or even threatened. One can attempt to attribute the state's interest in these cases as an effort to prevent future crime. But the society has always been properly wary of giving the state too much power to prevent crime, because it understands how broad and preemptive that justification could become.[28] In fact, from the vantage point of the police powers model, the response in these cases seems strikingly inappropriate. It extends state power over individual conduct beyond appropriate limits. And it focuses attention on the children rather than on the parents, where the attention might more properly belong.

From the perspective of the state's use of civil powers over families, however, the response seems less anomalous. In both cases, parental supervision and care seem to be less than desirable, leaving the children exposed to both short- and long-term risks. Thus, there is reason to intervene. At the same time, this perspective does not view the child as necessarily at fault and the only focus of attention. It is the relationship of the parents to the child and their capacity to supervise the child that is the issue. Efforts should be made to motivate and equip the family to do its job more effectively.

In sum, if one views the juvenile justice system as concerned primarily with the short-run protection of the community against criminal offenses by children, one encounters some striking anomalies in the operations of the system. One cannot easily accommodate to short-run protection the system's interest in exploring the social background of offenders and fitting the disposition of their cases to the strengths and weaknesses of the social network surrounding them, or the system's extraordinary emphasis on provision of services to children and protection of the family even at the price of risk to the community's interest in security. Nor can the system's focus on abuse and neglect cases be conveniently justified.

If, however, one views the juvenile justice system as a civil court system that superintends families and parents' responsibilities in the raising of children, these anomalies can be easily accommodated. Indeed, this conception covers all the principal features of the juvenile justice system: an individualized response to criminal offenses by children; the qualification of the response by concern for the context of the offense, the history of the child, and the competence of caretakers; concern for instances of abuse and neglect by private and public agencies that take responsibility for the development of children; and interest in leaving as much as possible of the work of fostering the development of children to institutions outside the juvenile justice system.

A Graphic Illustration of Police and Civil Powers

There is a great deal of overlap and a great deal of difference between these two conceptions. Figure 1.2 attempts to clarify the similarities and differences. The circle on the left represents the police powers model—the idea that the state's interest is primarily in guarding against property and violent crimes by children and in employing police powers to minimize such offenses. A necessary condition for the invocation of police powers then is a property or violent crime, or more broadly, any act that would be a crime if committed by an adult. How state power is used in juvenile cases, however, is not shaped entirely by the offense, as it would be in an adult system of retributive justice. Nor is it determined entirely by the blameworthiness of the child. It is also influenced by the capacity of private and public agencies to provide the supervision, guidance, and care that are necessary to protect the community from criminal acts by children in both the short and the long run. The smaller the threat the child represents and the stronger the private arrangements, the less the necessity for public intervention. In this conception, only a criminal act by a child engages the state's intervention, and the condition and background of the child are important only as qualifiers to the response.

The circle on the right side of Figure 1.2 represents the less familiar second conception—the civil powers model. The state's interest in this model is principally in ensuring minimal conditions for the development and socialization of children. Specific acts by children or their caretakers, such as crimes committed by the children or abuse and neglect by parents, signal breakdowns in these minimal conditions. In this conception, both

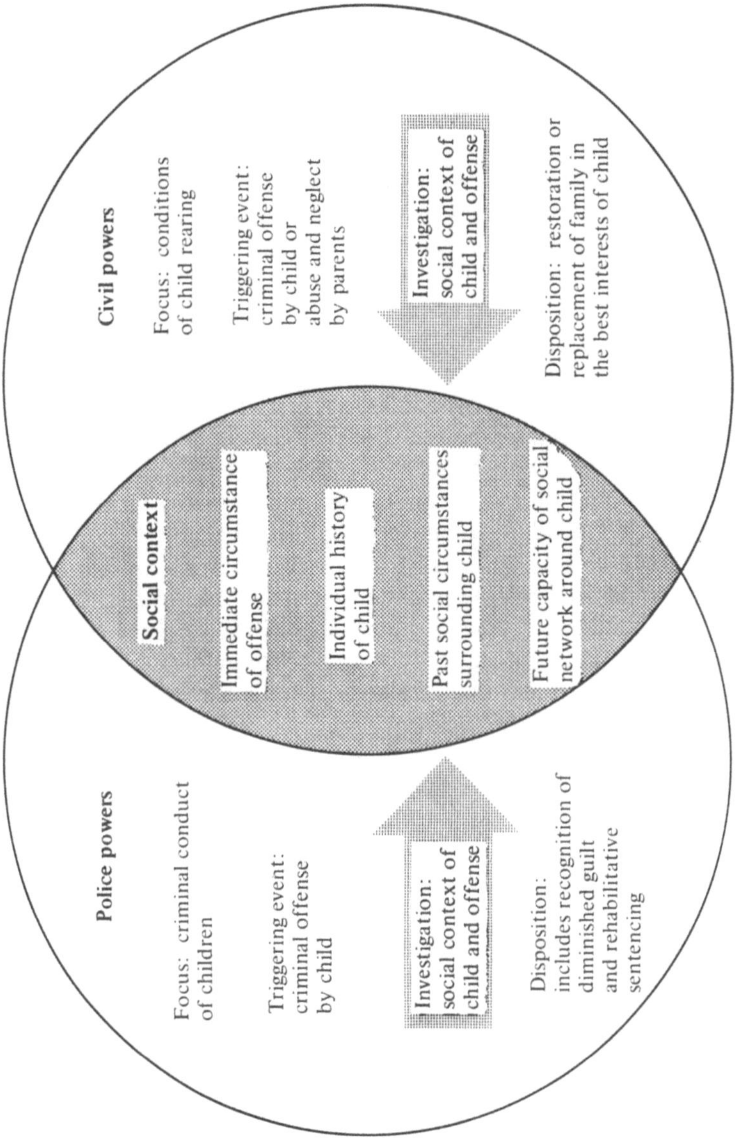

FIGURE 1.2. Police powers and civil powers: areas of separate and mutual intervention.

the act and a detailed investigation into the context of the act are important: It is the act that brings the case to public attention and the background investigation that guides the public response. The crucial difference between this conception and the police powers model is that the background investigation in this model is not a *qualification* of the state's primary interest, but an *exact expression* of it. The state's interest is in doing what it can to guarantee minimal conditions under which children are raised. It uses the conduct of children and parents as a way of focusing and limiting its concerns.

Figure 1.2 reveals that the two models overlap in the interpretation of the system's response to crimes by children. Both conceptions acknowledge criminal offenses by children as a problem that merits a public response. Both look behind the offense. Both condition the response on the basis of what can be observed about the context of the offense, the individual history of the child, and the strength of the child's private and public caretakers.

The principal difference between the two is in the principle that serves as the mandate for public response. The first conception, the one rooted in police powers, is guided by narrow, well-defined interests in doing justice to the child and the community and in preventing future criminal conduct by the child. The second conception, the one rooted in civil powers, is guided less by an interest in controlling crime than in making sure that the child is receiving minimally satisfactory levels of supervision, care, and guidance. The aim is not only to provide short-run protection from criminal offenses but also to protect community norms governing the care of children and to guard against both criminal offending and economic dependence in the future.

The response to criminal offenses is also different. The police powers model excludes cases in which there is a more or less significant breakdown in the development and socialization of children but in which no criminal acts are committed. If this model were to include these cases, it would have to deal with them as crimes committed against the child. It would have to explain why these crimes against children (but not by children) should be handled within the juvenile court or juvenile justice system. The second conception does not have this difficulty. The civil powers model easily embraces cases in which there are indications of a breakdown in the process of development and socialization; a crime does not have to have been committed for a case to arouse interest. Moreover, this model can justify its concern about these breakdowns in terms much broader than the society's crime control interests. It can talk in terms of minimizing future economic and social dependence of disadvantaged children.

A graphic illustration may be helpful in setting out this distinction. Figure 1.3 superimposes on Figure 1.1 the two alternative conceptions of the juvenile justice system. As Figure 1.3 (top) illustrates, cases in the top part of Figure 1.1 are at the center of the model based on police powers. Here the threats to the physical and economic well-being of the community are most obvious. Cases that fall in the upper left are included on the grounds that they represent criminal conduct by parents or that abuse and neglect are so strongly linked to future criminal offending that interest in preventing criminal offenses justifies the intervention.

From the point of view of a conception rooted in police powers, however, these arguments seem tendentious. The crime committed by those who abuse and neglect their children is not simply a crime against the lives and property of others. It is an offense against their children and the society. This sort of offense seems much more closely related to the second concept of the juvenile justice system. If the principal virtue of the first conception is to focus public attention narrowly on crimes committed *by* children, there is no reason to confuse the issue with crimes committed *against* children.

The concept of juvenile justice tied to broad civil powers governing family relationships covers a different part of Figure 1.1. Specifically, it covers quite comfortably both risks to the society and risks to the child. Since risks to the child are its principal concern, and since it interprets most kinds of criminal conduct as indications of risks to the child as well as risks to the community, it includes cases on the left side of Figure 1.1 as well as those on the right (Fig. 1.3, bottom). It may exclude some criminal conduct, such as that exhibited by Kevin and Royce, on the grounds that the perpetrators have reached a level of threat and maturity where their acts can no longer be viewed as the consequences of external influences. But many other criminal offenses are easily embraced by the civil powers model.

This second conception of juvenile justice is extremely suspect both among those who would like to economize on the use of public authority and among those who would like to economize on the use of public money. One problem is that the powers it confers are so broad that they seem to license extensive state interventions into the affairs of families, schools, and social work agencies. A second problem is the risk that these broad powers might be exercised on behalf of too narrow and ethnocentric a view of the conditions that are proper for raising children. In effect, the court might become the instrument of middle-class values in child rearing with disastrous consequences for the freedom and cultural diversity of the society. A third problem is that a half century of experience with such interventions has led to doubt of their efficacy. For all of these reasons, the society is now exceedingly reluctant to concede any broad interest of the community or the state in overseeing the conditions under which children are raised.

Yet we do not seem quite able to wash our hands of this problem either. In responding to instances of abuse and neglect, and even in responding to criminal offending by children, we seem to have some interest in the

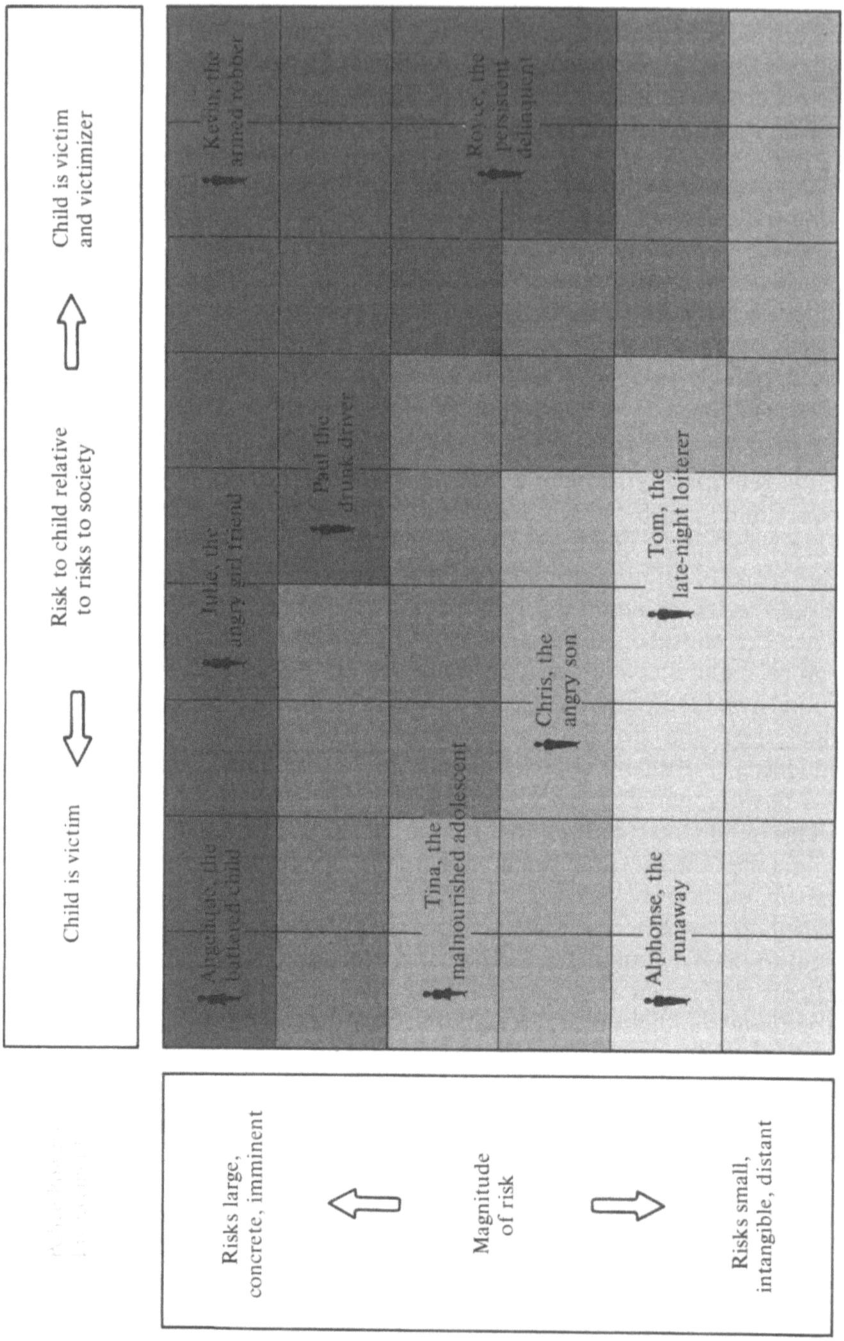
Child is victim
Risk to child relative to risks to society
Child is victim and victimizer
Risks large, concrete, imminent
Magnitude of risk
Risks small, intangible, distant
Angelique, the battered child
Julie, the angry girl friend
Kevin, the armed robber
Paul the drunk driver
Tina, the malnourished adolescent
Chris, the angry son
Royce, the persistent delinquent
Alphonse, the runaway
Tom, the late-night loiterer

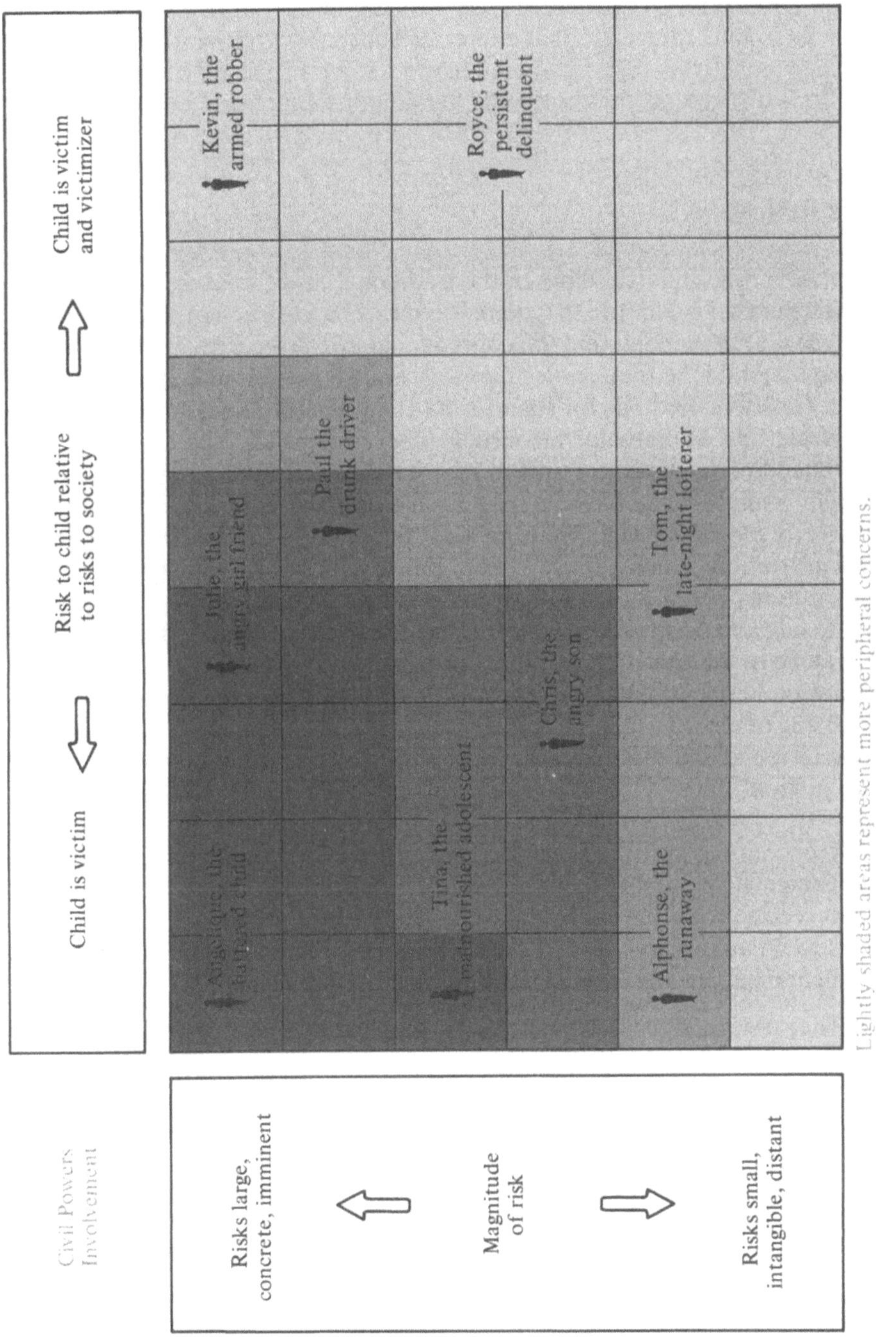
Child is victim
Risk to child relative to risks to society
Child is victim and victimizer
Kevin, the armed robber
Royce, the persistent delinquent
Paul the drunk driver
Julie, the angry girl friend
Tom, the late-night loiterer
Chris, the angry son
Angelique, the battered child
Tina, the malnourished adolescent
Alphonse, the runaway
Lightly shaded areas represent more peripheral concerns.
Civil Powers Involvement
Risks large, concrete, imminent
Magnitude of risk
Risks small, intangible, distant

social circumstances under which the children are being raised, and we seem willing to intervene. Moreover, viewing the enterprise of juvenile justice as a civil enterprise that exercises supervisory powers over children and those who care for them answers some of the most important objections directed at the traditional version of the juvenile court.

Conclusion

In my view, the principal flaws of the traditional juvenile court are not in its basic purposes. Nor are they in the scope of its jurisdiction. Rather the errors are (1) in thinking that the court can do all the work by itself, (2) in making the child the focus of legal power, and (3) in failing to experiment with a variety of methods for supervising children that draw more heavily on private and community resources. The conception of a civil court superintending families (and others who have responsibility for children) seeks to remedy these flaws by putting the court at a distance from the actual process of raising children. The conception operates by holding other institutions responsible for their part in child rearing. It thus draws in institutions better situated than the court to do the essential work of supervising and caring for children, shifts the focus of the court from the child alone to the child in the context of those who can supervise and care for him or her, and makes it natural for the court to think in terms of mobilizing others to support the natural family and community rather than trying to replace it. Because this form of court engagement is loose and more indirect than that of the traditional court, it seems to use less state authority, to run fewer risks of establishing narrow conceptions of virtue, and to encourage more experimentation with different community-based arrangements for supervising children.

This second conception of the juvenile court and juvenile justice system seems to be a more just and useful conception of the enterprise than the first. More specifically, my conclusions are the following:

1. The subject of juvenile justice is as much concerned with the conditions under which children are raised as it is about the criminal conduct of children. More provocatively, the juvenile court and the juvenile justice system are more properly concerned with superintending the conditions under which children are prepared for citizenship than they are with guarding the society from the criminal conduct of children or rehabilitating the children once they have committed crimes.

2. The principal role the juvenile court can play in managing the process of socialization is to lend its authority to overseeing the process as it is carried on by parents and children and by other private and public agencies. The court's job is to stand for the public importance of the task, to establish and maintain minimal standards of performance, and to hold

both those who care for children and the children themselves responsible for their performance. Moreover, when it is clear that existing arrangements for caring for children are inadequate, the court must redistribute the responsibilities so that performance can be improved.

3. The family is not just a private institution. It is also importantly a public institution with an important public function: to help its children reach the status of resourceful and responsible citizenship. In doing this it must protect, supervise, and guide its children.

4. Children, too, have public responsibilities. Like adult citizens, they must respect the lives, property, and physical well-being of other citizens. In addition, children have special public responsibilities, namely, to equip themselves for effective citizenship. As a practical matter, this means taking the advice of parents and guardians, going to school, and avoiding activities where their inexperience and untested judgment would expose them to substantial hazards.

5. The community's interest in the care and socialization of its children is large enough to make it worthwhile to develop and use a great many specialized, publicly supported institutions to help with this task. Fortunately, in virtually every community history has produced many such institutions, some of them privately supported, some publicly; some devoted to assisting parents, some devoted to the children; some providing financial assistance, others devoted to education or employment, still others devoted to psychological or medical treatment. The important objective is to deploy and use these institutions to buttress the family rather than to substitute for it or replace it.

To justify these conclusions, I and my coauthors have taken the following approach. In chapter 2 we explore the history of America's policy toward children and the development of its institutions for dealing with children who are at risk and creating risks, in order to determine what values have remained constant and which have changed over three centuries of experience. In chapter 3 we examine the political and legal mandate for the juvenile justice system, to discover whether, and if so how, the values of the community are changing with respect to the juvenile justice enterprise and what the court is being authorized to do for the society. In chapter 4 we analyze the current operations of the system, to fix the boundaries of the system, understand how it currently operates, and explore its strengths and weaknesses. In chapter 5 we look at the current work load of the systems and project the work load for the future, to test whether the system should be scaled up or down to deal with a different set of problems than it has dealt with in the past. In chapter 6 we set out and evaluate some alternative futures for the court and the juvenile justice system, in order to understand what kinds of enterprises society can create to carry out its responsibility to families. In chapter 7 we draw conclusions about the most appropriate and valuable future uses of the juvenile court and the juvenile justice system and about what investments should be made now to position them for that future.

Notes

1. These cases come from the Boston Juvenile Court. The names and a few of the nonessential facts have been changed for stylistic reasons and to protect the anonymity of the people. I am indebted to Dr. Richard W. Barnum of the Juvenile Court Clinic for assistance in locating and analyzing these cases.
2. Throughout this analysis I will distinguish between two different kinds of interests and arguments. One kind emphasizes practical or utilitarian interests and arguments. The other kind emphasizes issues of justice. The practical arguments are concerned about ends such as crime control and rehabilitation. The justice arguments are concerned about preserving proper relationships in the society: the just distribution of rights and duties across people in the society, the importance of due process protections to preserve proper relationships between the individual and the state, and the importance of holding people accountable who fail to live up to their duties. I will signal the first kind of argument through words such as *practical, wise,* and *useful.* I will signal the second kind of argument with words such as *just* and *principled.* Generally speaking, both kinds of concerns are involved in discussions of juvenile justice, but it is hard to join them. I have tried to give them equal standing in the discussion.
3. This body of law is generally taught in law schools under the heading of *Family Law*. An important text in this area is Judith C. Areen, *Family Law* (Mineola, NY: Foundation Press, 1978). Often, juvenile justice is taught as a different course. The criminal and sociological aspects of juvenile justice are sufficient to differentiate this subject from the broader subject of family law. An important text on the law of juvenile justice is that of Frank W. Miller, Robert O. Dawson, George E. Dix, and Raymond I. Parnas, *Juvenile Justice Process* (Mineola, NY: Foundation Press, 1976). A basic idea in this work is that these two fields of law need to be joined together to give a coherent account of the duties that parents and children have to one another and to the rest of the society. Once they were combined, we would discover that we had a more or less coherent body of law regulating family relationships.
4. See, for example, *McKinney's Consolidated Laws of New York Annotated,* Family Court Act, Art. 3.
5. Most curfew violations are established by local ordinance. Howard N. Snyder, John L. Hutzler, and Terrence A. Finnegan, *Delinquency in the United States, 1982* (Pittsburgh: National Center for Juvenile Justice, 1985), reported that 0.8% of delinquency referrals in 1982 were for curfew violations. For information on the general status of curfew laws see *American Jurisprudence,* 2nd ed., Vol. *42, Infants,* Sec. 19 (Rochester, NY: Lawyers Cooperative Publishing, 1969), pp. 24–25.
6. The prohibition against drinking by children may be represented in statute as a prohibition against the sale of alcoholic beverages to minors. See, for example, *Massachusetts General Laws Annotated,* Chapter 138, Sec. 34.

7. R. Hale Andrews, Jr., and Andrew H. Cohn, "Ungovernability: The unjustifiable jurisdiction," *Yale Law Journal 83*(7) (June 1974), note, pp. 1383–1409.
8. Massachusetts statute allows the court to intervene to prevent abuse regardless of which family member is the abuser and which the abused. See *Massachusetts General Laws Annotated,* chap. 209A.
9. The *Louisiana Statutes Annotated,* Civil Code Article 224, for example, mandates that parents are obligated "[t]o support, to maintain, and to educate their children according to their situation in life."
10. For a general discussion of the relationship between laws and normative practices in the society see Eugen Ehrlich, "Law and the inner order of social associations," reprinted in M. P. Golding, Ed., *The Nature of Law: Readings in Legal Philosophy* (New York: Random House, 1966), pp. 200–212.
11. There is a commonsense notion here that association with bad companions increases the likelihood of delinquency, and that delinquency increases the likelihood of criminal conduct in the future. This has been formalized into a powerful sociological theory. See Richard A. Cloward and Lloyd E. Ohlin, *Delinquency and Opportunity* (New York: Free Press, 1960). The theory is taken as axiomatic when the society considers the dangers of placing children in adult jails and prisons. The theory has less standing when it is used as a justification for giving the state power over "status offenses." In this context it is viewed as a hopeless effort to predict future criminality and a dangerous effort to extend state power over individuals on the basis of the erroneous prediction. For statistical evidence on the relationship between status offenses and future delinquency and criminality see David P. Farrington, "Early precursors of frequent offending," in volume 3 of this series. See also Solomon Kobrin and Malcolm W. Klein, *Community Treatment of Juvenile Offenders: The DSO Experiments* (Beverly Hills: Sage Publications, 1983). The basic conclusion of these studies seems to be that status offenses do increase the likelihood of future delinquency and crime, but the impact is small; that is, the likelihood of becoming an adult criminal offender is much higher if one has a record of "status offenses" in one's past, but the vast majority of "status offenders" do not become adult criminals.
12. Obviously, these are subjective judgments. Nonetheless, I think most people would agree with the ordering of these cases in this space. The Executive Session on Juvenile Justice, at least, accepted this ordering.
13. This notion that public interventions might change citizens' conceptions of their rights and responsibilities is one that has been neglected but is now coming into vogue. For an argument of this kind in the domain of welfare policy see Charles A. Murray, *Losing Ground: American Social Policy, 1950–1980* (New York: Basic Books, 1984).
14. This view is stated explicitly by the American Bar Association. See Institute of Judicial Administration–American Bar Association Joint Commission on Juvenile Justice Standards, *Juvenile Justice Standards* (Cambridge, MA: Ballinger, 1980).
15. This notion is fundamental to the theory of the liberal state. See John Stuart Mill, *On Liberty,* People's ed. (London: Longmans, Green, and Co., 1867). For a more modern discussion of the role of the criminal sanction see Herbert L. Packer, *The Limits of the Criminal Sanction* (Stanford, CA: Stanford University Press, 1968).

16. I am indebted to Martha Minow for giving me the courage to develop this perspective. For her discussion of this basic idea see Martha Minow, "The public duties of families and children," in volume 2 of this series.
17. Robert Jordan and William Warren, *Bankruptcy* (Mineola, NY: Foundation Press, 1985).
18. John E. Cribbet, *Principles of the Law of Property,* 2 ed. (Mineola, NY: Foundation Press, 1975).
19. Walter Gellhorn, Clark Byse, and Peter L. Strauss, *Administrative Law* (Mineola, NY: Foundation Press, 1979).
20. Thomas R. Bearrows, "Status offenses and offenders," in volume 2 of this series.
21. This point was made dramatically clear to me when I heard Judge Francis G. Poitrast of the Boston Juvenile Court comment on a term he served in the Boston Municipal Court. He complained about superficial treatment of the cases in the adult court. One case involved an assault in which the offender was clearly intoxicated by drugs, but no one seemed interested in that fact. Another case involved a college woman charged with prostitution, but no one seemed interested in the question of why she was hustling. His determination to look *behind* these offenses was treated as inappropriate by those in the "workgroup" of the adult court. I use the term *workgroup* in the sense developed by James Eisenstein and Herbert Jacob, *Felony Justice: An Organizational Analysis of Criminal Courts* (Boston: Little, Brown, 1977).
22. For a discussion of the role of intentionality in establishing criminal culpability see H. L. A. Hart, *Punishment and Responsibility: Essays in the Philosophy of Law* (New York: Oxford University Press, 1968), chap. 6.
23. For a discussion of how the law treats drunkenness see James F. Mosher, "Alcohol: Both blame and excuse for criminal behavior," in Robin Room and Gary Collins, Eds., *Alcohol and Disinhibition: Nature and Meaning of the Link,* Proceedings of a Conference, February 11–13, 1981, Berkeley/Oakland, CA (Washington, DC: U.S. Government Printing Office, 1983), pp. 437–478. Also see James W. Jacobs, "Putting drunk driving in perspective," unpublished mimeo, New York University School of Law, July 1985.
24. This argument has been made frequently by members of the Executive Session. (See Preface to this volume.)
25. On this notion that offices with special duties exist see Michael Oshima, "Towards a jurisprudence of children," in volume 2 of this series.
26. Susan Guarino, "Delinquent youth and family violence: A study of abuse and neglect in the homes of serious juvenile offenders" (Boston: Commonwealth of Massachusetts, Department of Youth Services, May 1985). Also see Donald Black, *The Behavior of Law* (New York: Academic Press, 1976).
27. On the issue of whether status offenders become adult criminals see note 11.
28. On the dangers of using predictions as a basis for state intervention see Alan M. Dershowitz, "The law of dangerousness: Some fictions about predictions," *Journal of Legal Education 23* (1970), pp. 24–47.

2
The Historical Legacy

With George L. Kelling

Resourceful, independent, and responsible citizens are the basic elements of a liberal society. Such a society assumes that its citizens have well-formed tastes and values, are capable of expressing and advancing their interests, and are fully responsible for their conduct and condition. In short, its citizens are on their own. These assumptions justify many of the basic institutions of the liberal society such as voting, free speech, private property, a free market in labor, and the criminal law.

Children have always been an anomaly in the liberal system. Children are vulnerable, rather than resourceful; developing, rather than independent; and, by virtue of their inexperience, not fully responsible for their actions. In short, they are dependents. They need care and supervision in the short run (lest they put themselves or others at risk) and investment and guidance over the long run (lest they fail to become resourceful citizens).

A liberal society prefers to rely on private institutions and motivations to accomplish public tasks. Consequently, in providing for the care, protection, and supervision of its children, such a society relies almost exclusively on the family. No other course is consistent with a liberal society's respect for the privacy and freedom of its citizens. No other course accepts and fosters the cultural diversity that is the hallmark of a liberal regime. And no other course is as well designed to exploit the natural advantages that parents have as guardians, supervisors, and developers of their children.[1]

For the most part, this institutional arrangement works harmoniously. Parents and children work out relationships with one another that seem just and fair. The relationships accomplish the task of preparing the children for full citizenship in the society. The issue of the society's role in managing these relationships never arises.

Occasionally, however, the relationships break down. Parents separate or die, leaving children exposed to natural hazards and the demands of the society. Parents sometimes lack the economic or psychological resources necessary to supervise or raise a child effectively. Or, instead of protecting and guiding their children, parents sometimes abuse and neglect them. On occasion, children find their relationships with their parents so difficult that they flee.

In such circumstances, society's responsibility toward families and children becomes an issue. The issue is problematic because it requires the society to address ideologically painful questions, specifically, whether children have a special status in the society and if so, what the substantive content of that special status is. What special rights and privileges do children have? What special responsibilities? The society must also decide what powers it has with respect to supervising parents and others who have assumed responsibilities for caring for children. It must further determine whether it has a particular substantive idea of what constitutes a good child or appropriate child care and supervision. Such questions are extremely threatening because they seem to entangle the state in intimate relationships and conduct on the basis of a subjective conception of virtue. And this seems profoundly illiberal. On the other hand, if the society fails to involve itself it risks the future of some of its children and consequently the justice and security of the society at large.[2]

Over time, the American society has responded to this recurrent dilemma in different ways. In organizing its response, the society has been guided by shared ideas about the status of children in families and society, the nature of children's needs, and the role of community or public institutions in responding to children who are needy, at risk, or committing crimes.

This chapter reviews these ideas over three centuries of American experience.[3] Inevitably, the review will be superficial. Moreover, given the regional, cultural, and class diversity of the American society, any effort to characterize the American view of children and of public responsibilities to children will inevitably fail to capture the real variety of America's experience. Nonetheless, by examining the broad ideas that guided America's public responses to children during the colonial period, the revolutionary period, the Jacksonian period, the post-civil-war period, and the progressive era, we might be able to see what is durable, what seems to change, and which of the changes seem likely to endure.[4]

Basically, five concepts have remained constant over this period: (1) Throughout our history, the society has seen children as dependents, not as rights-bearing, responsible adults. (2) This view has always mitigated the criminal responsibility of children. (3) The society has always acknowledged its prudential interests in the successful development of its children. (4) It has always relied on natural parents or other legal guardians to accomplish this job. (5) The society has always been willing to intervene if the parents were absent, incapacitated, or unmotivated. In essence, the society has always taken some responsibility for superintending the conditions under which children are raised.

Within this general set of relationships, much in particular has changed. The economic and social development of the society has transformed the tasks and social relations of children. In the past, children were deeply enmeshed in the family. They had relationships with few other social institutions. They made important economic contributions to the family at a young age. And their vocational, general, and moral education was integrated with the work and relationships in the family. Over three centuries, however, the grip of the family loosened. Children began to work outside the home, to go to public schools, and to associate with their peers. Their economic contributions came when they were older, after a long period of general education. These changes gave children a modicum of individual liberty earlier in life than before. As a result they began to have relationships with the rest of the society that were unmediated by their parents. At the same time, their economic dependence began to last longer, and they did not achieve the full status of citizenship until a much older age. Thus, children began to have a more complex and abstract set of relationships. The role of parents changed from one of social and economic power to that of a coach who tries to give meaning and coherence to a complex set of relationships outside the coach's control.

This new set of relationships created more room for public interventions. Originally, the community intervened when the parents were absent, when the child committed crimes, or when the parents complained about the child. The intervention aimed generally to create or restore effective parental control. However, once the child attained a somewhat independent status vis-a-vis the parents, society could begin to view parents as a potential threat to their child as well as the guarantors of his or her welfare. This created a new justification for intervention: protection *from* parents and legal guardians.

Interest in children spawned the development of many specialized institutions such as schools, child protection societies, and welfare agencies. These institutions changed the form and content of public interventions. In one dimension, the form changed from moral exhortation (or the use of coercive authority) to a greater reliance on provision of assistance and resources to children or their families. In a related but different dimension, public interventions changed from informal community pressure backed by the threat of court action to interventions mounted by private and public child assistance bureaucracies. These new agencies and forms of intervention also provided new platforms from which to observe the conduct and condition of children, and thereby widened the front for public intervention. Thus the justifications, form, and content of public interventions into the lives of children have all changed with great significance for the current choices the society must make.

The Colonial Period: 1600–1730

Colonial Americans viewed the family as having the (nearly) exclusive right and responsibility for raising children. As Thomas Hobbes explained: "The Father and Master, being *before* the Institution of Common-wealth, absolute Sovereigns in their own Families, they lose afterward no more of their Authority than the Common-wealth taketh from them."[5] This institutional arrangement was particularly well understood and important in the northern colonies, to which the colonists came in intact families organized around church and family. It was more an abstract ideal in the south, to which many colonists came as unattached individuals.[6]

The reliance on the family as the basic social unit was entirely consistent with the economic arrangements of the time. From a young age, children were valued for their economic contributions. On colonial farms there were a great many household chores that 10-year-old children could perform successfully with minimal guidance from parents. Such work was seen as a benefit to the child as well as to the family. As one commentator observed:

> [A] common social idea [of this period] was that the family or household served as the principal educator of children. Church and school, though valued for their contributions, were subservient to the family in turning unruly, immature children into dutiful subjects. The family introduced children to social customs and both cultivated and tested their ability to perform worthwhile services.[7]

The family's efforts to educate through work were supplemented in three ways. First, a few colonies laid the foundation for a system of public education. An authoritative historian noted the following example:

> In 1647 the [General] Court [of the Commonwealth of Massachusetts] required towns of fifty households to maintain a schoolmaster for elementary skills, and required larger towns of one hundred households to maintain a grammar schoolmaster. . . . Fines were to be exacted from the selectmen for failure to comply. It was left to the town to choose the means of supporting the school.[8]

Second, the apprenticeship system, which bound children to do economic work for masters, included requirements that the master provide useful education for the apprentice. Indeed, the main distinction between an apprentice and a servant was the master's obligation to teach the former a specific trade. The main distinction between the English and American apprenticeship system was the American emphasis on general education.[9] Finally, provision was made for poorer families to apprentice their children to wealthier families to take advantage of the superior opportunities the wealthier families presented. As one historian noted:

Two types of apprenticeships developed side by side: voluntary, where the child and his parents or guardians entered into the agreement on their own initiative, and compulsory, where orphan or poor or neglected children were bound out by the authorities.[10]

The family was considered such an important institution that those who did not live in families were encouraged to do so. Indeed, in a few colonies, laws were passed requiring single people to live within families.[11] Orphaned children were placed in families by church or town officials. The contracts written in such cases give a remarkably clear picture of the publicly sanctioned structure of relationships among parents, children, and the society. For example:

I, Thomas May, clerk of Petsworth Parish in Gloucester County [Virginia], do firmly in the name . . . of the vestry of parish above said bind unto Ralph Bevis of the said parish and county a mulatto boy named George Petsworth of the age of two years old . . . to serve him, the said Ralph Bevis . . . in all manner of lawful services and employments that he shall set him about. And the said Ralph Bevis doth bind and oblige himself [and] his heirs, etc. to give the said mulatto boy three years of schooling and to carefully instruct him afterwards that he may read well in any part of the Bible; also to instruct and learn him . . . such lawful way or ways that he may be able after his indent time expired to get his own living, and to allow him sufficient meat, drink, washing and apparel until the expiration of said time.[12]

Although the family was viewed as the predominant socializing institution, and parents' rights were considered quite sacred and inviolable, the community sought to bolster families through moral exhortation from the pulpit and occasionally through public laws. As a historian noted:

More important [than draconian laws for disobedience by children] was a series of laws designed to encourage parents to meet the responsibilities that social theory and biblical injunction placed upon them. Beginning with the Massachusetts law of 1642 that required parents to see that their children and other dependents were taught reading and a trade, the New England colonies tried to make the family function as a broadly educational and socializing institution.[13]

Although children played an important economic role, they were viewed as being entirely subservient to their parents or other legal guardians. Consistent with this philosophy, the children were judged to be incapable of criminal offenses before the age of 7.[14] Between the ages of 7 and 14, they were presumed innocent unless evidence of a criminal state of mind could be presented. Punishments for crimes were draconian but rarely applied.[15] Public humiliation was the most common sanction.

Thus, in the colonial period the society dealt with the issue of socializing children largely through the family. The family was sovereign as long as it met its responsibilities to supervise and raise its children. If it failed, it was subjected to public intervention—sometimes the stocks.

The Revolutionary Period: 1730–1820

The institutional arrangements for socializing children that characterized the colonial period were shaken, but only slightly, by the trends of the revolutionary period. The era is more interesting for what it presaged for the future than for the changes that occurred during it. All of the trends that were important in this era quickened in the Jacksonian era.

Perhaps the most significant developments concerned changes in the perceived status of children within the family. No doubt the revolutionary spirit had its impact: If fathers could become free of the burden of the crown, it was only natural to think that children, too, might breathe the air of freedom. This view was exemplified by John Locke's solicitousness of the standing of children. Whereas Hobbes would have emphasized the child's need of restraint and control, and parental sovereignty over children, Locke found room in his theories of education and child rearing for development of the child's capacity for self-restraint and reason:

> He that has not a mastery over his inclinations, he that knows not how to resist the importunity of pleasure or pain, for the sake of what reason tells him is fit to be done, wants the true principle of virtue and industry; and is in danger of never being good for anything. . . .
>
> On the other side, if the mind be curbed and humbled too much in children; if their spirits be abased and broken much, by too strict a hand over them, they lose all their vigor and industry. . . .
>
> To avoid the danger that is on either hand is the great art: . . . he, I say, that knows how to reconcile these seeming contradictions, has, in my opinion, got the true secret of education.[16]

The increased tolerance for the independence of children was obvious to observers from Europe, who noted the relative informality of relations within the American family. American children were seen as more independent, more willing to challenge the authority of their parents, and more given to expressing their own views—even to the point of contradicting their parents. As de Tocqueville noted in 1835: "In democratic countries . . . the language addressed by a son to his father is always marked by mingled freedom, familiarity, and affections which at once show that new relations have sprung up in the bosom of the family."[17]

Indeed, this tolerance for independence extended even to so important a domain as religion. The revolutionary period included the era of the "great awakening."[18] Previously, the authority of parents included the right to define the religious views and activities of their children. During the great awakening, however, children were seen as having emotional, religious experiences of their own, which provided the basis for religious conversion. For the first time, children were seen as having some independent voice in choosing their own religion.

The loosening of the tight bonds between parents and children was reflected in economic relationships as well. In the revolutionary period, manufacturing enterprises began to appear, challenging the relationships that were built around family farms and the apprenticeship system for trades. This was particularly important, because work relationships had previously been seen as the principal means for educating children into responsible citizenship. If those relationships were transformed, the society had lost a main mechanism for educating and socializing children. As a result, the issue of whether factories were good or bad places for children appeared on the public agenda. One commentator described the issue in the following terms:

> In principle, the employment of children in factories was not drastically different from the colonial precedent of child labor. . . . In reality, the labor of children in factories introduced novel conditions and required special adjustment. In the earlier practice of household production, children were not distinguished from adults. They shared in the burden of domestic chores. In the factory system, . . . the household ceased to be a self-governing economic unit. Paternal authority became separate from labor instruction and supervision. The father still had to decide whether his child should be employed . . . but in the factory room, the members of the family became part of a crowd.[19]

The society seemed perplexed by this situation. On the one hand, advocates of manufacturing stressed the potential advantages of the new economic arrangements. An observer in 1794 noted:

> It was perceived that children, too young for labor, could be kept from idleness and rambling, and of course from early temptations to vice, by placing them for a time in manufactories, and that the means of their parents to clothe, feed, and educate them, could be thereby increased.[20]

On the other hand, there was deep suspicion about the adequacy of these arrangements for educating children. Children working in factories had none of the legal protections that apprentices had because the relationship between the factory owner and the child laborer differed from that between the master and the apprentice.[21]

To restore the link between child labor and moral and general education, the society tried to force the factories to provide these services. An 1813 Connecticut statute mandating the education of children in factories read:

> The . . . directors of all factories which . . . are . . . legally incorporated . . . shall cause that the children employed in such factory or establishment, whether bound by indenture, by parol agreement, or in any other manner, be taught to read and write, . . . and that due attention be paid to the preservation of their morals.[22]

In addition, in response to such legislation or to the promptings of their own conscience, some factory owners established Sunday schools for the education of the children who worked in their factories. Initially, these were charity schools devoted to general education. Eventually, however, they were taken over by religious societies that wanted to use them for biblical instruction as well.[23] Such arrangements reached only a small fraction of those employed in manufacturing, however, so the public concern about children's education remained.

Indeed, public concern about education was expressed in the development of institutions outside the home and factory as well as within. The basis for public education was gradually expanded. The institutional innovation was the "academy": an institution for secondary education.[24] Academies were managed by private boards but were publicly chartered and subsidized. More important than the appearance of these quasi-public schools, however, was the fact that elites of this period, including Thomas Jefferson, began advocating that the public assume responsibility for general education.[25] They argued that a democratic government had to rely on an educated citizenry, and that the only way to ensure such citizens was to provide education on a public basis. Although this principle was not widely adopted due to insufficient public resources, it was accepted as an ideal for a new democracy.

The emerging social and economic autonomy of children, and the gradual urbanization of the society, brought the issue of crimes committed by children into a different focus. Although colonial laws made a clear-cut distinction between children and adults with respect to crime, one has the sense that the cases were dealt with quite informally in the context of well-established community relationships. Social control was exerted through informal community means rather than through formal institutions of justice. As the cities developed, however, the informal arrangements operating beneath the laws gave way. As they did so, children who committed crimes began to be exposed to the full force of a developing criminal law. Since at the time the society as a whole was engaged in a revolution against unjust laws, the justice of exposing children to the criminal law without the mediation of family, church, and community began to raise concerns. As one civic group working in New York complained in 1819:

> Those unfortunate children from 10 to 18 years of age, who from neglect of parents, from idleness and misfortune, have . . . contravened some penal statute without reflecting on the consequences, and for a hasty violation, been doomed to the penitentiary by the condemnation of the law . . . [deserve better treatment].[26]

The society's solution for this injustice was to take the children out of jail and bind them over to people who needed work done.[27] In effect, the old apprenticeship system was used for crime control and punishment.

Thus, in the revolutionary period, the public response to children changed in subtle ways in response to currents broader than just those shaping the society.

The Jacksonian/Antebellum Period: 1830–1860

The social and economic quickening of the revolutionary period became chaotic by the mid-19th century. Under the pressures of economic growth, urbanization, and the first large wave of immigration, the initial diversity of the American population was stretched to the limit. As Bremner observed:

> What did slave children, immigrant children in city slums, children of pioneer farmers, children of a doctor or minister in a comfortable home, and the children of a proud aristocrat on a plantation or those of a wealthy New England merchant really have in common? . . . Little wonder then that experiences of childhood and youth are so elusive. At that early point in life when social institutions have had little opportunity to produce some semblance of uniformity, the spectrum of potential experience stretched wider than at any other time.[28]

Such a heterogeneous society required a philosophy that gave standing to individual freedom and revered the capacity of each individual to make his or her own destiny. Thus, rationalism (especially that of John Locke) began to replace traditional Protestant theology as a dominant social philosophy. These trends inevitably invaded the family. Bremner observed:

> The processes and principles of an individualistic, laissez-faire, white democracy were penetrating government, the economy, churches, and even so traditionally aristocratic an institution as the family. . . . The hierarchical family, reaching its apex in the father, was undermined and finally levelled by the force of democratic social principles. . . . American children were more independent, individualistic, and socially precocious than their European counterparts; they were less polite and deferential to adults.[29]

To create some order in these conditions, the society was forced to rely increasingly on the law. But it was not the common law rooted in custom and enforced by community institutions. Increasingly it was an abstract law established by legislatures and legal commentators, who sought to rationalize a crazy-quilt pattern of case dispositions concerning the custody of children and the rights and responsibilities of children to parents and parents to children.[30] These relationships were set out in clear, if not precise, legal language. James Kent, an early commentator, described them in these terms:

> The duties of parents to their children . . . consist in maintaining and educating them during the season of infancy and youth, and in making reasonable provision for their future usefulness and happiness in life. . . .
>
> In consequence of the obligation of the father to provide for the maintenance, and, in some qualified degree, for the education of his infant children, he is entitled to the custody of their persons, and to the value of their labor and services.[31]

The aim of these laws was to arrange relationships so that ideal children could be produced: children who in Bremner's words "would be independent but in agreement on essentials with parents as a result of free choice."[32]

Inevitably these efforts failed, for they were abstract words directed at an enormous social problem. As Bremner observed:

> An unprecedented wave of migrations in the middle of the nineteenth century confronted America with new social problems. From 1790 to 1820 only about 250,000 immigrants entered the United States, while from 1815 to 1860 5,000,000 immigrants poured into a population which in 1820 numbered about 10,000,000 and in 1860 31,000,000. . . . The immigrant child did not import delinquency and dependency to America. Yet, the staggering influx of immigrant poor aggravated existing conditions of destitution.[33]

To deal with this problem, the society reached for more powerful institutions.

In the past, the bulwarks of child development had been protective parents, productive work, and moral and general education provided in the home or work place. Now, all of these were crumbling.

The influence of parents was weakened by the general liberalizing trend, by the growing economic independence of children, and by growth of cities. Rural parents found it increasingly difficult to keep their children in traditional occupations at home. Immigrant parents found themselves unable to maintain their families as viable economic and social units in the midst of alien cities. Thus, the cities accumulated children who were separated from their parents.

To deal with this problem, voluntaristic organizations organized along sectarian religious lines made their appearance. Organizations such as the American Bible Society (1816), the American Sunday School Movement (1824), the American Tract Society (1825), and the Young Men's Christian Association (YMCA) (1851) sought to supplement the family as supervisors, protectors, and socializers of children.[34] These organizations offered programs for children that emphasized discipline, order, and respect for authority. The values they stood for included piety, obedience, chastity, industriousness, and sobriety.[35]

Such programs were based on a new idea: that the general environment surrounding a child had an important effect on his or her development. The child's destiny did not lie in fate or in personal moral character: It lay in the social environment. When environmental influences were corrupting (as they were in the cities), and when parents were ineffective in shielding the child from these influences, there was an important problem to be managed. The residential and recreational programs offered by organizations like the YMCA were one response. The most extreme expression of this idea was Charles Loring Brace's program to take poor and delinquent children from the streets of New York City and ship them to families on the western frontier where they would be free of the evils of city life.[36] This program formed the core of the Children's Aid Society founded in 1853.

The other response was to seek to regulate social conditions in the key institutions in contact with children that might threaten their future. Thus, judges were increasingly willing to intervene in family affairs to protect the interests of the children. As Bremner observed:

> During the first half of the nineteenth century, the judges' determination of the welfare of the child . . . began to override the formal rights of parents. . . . This trend was most apparent in custody cases. Courts began to favor mothers . . . on the grounds that the child's future welfare depended on a mother's care.[37]

In addition, the laws requiring factories to provide educational opportunities for children or to give them time to attend school were expanded, but were rarely enforced.[38] Finally, laws regulating, sometimes even prohibiting, use of liquor and prostitution were passed to minimize the exposure of children to these vices. Thus, for the first time, the law was used not against parents and children who failed to meet their responsibilities to the society, but instead against those institutions that threatened the social environment in which children were growing up. Because the family was no longer so dominant, the law had to stretch wider to encompass the conditions that affected the growth and development of children.

An equally significant development occurred in the domain of public schooling. Previously, although everyone agreed on the importance of both general and moral education for children, it was thought best to leave this education in private hands—in the bosom of the family for traditional families, and in special academies for those wealthy enough to be able to afford them. In this period, however, new support appeared for publicly supported education of children. If pluralism was to be overcome and traditional American values protected against the onslaught of immigration, public education was essential.

Indeed, two principal justifications for public schools were offered and established during this period. One justification, a narrow one focused on security issues, was expressed by Daniel Webster:

> I must yet advert to another most interesting topic,—the Free Schools. In this particular, New England may be allowed to claim, I think, a merit of peculiar character. She early adopted, and has constantly maintained the principle, that it is the undoubted right and the bounden duty of government to provide for the instruction of all youth. *That which is elsewhere left to chance or charity, we secure by law. . . . We regard it as a wise and liberal system of police, by which property, and life, and the peace of society are secured.* We seek to prevent in some measure the extension of the penal code, by inspiring a salutory and conservative principle of virtue and of knowledge in an early age. . . . We hope to continue and prolong the time, when, in the villages and farm-houses of New England, there may be undisturbed sleep within unbarred doors.[39]

The other principle is a broader one aimed at producing virtuous rather than simply law-abiding citizens. That principle was articulated by Horace Mann:

Under a republican government it seems clear that the minimum of this education [the one to which every human being has an absolute right] *can never be less than such as is sufficient to qualify each citizen for the civil and social duties he will be called to discharge*—such an education as teaches the individual the great laws of bodily health; as qualifies for the fulfillment of parental duties; as is indispensable for the civil functions of a witness or a juror; as is necessary for the voter in municipal affairs; and finally for the faithful and conscientious discharge of all those duties which devolve upon the inheritor of a portion of the sovereignty of this great republic.[40]

The result of these ideas was the common school movement, based largely on the ideas of Jefferson and including a commitment to common textbooks, separation into classes, and grading of students.[41] This movement established a foothold in the East and spread rapidly through the Midwest.

Thus, the society became much more active in creating attractive environments for children. It used the law to regulate the family and work place to this end. It used voluntary associations to find or create such environments when parents were absent or ineffective. And it began spending public money on an educational system justified in terms of promoting security or of increasing the quality of citizenship offered by children. Nonetheless, some children continued to fall through the cracks as a result of poverty, mental disease, or moral turpitude. To deal with children and also adults in these categories, the society explored new institutional arrangements.

The basic options for public care of the poor were clearly set out by an analyst of Rhode Island's practices in the mid-19th century:

Four different modes are pursued by the towns in maintaining their poor.
1st. By vending them to the lowest bidder;

2d. By contracting for their maintenance, with an individual, or individuals, through the agency of a committee or otherwise.

3d. By placing all the poor in one Asylum owned by the town;

4th. By placing all such in an Asylum as are bereft of home and friends, and administering out-door relief to such as have.[42]

The new ideas in this analysis are that the public should take responsibility for the poor, that the poor should be supported with public funds, and that one of the options is publicly supported asylums.

Indeed, one of the important social inventions of this period is the public institution as a device for dealing with the insane and also the criminal. For the first time in the United States, asylums and penitentiaries were built with public funds to house these populations away from communities. These facilities were seen as a humanitarian reform of previous practices which, in the case of the insane, included simple neglect and, in the case of crime, included corporal punishment and public humiliation.[43] On the assumption that the causes of crime were to be found in lack of discipline and obedience, the institutions for criminals emphasized these virtues. The prison was a place of solitude, silence, industry, obedience, and quick punishment for infractions.[44] Prisoners were isolated from their community and family.

The first institution for juvenile offenders, New York City's House of Refuge, was opened in 1825.[45] In 1847, Massachusetts opened the first state reform school for "changeable delinquents."[46] The emphasis in such institutions was on obedience, tidiness, punctuality, and so on. After a year in residence, youths could be bound out as servants or apprentices—an option that was less expensive to the state and potentially more valuable in the reformation of the child.

Thus, in this period, public concern for the conditions under which children were being raised and the role the public played in their supervision, care, and protection increased dramatically.

The Post-Civil War Period: 1860–1890

Two problems with society's role emerged following the Civil War. First, urban reformers became discouraged by the ineffectiveness of tract and Sunday school movements. Second, institutional programs started to take on the characteristics that are deplored today: abuse of inmates, overcrowding, and failure to prepare inmates to return to the community. Each problem stimulated important changes in the society's response to children at risk or creating risks.

From the point of view of urban reformers, conditions in the cities continued to deteriorate. In political terms, the cities were increasingly dominated by politicians representing non-Protestant immigrants. Their values seemed threatening to the Protestant establishment.[47] Moreover, urban violence was becoming much more common. Some urban disorder took the form of labor unrest, a much more fundamental threat to the society than street crime. The tract movement waned. Sunday schools continued, as did YMCAs. But to meet the new challenges, reformers developed two original, but quite distinct, voluntary organizations.

The first was the Charity Organization Society. For adherents of this approach, the roots of urban poverty were to be found in the character flaws and moral deficiency of the individual.[48] The basic goal was to get the poor to recognize their flaws and deficiencies and take steps to correct themselves. The vehicle for this education was the "friendly visitor"—a middle- or upper-class woman volunteer who would visit the individual and provide the elevating influence of a moral superior.[49] In addition to befriending the poor individual (i.e., providing a moral example as well as advice on child rearing, morals, and the value of cleanliness), the friendly visitor developed a social history—data about the individual and family that ostensibly allowed diagnosis of the defects that led to poverty and prescription of treatment.[50]

This social history, developed without the knowledge of the subject, was the centerpiece of another innovation: linkages among social service organizations. Information about families was circulated among private agencies and between public and private agencies, so that efforts at reform could be coordinated and decisions made by public relief agencies about whether to provide financial assistance.[51]

During this era a conflict developed between Protestant reformers on the one hand and Jewish and Catholic leaders on the other. Reformers, perhaps with mixed motives but proclaiming that their interests were to keep children out of institutions, advocated placing children in proper foster homes.[52] "Proper" often meant Protestant. Jews and Catholics, instead, developed sectarian *institutions* as a mean of maintaining their religious and cultural identity.

Thus, the Charity Organization Society, with Mary Richmond as its most famous spokesperson, made three distinct contributions to future child welfare and social work: the friendly visitor (the antecedent of the social caseworker), the social history, and the social service network.

The second voluntary organization to develop during this era was the settlement house. The most famous, Hull House, was opened in Chicago in 1899 by Jane Addams.[53] Although sharing many common assumptions with the Charity Organization Society, the settlement house movement emphasized the environmental causes of poverty—primarily the slum—rather than individual causes.[54]

Foreshadowing community organization techniques, settlement workers concentrated their efforts on the community rather than on the individual. In contrast to friendly visitors, who collected data on individuals, voluntary live-in settlement workers collected data on neighborhoods and communities. These data were to be used to assist the community in exerting moral force on its members as well as in making claims on the broader community for resources and assistance. This approach laid the groundwork for the development of both community organization and political action as social work methodologies.

Regardless of the approach, however, positivist theories about the etiology of deviance, crime, and poverty came to dominate old-fashioned moral theories. Heretofore, theories of crime had emphasized the responsibility of the criminal. Positivists, so named because of their claim to the use of scientific methods, now stressed the power of physiological and psychological factors as causes of crime. This change had marked implications for the moral status of offenders and the proper target of social interventions. Although *physiological* determinants of criminal behavior were emphasized by early positivists, following the tenets of Lombroso and others, *psychological* theories quickly came to the fore, especially in the thought of new penologists. These theories, less deterministic than physiological ones, suggested that the cause of crime was to be found in the upbringing and socialization of children. Consistent with this thinking, treatment rather than punishment seemed the most reasonable way to overcome these social problems.

These theories had an important effect on the way public institutions for criminals and delinquents were managed. Indeed, they formed the basis for a "new penology" that saw the causes of crime in individual pathology and their cure in psychological treatment. Youth crime was seen as temporary and reversible. Programmatically, youths were to be separated from adults and placed in reformatories rather than prisons, indeterminate sentences were to replace fixed sentences, and nurture was to replace coercion as the basic mode of changing offenders. No intrinsic conflict was seen between custody and rehabilitation. The Elmira reformatory, opened in 1874, was an expression of this new philosophy of managing delinquent children within public institutions.[55]

This period also produced a sharp break with the past in that doubts began to be raised about the value of work for children. In 1890, reformers, influenced by new psychological and physiological theories of development, began to challenge the idea that children should have a significant economic role in the family.[56] Indeed, many middle- and upper-class persons criticized immigrant families for exploiting children for economic purposes. Reformers began to charge that children were exploited in a variety of ways: being paid low wages, having prolonged apprenticeships, and not being provided education as required by laws in most states.[57]

During this period the educational system began to differentiate into the patterns we are familiar with today. The academy gave way to the publicly funded high school, as the need to educate those too poor to pay their way in academies grew.[58] The number of private colleges continued to increase, and the Morril Act of 1862, which provided land grants to states, accelerated the growth of public colleges and universities.[59] Compulsory attendance in grade and high school, however, was to wait until the progressive era—until the enforcement of compulsory attendance laws in those states that had them, and the adoption of such laws in those that did not.

The Progressive Era: 1890–1920

The creation of the Urban Municipal League in New York City in 1894 by the Reverend Charles Parkhurst is generally identified as the symbolic beginning of the progressive era.[60] Parkhurst and his followers were concerned about political corruption, vice, liquor use, and maintenance of middle-class morality. They looked back at the major reform efforts of the 19th century with considerable frustration: Despite the efforts of two generations of reformers, conditions in the cities were, from their point of view, deplorable.

Government itself, influenced by "machine" politics, was corrupt. If reform were to be reality, it would have to be achieved through political action. Thus, the battleground shifted. Although private sector efforts at reform continued through the activities of organizations like settlement houses and the Charity Organization Society, attempts at reform now concentrated on the public governmental sector. Progressives entered politics and tried to combat vice and corruption by revamping public employment through establishment of the civil service system, opposing machine politics (often dominated by ethnic groups with different perceptions of morality), transferring city authority to state government (control of the police, for example), and successfully pushing for legislation to control drinking and prostitution (resulting in the Volstead and Mann Acts). Social legislation began to define public and private morality, and the machinery of government enforced adherence to the definitions. Private collective efforts thus began to yield to public policies and programs.

There were trends in Progressivism that did not emphasize coercion, however. The means to moral goals were not to impose duties on individuals, but instead to eliminate bad conditions that adversely affected individuals. Positive environmentalists rejected the Jacksonian assumption that cities were inherently evil. They believed instead that an attractive and nourishing environment would prove to be far more powerful in shaping behavior than either personal contacts with "moral superiors" or legal coercion. Rejecting individualistic and group theories about the etiology of deviance and locating it instead in an impoverished environment, they believed that vice met certain unfilled human needs. Consequently, their solution to vice was an enriched urban environment: parks, playgrounds, public housing, and other urban amenities.

In 1904, G. Stanley Hall published *Adolescence,* symbolizing the culmination of a developing line of thought regarding youth.[61] It expanded and gave expression to a view of youth in which adolescence was defined by a biological maturation process and accompanying social and psychological "storm and stress." Adolescence became a "time between" childhood and maturity during which the child was reformed with new drives, energy, and values.[62] In itself, the idea that changes occurred at puberty was not new to this era; indeed, romantic ideas about adolescence existed long before the invention of adolescence as a discrete period of life. What was new was the idea that all aspects of a youth's life should be viewed in terms of this period: social development, education, values and interests, relations with parents, vocational development, and relations with the other sex. Moreover, it was during this era that adolescence was to become a universal experience for all young persons, not just upper- or middle-class youth. Educational and child-supporting institutions, including the juvenile court, developed their programs around this invention.

It was also during this era that the child-saving movement reached its apex. Although the term *child saving* may have a derisive tone today, the movement itself was a greatly respected enterprise in its time. Platt traced its intellectual origins:

> The child-saving movement, like all moral crusades, reaffirmed ideal values and stressed the positive capacities of traditional institutions. The child savers' ideology was an amalgam of convictions and aspirations. From the medical profession, they borrowed the imagery of pathology, infection, immunization, and treatment; from the tenets of social Darwinism, they derived their pessimistic views about the intractability of human nature and the innate moral defects of the lower classes; finally, their ideas about the biological and environmental origins of crime can be attributed to the positivist tradition in European criminology and anti-urban sentiments associated with the Protestant, rural ethic.[63]

To a large extent it was a movement dominated by middle- and upper-class women. At its roots, it was prepared to use governmental authority to enforce certain moral standards: Neither parents nor children who were to be targets of reform would be able to withdraw from efforts at their reformation. The goals of child savers were complex. They included maintenance of traditional middle-class values, protection of children from abuse, restriction and regulation of child labor, supervision of children, efficient law enforcement, universal education, and elimination of sources of corruption (liquor and prostitution). Although defining itself as above politics, the movement used its influence to obtain social legislation and create professional institutions to carry out its goals. The moral authority of the state and its resources were harnessed for the problem of socializing children.

Some have seen laws regarding child labor as the most important social gain of child savers. Fed by ideas of child development, adolescence, the need for universal education, and exploitation of children, reformers obtained legislation in most states in the early 1900s restricting child labor. Although loopholes allowed wide-scale evasion of the intent of the laws, by the 1930s all child labor was strictly regulated in the United States.[64]

Others have believed that the creation of the Illinois Children's Court in 1899 was the most significant achievement of child savers, the culmination of social reform movements that dominated the 19th century.[65] This court inherited the concern for the social control of youth and children that initially was expressed during the Jacksonian era. From that era as well, the children's court concept derived beliefs that inadequate families and environment, especially the urban environment with its vice, gave rise to the maltreatment of children as well as to children who were obstreperous or delinquent.[66]

The children's court also inherited ideas from the new penology about pathology and disease in the etiology and handling of youths who were at risk or delinquent. Children were seen as redeemable and vulnerable to positive change efforts, whether nurturing or coercive. Custody and institutionalization were not seen as antithetical to nurturing rehabilitation.[67] All youths were portrayed as in the throes of adolescent turmoil and in need of particular forms of institutional and moral guidance—schools, for example—whether or not they or their parents felt they needed such guidance. Progressive legislation during the early 20th century gave legal status to the social invention of adolescence and defined it as a period of dependence. Additionally, adolescence was a period during which the state would have to compensate for both weaknesses in families and the inability of private efforts to overcome those weaknesses.

Furthermore, the children's court inherited ideas from child savers about what goodness in youth consisted of: obedience, punctuality, hard work, abstinence from liquor, modesty, chastity, thrift, attendance at school, studiousness, respect for authority, cleanliness, and other such virtues.

From the Charity Organization Society the children's court derived ideas about the beneficent influences of moral superiors acting in a one-to-one relationship, the value of social histories in diagnosing the etiology of problems, and the wisdom of linking social agencies into a coordinated system.[68]

Where a century of reform had failed, the architects of the juvenile court system now believed they would succeed. The court would focus on the "state" of the delinquent rather than on his or her act. Delinquency petitions replaced criminal charges. Similarly, the procedure was primarily civil, not criminal. Because state interests naturally coincided with the juvenile offender's, the hearing itself lacked procedural safeguards found in the adult court such as a jury of peers, defense counsel, and the formal rules of evidence.[69]

Moreover, the court's emphasis on saving the child (rehabilitation) meant a change in fact-finding focus from a determination of the accused's guilt or innocence to the needs of the child, based upon his or her moral character and life-style. As a result, the court enjoyed unfettered power for both presentencing investigations and postsentencing supervision.

The movement swept the country. By 1920, all but three states had created juvenile courts. These courts functioned unchanged until the early 1960s, when several Supreme Court decisions signaled a change in attitude toward individual rights and state action.

Many believed the creation of the juvenile court established the best of all possible circumstances. The interests of the individual child and the state were one and the same. The court, armed with a vision of adolescence and how adolescents and parents should and should not behave, with legal definitions of adolescence, with legal jurisdiction to intervene, and with technologies of intervention, was in place.

Conclusion

This review of America's experience in responding to children at risk or creating risks for others reveals some constant features and some that have changed as the material and social conditions of the society have changed. The constant features can be thought of as the axioms of America's response to children. Four seem particularly important.

The first concerns the status of children: Basically, children are different from adults. They are in a dependent status. This is reflected in the legal fact that no child can be without a parent or legal guardian. If a child does not have a natural guardian, the state will provide one. Children are given dependent status because they have special needs. They need protection from starvation and violence. They need instruction not only in skills for making a living but also in the moral values that guide the society. They need supervision and discipline not only so that they learn the rules of the society but also so that the society is guarded against their negligent or willful misconduct. Within this structure of care, investment, and supervision, children also need recognition of their partial autonomy. This is consistent with the demand on them to become responsible members of a free society. But having some autonomy, they also need protection against the full liabilities of such autonomy, for they are not yet knowledgeable enough or skilled enough to take their places as adults. Finally, and perhaps most importantly, they must be guided by the prospect and duty of citizenship in the society. Eventually the society will treat them as autonomous, responsible citizens even if they are not yet ready to assume the consequent duties. This reckoning must be kept in mind.

The second axiom is that the society prefers that families assume the responsibility for raising children to become successful citizens. This is consistent with a theory of justice based on ideas of rights and responsibilities of parents and children. It is also consistent with a practical observation that no other institution is as highly motivated or capable of performing this task. Families who accept the responsibility in good faith must be allowed to discharge it as they see fit in the interest of freedom and diversity throughout the society. Families that shrink from the responsibility must be challenged to accept it. Otherwise, one of the crucial institutional underpinnings of the society will be lost.

The third axiom is that the society has a broad and significant interest in the conditions under which children are reared. Indeed, it would be only a slight exaggeration to say that raising children is fundamentally a public responsibility. This is partly a matter of justice, that is, a concern to establish and maintain a proper ordering of relationships and duties throughout the society. This concern is evident in the fact that the state acts to structure the relationship between a child and a parent or legal guardian. Such action is largely automatic and therefore invisible when the natural parents are present and motivated to assume their duties. It becomes much more visible when the parents separate or when the child is put up for adoption. Then the state's role in assigning responsibility for the child is clear. It also becomes visible when parents seem unmotivated or incapable of discharging their duties. Then the state becomes involved in regulating the content of the relationship between the parents and child. This happens when either party, or a third party, judges that the parent or the child is not living up to his or her responsibilities. In the case of such disputes, the court must step in and say what is justly owed by one party to the other.

In addition to its concerns for the just ordering of relationships between parents and children, the society has a practical interest in the development of its children. If the children are not successfully habilitated, the society risks future crime, social dependence, or other less dramatic forms of failed citizenship. If the children are not protected, the society risks its own standing as a decent society that cares for its children. If the children are not given a good chance to develop, the justice of holding them accountable for acts committed when they become adults may be undermined. For all these reasons, the raising of children is importantly a public as well as a private responsibility. This has been true since parents were tutored in responsible parenting from colonial pulpits.

The fourth axiom is that the criminal responsibility of children has always been mitigated by virtue of their immaturity. This also is partly a matter of justice and partly a matter of prudence. As a matter of justice, it has always seemed wrong to hold someone criminally responsible for an act when his or her intention to commit the act was uncertain and when the person was under the supervision and influence of others. As a matter of prudence, it has often seemed wise to take advantage of the malleability of children to lure them back into a proper relationship with the society before they become committed to a life of crime. Thus, a certain amount of leniency and tolerance of the acts of children has been a constant in our history.

Within these axioms, much has changed. Indeed, one might say that each generation has given different answers to how these basic axioms are reflected in particular social arrangements.

Some of the most striking changes have occurred in the society's conceptions about what children need to become responsible citizens. At the outset, childhood was viewed as a fairly short period lasting from infancy to the age of about 10 or 12. There was little sense that children needed protection from their parents, and great confidence that informal social arrangements would operate to keep children from being intolerably victimized. Work was regarded as beneficial, as an occasion for practical and moral education and a path to increased status within the family and the society at large.

Over time this perception has changed markedly. The period of childhood has gradually lengthened. Currently, childhood is seen as lasting at least until age 16 and perhaps until age 18 or 21. Children, particularly infants, are seen much more as at potential risk from their parents, and thus have a relationship to the society independent of their parents. Work has gradually come to be viewed as exploitative and as interfering with education, rather than as part of an educational experience. Adolescents are seen as having much greater legal independence from their parents.

Thus, the view of childhood has changed from its being a short period in which the child is entirely dependent but with a significant economic role to its being a long period in which the child has formal independence early but remains economically dependent. Education has changed from work-related moral education to abstract education unconnected to immediate work tasks and social values. No doubt these changes reflect the economic and social conditions of our times. But they complicate the relationships among parents, children, and the state and leave much more room for public regulation and intervention.

Other changes have occurred in the occasions and forms of public intervention. In the past, public interventions into the lives of families and children were triggered when the formal arrangements for the care and custody of the children collapsed as a result of the death or separation of the parents or when the child's unruly conduct threatened the community. Informal public interventions in the form of advice and gossip from neighbors and clergy undoubtedly occurred in less dramatic circumstances but were not explicitly sanctioned by law. More recently, public interventions have been triggered by concern that children were being abused and neglected by their parents or that the children were failing to go to school and obey their parents. This is obviously a broader conception of formal public responsibility.

The forms of public intervention have changed as well. At the outset, interventions came from informal community agents, for example, relatives, neighbors, clergy. Occasionally a secular official such as a selectman was involved, but even he was tied closely to the community. Intervention took the form of moral exhortation and of limited assistance to deal with problems that were viewed as temporary. (If the problem was viewed as permanent, it became the responsibility of the person being assisted, not that of the agent.) Soon, however, the intervenors became more impersonal. First, private voluntary agencies appeared. They were followed by publicly supported bureaucracies. Interventions from private and public bureaucracies increasingly took the form of services and assistance rather than moral exhortation. Their relationships to the children and families were increasingly regulated by procedures and law rather than informal agreements. Thus, while public interventions became broader and deeper, they were carried on by institutions whose purposes became more obscure and whose relationships with the families and children became more distant and impersonal. It is not surprising, then, that the society is currently confused about its responsibilities for children who are at risk or creating risks. Society seems to be moving toward greater intrusions into the lives of families and children, with less understanding about why it is intervening and with less confidence that intervention can be successful.

Notes

1. The municipal laws of all well-regulated states have taken care to enforce this duty [in this case, the maintenance and support of children]: though providence has done it more effectually than any laws, by implanting in the breast of every parent that . . . insuperable degree of affection, which not even the deformity of person or mind, not even the wickedness, ingratitude, and rebellion of children, can totally suppress or extinguish. (William Blackstone, *Commentaries on the Laws of England, Book 1,* Oxford: Clarendon Press, 1765, p. 435)
2. For an elegant treatment of the problems that derive from the collision of these basic liberal premises see James S. Fishkin, *Justice, Equal Opportunity, and the Family* (New Haven, CT: Yale University Press, 1983).
3. In writing this chapter we relied heavily on two seminal works. One is the comprehensive and thoughtful work of Robert H. Bremner and his associates—Robert H. Bremner, John Barnard, Tamara K. Hareven, and Robert M. Mennel, Eds., *Children and Youth in America* (Cambridge, MA: Harvard University Press, 1974). The other is an elegant volume of essays edited by LaMar Empey: LaMar T. Empey, Ed., *Juvenile Justice: The Progressive Legacy and Current Reforms* (Charlottesville, VA: University Press of Virginia, 1979).
4. In distinguishing the periods, we are following Bremner et al. (see note 3).
5. Thomas Hobbes, *Leviathan* (London, 1924) first published in 1651, p. 124. Quoted in Bremner et al., Vol. 1, p. 27.
6. Bremner et al., Vol. 1, p. 5.
7. Ibid., p. 27.
8. Ibid., p. 73.
9. Ibid., pp. 104–105.
10. Ibid., p. 104.
11. Ibid., p. 28.
12. From Edgar W. Knight, *A Documentary History of Education in the South Before 1860,* Vol. 1 (Chapel Hill, NC: 1949), p. 60. Quoted in Bremner et al., Vol. 1, p. 67.
13. Ibid., p. 28.
14. *In re Gault,* 387 U.S. 1 (1967), at 16.
15. Bremner et al., Vol. 1, p. 29.
16. John Locke, "Some thoughts concerning education," in *The Works of John Locke IX* (London, 1823) sections 40–46. Quoted in Bremner et al., Vol. 1, p. 134.
17. De Tocqueville, *Democracy in America.* Quoted in Bremner et al., Vol. 2, p. 206.

18. Joseph F. Kett, *Rites of Passage: Adolescence in America 1790 to the Present* (New York: Basic Books, 1977), pp. 63–64.
19. Bremner et al., Vol. 1, pp. 147–148.
20. Trench Coxe, *A View of the United States of America* (Philadelphia, 1794), quoted in Bremner et al., Vol. 1, p. 172.
21. Bremner et al., Vol. 1, p. 149.
22. "An act in addition to an act, entitled 'An act relating to masters and servants, and apprentices,' " 1813, chap. 2, *Public Statutes of Connecticut*, Oct. 1808–May 1819, May Session, 1813 (Hartford, 1813), pp. 117–118. Quoted in Bremner et al., Vol. 1, p. 179.
23. George S. White, *Memoir of Samuel Slater*, 2d. ed. (Philadelphia, 1836), pp. 107–108. Quoted in Bremner et al., Vol. 1, p. 177.
24. Kett, *Rites of Passage*, pp. 18–20.
25. Bremner et al., Vol. 1, p. 187.
26. Society For the Prevention of Pauperism in the City of New York, *Second Annual Report, 1819* (New York, 1820), p. 32. Quoted in Bremner et al., Vol. 1, p. 308.
27. According to Bremner et al., Vol. 1, p. 307: "In the eighteenth century, no special facilities existed for the correction or reformation of young offenders. . . .Colonial authorities recognized the inadvisability of incarcerating youths with adult criminals but they could not even afford to maintain the children, much less to establish separate institutions for them. Instead of holding delinquents in jail, town officials bound them out—in effect, sold them for their keep."
28. Bremner et al., Vol. 1, p. 343.
29. Ibid., pp. 343–344.
30. Ibid., p. 345.
31. James Kent, *Commentaries on American Law*, 11th ed. (Boston, 1867), Vol. 2, pp. 189–205. Quoted in Bremner et al., Vol. 1, pp. 363–364.
32. Bremner et al., Vol. 1, p. 344.
33. Ibid., pp. 398–400.
34. Paul Boyer, *Urban Masses and Moral Orders in America, 1820–1920* (Cambridge, MA: Harvard University Press, 1978), chaps. 2, 3, 7.
35. Ibid.
36. Ibid., pp. 94–107.
37. Bremner et al., Vol. 1, p. 345.
38. Bremner et al., Vol. 2, p. 601.
39. Daniel Webster, "First settlement of New England," in Edward Everett, Ed., *The Works of Daniel Webster* (Boston, 1851) Vol. 1, pp. 41–42. Quoted in Bremner et al., Vol. 1, p. 451.
40. Horace Mann, *Massachusetts Board of Education, Tenth Annual Report* (Boston, 1847), pp. 111–113, 119–120, 124–125. Quoted in Bremner et al., Vol. 1, pp. 455–456.
41. Anthony M. Platt, *The Child Savers/The Invention of Delinquency* (Chicago: University of Chicago Press, 1969).
42. Thomas R. Hazard, *Report on the Poor and Insane in Rhode Island* (Providence, 1851), pp. 85–89. Quoted in Bremner et al., Vol. 1, p. 637.
43. Empey, Ed., *Juvenile Justice*, pp. 25–28.
44. Ibid.

45. Platt, *The Child Savers.*
46. Ibid.
47. Ibid.
48. Boyer, *Urban Masses,* p. 144.
49. Ibid., p. 151.
50. Ibid., pp. 149–150.
51. Ibid., p. 153.
52. Ibid., chap. 8.
53. Ibid., p. 158.
54. Ibid., p. 156.
55. David J. Rothman, *The Discovery of the Asylum: Social Order and Disorder in the New Republic* (Boston: Little, Brown, 1971).
56. Bremner et al., Vol. 2, pp. 601–604.
57. Ibid.
58. Ibid., p. 1383.
59. Arthur J. Klein, *Survey of Land-Grant Colleges and Universities,* in U.S. Office of Education, *Bulletin,* 1930, No. 9 (Washington, DC, 1930), Vol. 1, pp. 8–33. Quoted in Bremner et al., Vol. 2, pp. 1480–1487.
60. Boyer, *Urban Masses,* p. 162.
61. Ibid., p. 185.
62. Kett, *Rites of Passage,* p. 62.
63. Platt, *The Child Savers,* p. 18.
64. Bremner et al., Vol. 2, pp. 601–604.
65. Julia Lathrop, "The Background of the Juvenile Court in Illinois, in *The Child, the Clinic and the Court* (New York: New Republic, 1925), pp. 290–295. Quoted in Bremner et al., Vol. 2, pp. 504–506.
66. Sophonisba P. Breckinridge and Edith Abbott, *The Delinquent Child and the Home* (New York, 1912), pp. 170–174. Quoted in Bremner et al., Vol. 2, pp. 513–515.
67. U.S. Bureau of Education, *Circulars of Information, Number 6* (Washington, DC, 1875), pp. 42–45, 49–50. Quoted in Bremner et al., Vol. 2, pp. 464–468.
68. Bremner et al., Vol. 2, pp. 439–441.
69. For an early criticism of the juvenile court, see Timothy D. Hurley, "Necessity for the Lawyer in the Juvenile Court," *Proceedings of the National Conference of Charities and Correction* (1905), pp. 173–177. Quoted in Bremner et al., Vol. 2, pp. 539–540.

3 The Contemporary Mandate

With THOMAS BEARROWS, JEFFREY BLEICH, and MICHAEL OSHIMA

History has brought society to reconsider its responsibilities to children who are at risk or creating risks. The debate is carried on within separate policy domains concerned with welfare, education, youth employment, drug abuse, and so on. An important part of the debate concerns the basic purposes and authority of the juvenile court and the associated juvenile justice system. These institutions might seem relatively significant compared with such social behemoths as the welfare system, the public schools, or statutes regulating child labor and minimum wages. After all, millions of Americans interact with the larger institutions, while only a tiny fraction of the nation's children and families appear before the juvenile court.[1] Yet, three observations establish the key importance of the juvenile justice system.

First, the system must deal with the most difficult cases: the ones in which the children are most threatening or threatened and in which the natural, private arrangements for the care and guidance of the children are the weakest. If the mark of a society's commitment to its children is how it handles the children who are least fortunate, then the juvenile justice system is the institution that will set that mark.[2]

Second, the system sets minimum standards for the proper conduct of children and their responsible care. This is done explicitly for individual cases that come before the court but is also done implicitly for all others by the general force of law expressed through the juvenile court's decisions.

Third, the system often decides who has the socially recognized responsibility for a particular child. Mostly that responsibility stays with parents or other legally established guardians. But sometimes it reverts to the state through the agency of temporary foster care or "youth authorities." Thus, the juvenile justice system sets the context within which many children—particularly many disadvantaged children—will be raised.

Unfortunately, the central importance of the juvenile court and the juvenile justice system is reflected neither in their current social standing nor in the public debate about their past and future. For the most part, juvenile courts are seen as unimportant, low-status enterprises within the nation's legal system.[3] Little new authority or money is channeled through them to accomplish important social objectives. Instead they are subjected to criticism and increasingly heavy demands for accountability—sure signs of fading public credibility.

The public debate views juvenile courts as unjust and ineffective adjuncts to the nation's adult criminal justice system. From one perspective they are too overreaching and arbitrary to satisfy the demands of justice.[4] From another their response to juvenile crime is too flaccid to produce a form of justice that acknowledges the suffering of victims and properly accommodates the community's legitimate interests in controlling crime.[5]

Much of the explanation for juvenile justice's low estate is an (historically justified) impression that the system has failed to produce promised results.[6] That is, the system is criticized for its performance rather than for the appropriateness of its mission. Another part of the criticism, however, has focused on the legitimacy of the enterprise more or less independent of its performance. The system is criticized for pursuing narrow interests in security and social control behind a mask of good intentions, and for intruding in areas where state authority should not be used.[7] In short, the system is criticized for being ill-founded as well as ineffective.

This chapter seeks firmer ground on which to build the future juvenile justice system. More specifically, it aims to discern the contemporary political and legal mandate for juvenile justice. By the mandate for juvenile justice we mean the shared understandings about the purposes the society means to pursue through the juvenile justice system and the powers it grants to the enterprise. We leave the issues of the system's performance to the next chapter.

The function of a mandate is to legitimate and guide a public enterprise. Consequently, it is constructed of three basic materials: fundamental social values, the politics that reflect and balance those values in accord with the times, and legal thought about the proper uses of state authority in a free society. The method for discovering the contemporary mandate, then, is to go to these sources: to probe the basic social values that guide, or are at stake in, the enterprise of juvenile justice; to assess the balance of political forces that now sustain and shape the system; and to see how legal doctrines about important issues in juvenile justice are now developing. That is what we will do.

Our basic contention is that, in thinking about the mandate for juvenile justice, the society has been misled by perceiving the juvenile court as an adjunct to the adult criminal court. In our view, society would be far better served by viewing juvenile justice as an enterprise more akin to a civil court concerned with maintaining proper relationships among children, caretakers, and the society than as a criminal court focusing on the misconduct of children. What we mean by "better" is that viewing the court in these terms is more consistent with our social history, our shared values, our current politics, and emerging legal doctrines than the alternative. Moreover, in subsequent chapters we will show that this perspective is also better for understanding the current operations of the system and for guiding investments to position the system to deal with emergent problems.

Politics, Social Values, and the Legislative Mandate

An obvious way to explore the mandate for juvenile justice is to examine the statutes that authorize the enterprise. Since 70% of the state statutes seem to be modeled on the 1899 Illinois statute, it is useful to begin our analysis with that statute.[8]

The Original Legislative Mandate

The key provisions of the 1899 Illinois statute are the following:

Section 1. . . . For the purposes of this act, the words "dependent child" and "neglected child" shall mean any child who for any reason is destitute or homeless or abandoned; or dependent upon the public for support; or has not proper parental care or guardianship; or who habitually begs or receives alms; or who is found living in any house of ill fame or with any vicious or disreputable person; or whose home by reason of neglect, cruelty or depravity on the part of its parents, guardian or other person in whose care it may be, is an unfit place for such a child; and any child under the age of 8 years who is found peddling or selling any article or singing or playing any musical instrument upon the streets, or giving any public entertainment. The words "delinquent child" shall include any child under the age of 16 years who violates any law of this State, or any city or village ordinance.

Section 7. . . . when any child under the age of sixteen (16) years shall be found to be dependent or neglected within the meaning of this act, the court may make an order committing the child to the care of some suitable State institution, or to the care of some reputable citizen of good moral character, or to the care of some training school or an industrial school, as provided by law, or to the care of some association willing to receive it.

Section 9. . . . In the case of a delinquent child the court may continue the hearing from time to time, and may commit the child to the care and guardianship of a probation officer duly appointed by the court, and may allow said child to remain in its own home, subject to the visitation of the probation officer; such child to report to the probation officer as often as may be required and subject to be returned to the court for further proceedings, whenever such action may appear to be necessary; or it may authorize the said probation officer to board out the said child in some suitable family home, in case provision is made by voluntary contribution or otherwise for the payment of the board of such child, until a suitable provision may be made for the child in a home without such payment; or the court may commit the child, if a boy, to a training school for boys, or if a girl, to an industrial school for girls. Or, if the child is found guilty of any criminal offense, and the judge is of the opinion that the best interest requires it, the court may commit the child to any institution within said county incorporated under the laws of this State for the care of delinquent children, or provided by a city for the care of such offenders, or may commit the child, if a boy over the age of ten years, to the State reformatory, or if a girl over the age of ten years, to the State Home for Juvenile Female Offenders. In no case shall a child be committed beyond his or her minority.[9,10]

This legislation chartered the *parens patriae* model of the juvenile court. Although this mandate was widely supported at the time of its creation, it has not escaped criticism. Quite the contrary. Criticisms from both the left and the right of the political spectrum have eroded the power of the mandate to stand as a social consensus or agreement about the focus and authority of the juvenile court.

The political left attacks both the justice and the effectiveness of the court. With respect to justice, the left criticizes the court's broad and ambiguous jurisdiction, its indifference to due process protections for those subjected to its judgments, and its potentially discriminatory practices.[11] With respect to effectiveness, the left argues that court interventions generally make matters worse by labeling children as delinquents and helping to create a delinquent subculture.[12] Finally, the left attacks the hypocrisy of justifying broad state powers to intervene in the lives of children in terms of a public interest in fostering the development of the children when the state is unwilling to supply the resources necessary to achieve that goal.[13] The left's agenda for the juvenile court, then, is to shrink its jurisdiction, focus it narrowly on the most flagrant juvenile crimes and instances of abuse and neglect, provide adequate due process protections for those who come before the court, and ensure the quality of the services made available to families and children who, on the basis of a fair court procedure, seem to be in need of public assistance.

The political right's attack on the juvenile court is different: Its criticism focuses on the court's leniency in handling juvenile offenders.[14] According to the right, it is fundamentally wrong to excuse the criminal conduct of children on the grounds of immaturity, circumstantial events, or social deprivation. It is right to hold children accountable for their actions.[15] Indeed, in this view, making children feel accountable for their actions is an important aid rather than an obstacle to their development. In addition, the right argues that court dispositions are too expensive and insufficiently protective of the community.[16] The right asks why the juvenile court continues to be tempted by the prospect of rehabilitation despite little evidence that rehabilitation programs succeed.[17] Finally, the effort to personalize justice and accommodate special features of the child's situation seems to risk the fairness of a system that holds everyone equally accountable for their actions. These observations have led the right to recommend the abolition of the juvenile court's criminal jurisdiction in favor of adult court processing.

The "Constitutionalized" or "Criminalized" Court

Surprisingly, there are several points of potential agreement between these two ways of looking at the juvenile court: (a) The principal focus of the juvenile court should be criminal offenses committed by children. (b) Status offenses and ambiguous cases of abuse and neglect could be excluded from the court's jurisdiction as irrelevant to its basic work. (c) Children who commit crimes should be guaranteed basic due process protections; this would enhance the seriousness and accountability of the proceedings. (d) At least some of the rhetoric and trappings of rehabilitative approaches could be stripped away in the interest of both candor and accountability.

Thus, juvenile crimes could be handled more effectively and decently in a straightforward "justice" court for juveniles. To the extent that the society wanted to concern itself with other matters such as status offenses or ambiguous cases of abuse and neglect, a different forum could be created that would make less use of coercive state authority.

The recent change in Washington state's approach to juvenile justice realizes the potential of these points.[18] The Washington state statute, passed in 1977, divides the jurisdiction of juvenile justice into two large pieces: crimes committed by children and everything else.[19] With respect to the crimes, the process is formalized with due process protections, clear penalties, intensive prosecutorial involvement, and so on.[20] There is an effort to channel cases involving status offenses and minor cases of abuse and neglect through informal mechanisms.[21]

The basic appeal of this approach is that it makes the juvenile justice system more like the adult criminal justice system. It moves the unfamiliar, disturbing, and discredited idea of a *parens patriae* juvenile court into a more comfortable niche in the public mind—a criminal court for children. This shift appeals to the left because it narrows the court's jurisdiction, "constitutionalizes" its procedures, and strips away the hypocrisy of paternalism. It appeals to the right because it promises to hold juvenile offenders accountable for their crimes and to emphasize the community's interests in security in juvenile dispositions.

Limits of the Criminalized Court

Despite the apparent appeal of the criminalized juvenile court, few states have followed Washington's lead. The problem is *not* the basic appeal of dealing more sharply with juvenile crime: Legislation has been enacted to establish separate categories of "dangerous" juvenile offenders to be waived immediately to the adult court.[22] Other legislation has widened the authority of juvenile court judges to waive cases to the adult court or has established concurrent juvenile and adult court jurisdiction over some crimes and allowed prosecutors from the adult system to decide in which court to proceed.[23] A few states have reduced the age of jurisdiction for the juvenile court and thereby shifted work from the juvenile court to the adult court.[24]

What seems to stop other states from following Washington's lead are two problems that the Washington statute does not resolve. The first is that, at the extreme, the idea of criminalizing the juvenile court leads to an argument for totally dissolving this court. Once one has made juvenile *crime* the principal focus of juvenile justice and has constitutionalized the procedures, it becomes difficult to see what distinguishes the juvenile court from the adult court—one might as well eliminate the juvenile court altogether. In continuing to protect juvenile court jurisdiction over criminal offenses committed by juveniles, the society's representatives are signaling a reluctance to start down this path.[25] Apparently, they wish to retain special features of the juvenile court even when this court is explicitly handling crimes committed by juveniles.

The second limitation is that there is some important work the society wants the court to do that is not fully captured by the concept of juvenile crime, nor is it captured when that concept is enlarged to include crimes committed *against* children. The crucial work consists of the "minor" problems: children who have run away, parents who are chronically neglectful or intermittently abusive, and parents who are absent. These problems all grow out of situations in which the structures for supervising, protecting, and caring for children are deteriorating but have not yet collapsed into violence.

It is significant that even the Washington state statute does not eliminate such things from state jurisdiction. They are simply shunted to a more informal procedure.[26] It also is significant that despite a decade or more of political lobbying to eliminate status offenses (as these problems are called), most states retain the category.[27] Finally, it is particularly significant that powerful new political forces are now appearing that focus attention on family relationships and the conditions under which children are being raised rather than on juvenile crime.

One can see the influence of these new political forces in three domains. The first is the increased, almost hysterical, concern about missing children and runaways. Over the last year or two, individuals, business groups, and social agencies have all participated in widespread activities to help identify and reclaim missing children. Indeed, the concern is so intense that during the 1984 hearings on the 1974 Juvenile Justice and Delinquency Prevention Act, a name change was proposed, to the "Juvenile Justice, Runaway Youth, and Missing Children Act."[28] The Act that finally passed explicitly mandated the Office of Juvenile Justice and Delinquency Prevention to explore alternative methods of strengthening families as an approach to delinquency prevention.[29]

The second domain where one can see evidence of these political forces at work is in the growing public concern about the foster care system.

Originally conceived as a stopgap measure to deal with family emergencies, the foster care system has grown into a vast enterprise in which hundreds of thousands of children remain in limbo for long periods of time.[30] Increasingly, through the mechanisms of "permanency planning," the nation's juvenile courts are being drawn into the ongoing management of the foster care system as well as into the initial placement decisions.[31]

Behind the issue of foster care lies a still larger and more significant political concern about the weakening of the family as an important institution within the society. Sometimes the issue is seen as a problem of frequent divorces, working mothers, and latchkey children.[32] At other times it is viewed as a problem of pregnancies among unmarried young, urban poor.[33]

These issues—runaways, foster care, and weakened families—prevent the politics of juvenile justice from becoming too narrowly focused on crimes by children. Indeed, it does not seem accidental that just when the debate about juvenile justice seemed to turn decisively in the direction of controlling juvenile crime through criminal court processes, the society rediscovered its concerns about runaway children, the foster care system, and the state of the family. The society cannot seem to disentangle the issue of juvenile crime from the issue of the conditions under which children are reared. The question is how these issues will be integrated within a legislative mandate for juvenile justice.

The Legislative Options

The original legislation that authorized broad public interventions to save children and the society from the consequences of parental failures still survives, but in damaged form. The society has come to be more cynical about the state's motives in intervening, more attentive to the rights of children and parents in such interventions, and more skeptical about the state's ability to fashion alternative living arrangements for children that are superior to their original ones, however desperate the children's situations seem to be. Thus, society is less willing to grant juvenile justice the necessary powers and financial resources to perform the job it has apparently been given.

New legislation designed to enhance the accountability of juvenile offenders by shrinking the juvenile court's jurisdiction over their crimes or by importing into the court the style and procedures of the adult criminal court presents an alternative to the traditional *parens patriae* model. Such legislation satisfies some, who believe that the most important part of the juvenile justice problem is finally being handled well. But it worries others, who believe that neither community security nor justice is being much improved and that important areas of court concern (such as abuse and neglect of children) will be insufficiently emphasized.

A third alternative may now be coming into view: It mandates a juvenile justice system with the principal responsibility of using state authority and resources to strengthen and oversee families. In this alternative, the system's job is not to assume direct responsibility for children (as it does in the *parens patriae* model). Nor is it to control crimes committed by children (as in the criminalized model). Instead, the task is to hold children and those who care for children responsible for the children becoming responsible citizens.

The strength of this third alternative is that it retains the juvenile court (and juvenile justice system) to do the work the society wants it to do but avoids the hubris and errors of the original court concept. From the perspective of this third alternative, the crucial error of the original legislative mandate was not in the breadth of its purpose. The mandate was correct in viewing the overall objective as the socialization of children. Instead, the error lay in allowing the state to shoulder parents aside and do the job by itself. The error in viewing the juvenile court as a criminal court for children is not in wanting to hold juveniles accountable for their crimes—they *should* be held accountable. It is also right to make dispositions that protect the society from their future criminal conduct. The errors in this conception lie in construing society's interests in the development of its children too narrowly and in failing to view parents, legal guardians, and public agencies as both part of the problem and part of the solution for children's misconduct.

Whether the society is prepared to establish a juvenile justice system that helps families discharge their duties to raise socialized children remains unclear. Initially, the notion seems too radical in both political and legal terms. Yet, in looking closely at the politics of children, the idea of moving families toward greater social prominence and responsibility seems quite plausible. No alternative seems to balance the society's competing interests in these areas as well.

Moreover, when one examines the broad trends affecting state legislation, one sees a growing concern for family autonomy and responsibility. The Illinois statute itself has recently been revised and has a new preamble that reflects a new balancing of values in the mandate for juvenile justice. The preamble now reads:

> The purpose of this Act is to secure . . . such care and guidance, preferably in his own home, as will serve the . . . welfare of the minor and the best interests of the community. . . ;
>
> . . .[T]o preserve and strengthen the minor's family ties wherever possible, removing him from the custody of his parents only when his welfare . . . or the protection of the public cannot be adequately safeguarded without removal.
>
> . . .[A]nd when the minor is removed to secure for him custody, care, and discipline as nearly as possible, equivalent to that which should be given by his parents.[34]

This preamble is interesting for two reasons. One is that it sets out nicely a contemporary statement of the basic values that must be recognized and balanced in establishing (and operating) a juvenile justice system.

First and most importantly, the preamble recognizes a state interest in securing the "care and guidance" of minors. Since the state does not recognize this interest with respect to adults, the statute implicitly creates a special status for children and a special relationship between them and the state. Second, the preamble justifies state intervention to protect not only the community but also the child. Hence it implicitly authorizes jurisdiction over not only *dangerous* children but also *endangered* children. Third, the preamble sets a minimum standard the state must meet in caring for the child if the State assumes the responsibility: It must provide "custody, care, and discipline" at the same level (and of the same type) as "that which *should* be given by his parents" (emphasis added). Fourth, in recognizing that the aim of the statute is "to preserve and strengthen the minor's family ties whenever possible," and in creating a preference for providing the necessary care "in [the minor's] own home," the preamble recognizes the preeminence of the family in providing appropriate care and guidance.

The second reason this new preamble is interesting is in what has been subtracted from and what has been added to the initial legislation. What has been subtracted is much of the descriptions of the particular acts that would define a child as delinquent. This reflects a greater contemporary tolerance for the diversity of conduct and conditions that are acceptable for children in a pluralistic society. What has been added are (a) an explicit concern for protecting children from abuse and neglect and (b) a desire to keep children with their own family in all but the most threatening circumstances.

In emphasizing the crucial importance of family integrity and responsibility, the Illinois statute lies within the mainstream. An analysis of changes in legislative preambles for juvenile justice indicates that statutes that emphasize crime control or the social development of the child were all drafted prior to 1959. Preambles that were drafted after 1969 emphasized family integrity and responsibility over these other values.

Thus, trends in the political and legislative mandate have not moved decisively in the direction of criminalizing the juvenile court. They have moved a little in the direction of making families more prominent.

Jurisprudence, the Law, and Juvenile Justice

Community values, and their reflection in statutory law, create one kind of legitimacy for juvenile justice. Another kind is created by nonstatutory law, for example, common law doctrines governing the conduct of parents and children and constitutional doctrines establishing the rights of children, parents, and the state. Consequently, if one seeks a legitimate basis for juvenile justice, it is important to go beyond the politics and determine how legal thought and judicial opinion are developing in this area.

Three legal issues profoundly influence the society's conception of juvenile justice. The most basic concerns the legal status of children: specifically, whether children should be regarded as autonomous, rights-bearing citizens or as dependents with special claims on the society by virtue of their dependent status. The second concerns the appropriate due process protections for children during legal action initiated by the state or the children's legal guardians. And the third concerns the proper jurisdiction of the juvenile court: whether it should continue to have jurisdiction over crimes committed by children or should relinquish that jurisdiction to the adult court, how abuse and neglect should be defined to minimize state intrusion into family life, and whether the so-called status offenses (e.g., incorrigibility, running away, truancy) should continue to be legal offenses.

The Legal Status of Children

Recently, juvenile justice jurisprudence has been dominated by the issue of "children's rights."[35] Advocates for children have drawn parallels between the status of children on the one hand and the status of women, minorities, the handicapped, and the mentally ill on the other.[36] In the advocates' view, these groups are alike in their dependent status in the society. Justice requires that the groups be restored to equality. This, in turn, implies that these groups should be granted due process protections from arbitrary action by government or private agencies and that their special needs for personal development; economic opportunity; and access to schools, employment, and public transportation should be accommodated even when the cost of such recognition is high. In the specific case of children, this means that children deserve due process protection against arbitrary action by their parents, legal guardians, and the state; that their special needs for schooling, medical care, counseling, and so on should be provided for, through public expenditures if necessary; and that their culpability for acts that would be criminal if committed by adults should be limited.[37] To achieve these goals, advocates frequently have relied on the courts rather than on politics and legislatures.

The generous spirit of justice and equality that lies behind these concepts is compelling. So is the hope implicit in them that if only children are given what they want and need, they will become resourceful citizens. In all likelihood, these broad, compelling visions will continue to animate the crusade for children's rights.

As a legal matter, however, the drive for the rights of juveniles seems to have reached a high-water mark in the Supreme Court decisions of the late 1960s and early 1970s that commenced the constitutionalization of the juvenile court (e.g., the *Gault* and *Winship* decisions).[38] A few other cases decided subsequently also seem consistent with the view that children are "rights-bearing" persons and that their due is "adult-like liberty" rather than "child-like dependency."[39] However, decisions about some cases were in the opposite direction. Only four years after *Gault,* the Supreme Court denied children in juvenile court the right to a jury trial in criminal cases against them.[40] Dramatically, in 1984 the Supreme Court ruled that a state can authorize the pretrial detention of children who pose a serious risk of committing a crime because, in its words, "juveniles, unlike adults, are always in some form of custody."[41] As one commentator interpreted this decision and others leading up to it: "The Court has revived a notion of custody, rather than liberty, as children's due, and thereby legally enforced a difference between children and adults."[42]

It is unclear how the Court will decide matters concerning the status of children in the future. Both the trend of Supreme Court decisions and the drift of legal commentary in this area, however, indicate disinclination to develop children's rights beyond their current limits.[43] Apparently, in the eyes of the law, children are more dependent than they are free. Their due is supervision and assistance more than independence and accountability.

Yet this conclusion hardly ends the matter of adolescent claims against the rest of the society. As one commentator forcefully argued:

> Failure to recognize any claims to liberty until the magic birthday of majority is a profoundly illiberal policy that is out of step with legal and social conditions of our age. Indeed, the theory that those who are not totally independent should be regarded as totally dependent is the most troublesome aspect of the legal theory of early adolescence associated with juvenile courts, public schools, and social services for most of this century.[44]

But if the child or adolescent is neither totally dependent nor totally independent, what is his or her status? One answer is that the adolescent is in a state of "semi-autonomy" in which there are strong moral and prudential reasons to recognize his or her "liberty interests"[45] but in which the child must always be seen as existing in a relationship with others who assume some responsibility for him or her.

If this is the child's legal status, what should guide courts in deciding whether the child's liberty interests should be protected or should be yielded to some other social interest in controlling the child's conduct? Two different concepts seem to be emerging as guides toward justice for juveniles in a world in which the concept of children's rights no longer provides the proper touchstone. One is captured by Franklin Zimring's view of the development of adolescents:

> Adolescence, in my view, is both a period in itself and a transition. It is a term of years when those not yet adult are engaged in the process of becoming adult, a rich but often stressful period of trial and error. As a period of semi-autonomy, it places special burdens on legal reasoning and public choice. As a transition to adulthood, it commands a future orientation in public policy: how we grow up is an important determinant of what kinds of adults we grow up to be.

Further, in these last years of the twentieth century, adolescence requires a peculiar mix of liberty and order that is anything but simple to achieve. Unlike the earlier stages of childhood, this is a time when the adolescent acquires a voice and a will that we can neither ignore, nor slavishly follow. In the jargon of the law library, contemporary adolescents possess "liberty interests" and voices to speak them; at the same time, they are prone to make mistakes that enlightened public policy cannot ignore in the name of civil liberty. A central theme in my analysis is that full maturity can only be achieved by what Wallace Stevens called "committing experience." But how do we get from here to there? If a person can't make choices without the experience of making choices, how can that person become an adult without being one? It is this need to learn one's way into maturity that makes growing up in a free society a process rather than an event.[46]

In line with this analysis, Zimring gave us the notion that we should think of the laws and policies regulating adolescent conduct as "learner's permits" given to "semi-autonomous" people who must "learn their way into adulthood."[47] In applying these principles in particular areas of public policy, the society has three different interests. The first is in advancing the maturation and social development of the child.[48] The second is in protecting the principle of family autonomy.[49] The third is in protecting itself.[50]

There is a price to be paid for advancing the first objective relative to the others. As Zimring noted,

We gamble when we extend choices to the not-yet-adult. If we win, the experience gained in decision-making becomes an integral part of a process of achieving adulthood. If we lose, harm can come to the adolescent and the community.[51]

Despite the risks, in Zimring's view the principal objective should be to maximize the child's chance for development. If we are to take losses in this endeavor, the goal of public policy should be to minimize the loss. In Zimring's words:

An important part of cutting our losses during this period of development is minimizing the harm young persons do themselves, and keeping to a minimum the harm we inflict on them when they have abused opportunities in ways that harm the community. Above almost all else, we seek a legal policy that preserves the life chances for those who make serious mistakes, as well as preserving choices for their more fortunate (and more virtuous) contemporaries.[52]

The adolescent must be protected from the full burden of adult responsibilities, but pushed along by degrees toward the moral and legal accountability that we consider appropriate to adulthood.[53]

This vision of managing a learner's permit in a way that maximizes the development of the child at the least cost to the child, the rest of the society, and the principle of "family autonomy" is one guide to legal actions in a world in which children's rights cannot be the touchstone. The other conception, offered in a somewhat sketchier form by Martha Minow, is more concerned with the quality of the relationships within which the adolescent will do his or her experimentation and learning.[54] In her view, the child should be seen not as an independent rights-bearing person but as a person who has a right and an obligation to affiliation with others.

Minow begins with a view that a liberal state recognizes two quite distinct legal statuses:

> [P]ersons under the law may be treated either as separate, autonomous, and responsible individuals entitled to exercise rights and obliged to bear liabilities for their actions, or else as dependent, incompetent, and irresponsible individuals denied rights and removed from liabilities, subjected instead to the care and protections of the state or a guardian.[55]

She interprets these distinct statuses as the result of an incomplete challenge to feudal institutions, a challenge that sought to free individuals from the authority of religious and political institutions. This challenge

> created an opening wedge for what has become the dominant set of conceptions about the relationship between the individual and the society: notions according rights to autonomous individuals against a state and notions imposing responsibilities on individuals for their willed actions.[56]

She contrasts this idea of rights with "earlier and persistent uses of the law to facilitate interpersonal relationships."[57] Indeed, she notes that the earlier notions of "status-based relationships and mutual obligation endured . . . [e]specially for people who continued to occupy special statuses even under the liberal order—persons like children, women and mentally incompetent people."[58]

What makes Minow's argument different from many others is that she does not deplore the incomplete emancipation of persons in such statuses, but instead sees that such people have a special form of rights—rights to *relationships* with the rest of the society.

> In this sense rights represent not only a social commitment to preserve individual freedom from the injuries and intrusions of others, but also individual freedom to form relationships with others. And the preconditions for relationships are not just bilateral, but also social; not just a subject for the parent and child, but also for the state and the community.[59]

She then takes the jurisprudence of the juvenile court to task for not focusing on the content of these relationships:

> The juvenile court offered rights in the form of child protection against parents in situations like charges of abuse; the juvenile court currently offers some forms of family protection against state power, and at times affords juveniles power to assert their own wishes. But it has not taken as its task the articulation or promotion of rights of care and connection, rights to affiliative relationships—or the preconditions for such relationships.[60]

She notes that this defect could be cured if the juvenile court "spelled out not just rights, but duties—including both the duties of adults upon whom the juvenile is dependent, and the duties of the juvenile to those entrusted with his care, to the state, and to the larger community as well."[61]

As to the future development of the jurisprudence of juvenile justice, she observes the following:

Perhaps efforts to bring the talk about children's rights in greater accord with the facts of children's double dependency, on parents and on the state, could begin to build a jurisprudence of children's rights of some use in current debate. Further, it is clear that there remains a role for an institution, perhaps still called a juvenile court, that engages in efforts to educate parents, children, and the broader community to their interdependent needs, duties, and yes, rights. Someday, such a court could bear the role of mender of the social fabric with which it is safe for children and adults to craft trusting relationships. Meanwhile, a richer debate over the rights for children, a debate joining goals of autonomy and goals of affiliation, would expose how our society neglects children by treating responsibility for children as a private matter while failing to meet adequately the preconditions for that private responsibility.[62]

In sum, the decisions of the Supreme Court and the commentary of legal scholars seem to be turning away from a jurisprudence of children's rights. Instead they seem to view the child as a dependent whose status as a dependent must be given a more refined definition. Zimring's definition emphasizes the recognition of the child's liberty interests, the importance of leaving room for experimentation, and the creation of institutional arrangements to minimize risks to the child and the society associated with the necessary experiments. Minow's definition, on the other hand, emphasizes the construction of relationships of mutual obligation within which the child might grow to productive citizenship, and the public's responsibility for guaranteeing both the relationships and the preconditions for the relationships. These views seem more likely to guide future court decisions than any simple notions of children's rights or adult-like autonomy.

Due Process and the Juvenile Court

A second area of legal controversy concerns due process protections for children. Due process protections can be viewed from two different perspectives: (a) as a reflection of the just and proper relationship between an individual and the state and (b) as an instrument serving practical purposes generally having to do with the development of facts to be used in court decisions.

The most familiar (and therefore most natural) way to think about due process protections is in the context of state action against adult criminal offenders. That is where they have their most visible and most powerful edge. Moreover, since many of the matters before the juvenile court concern criminal offenses by children, this perspective seems appropriate to the juvenile court and juvenile justice system. Finally, in many matters that do not concern crimes committed by children, the liberty of children is nonetheless at stake. Thus, since much of the action of the juvenile court resembles a state proceeding to deny children their liberty in the interests of protecting the community, it seems natural to assume that children's due process rights should resemble those enjoyed by adult criminal offenders.

This perspective essentially has been advanced through what some have called the constitutionalization and others have called the criminalization of the juvenile court.[63] The first major step in this direction was the *Gault* decision.[64] Indignant about the cavalier way in which Gault was committed to six years in a juvenile institution for nothing more than a lewd telephone call, the Supreme Court in 1967 proclaimed: "Under our Constitution, the condition of being a boy does not justify a kangaroo court."[65] Relying on the Fourteenth Amendment's "fundamental fairness" requirements, the Court granted rights to advance notice of charges, a fair and impartial hearing, assistance of counsel, and the opportunity to confront and cross-examine witnesses to all juveniles facing court action in the United States.[66] A year later, in *In re Winship*, the Court decided that delinquency must be established "beyond a reasonable doubt," a much higher standard than obtained in civil court proceedings.[67]

Although some see these developments as establishing strong due process protections for children analogous to those enjoyed by adults facing criminal prosecution, others see a much lesser outcome.[68] And the Court has given the latter much to point to.

First, the Court has been somewhat inconsistent in finding a basis for extending due process protections. *Gault* was based on the Fifth Amendment. *McKeiver* shifted the basis. *McKeiver* was based on the "fundamental fairness" requirements of the Fourteenth Amendment rather than on the special protections associated with criminal proceedings established in the Fifth and Sixth Amendments.[69] This inconsistency seems to reflect a basic confusion in the Court as to whether a juvenile delinquency proceeding is a civil or criminal proceeding. As the Court ruled in *McKeiver*, "The juvenile court proceeding has not yet been held to be a 'criminal prosecution' within the meaning and reach of the Sixth Amendment, and also has not yet been regarded as devoid of criminal aspects merely because it has been given the civil label."[70]

Second, the Court stopped short of granting all the adult due process protections to children before the juvenile court. In *McKeiver v. Pennsylvania*, the Court declined to grant the right to a jury trial to juveniles.[71]

Third, the Court has limited its interventions in this area to juvenile delinquency proceedings, leaving many of the other proceedings untouched. As the Court stated in the *Gault* decision, "We do not in this opinion consider the impact of these constitutional provisions upon the totality of the relationship of the juvenile and the state. We do not even consider the entire process relating to juvenile 'delinquents.' "

Fourth, in the *Gault* case it seems clear that the Court was as concerned about the conditions under which Gault was being held as the fact that he was being held.[73] If a plausible case could have been made that his commitment to a training school did in fact provide for his best interests or prevent recidivism, or if the conditions under which Gault was being held granted him more freedom, was more importantly connected to the community from which he came, or was more generously endowed with therapeutic resources, perhaps the Court would not have intervened. As it was, the terrible conditions in the juvenile institution invited a comparison with adult jails and prisons. Further, if no more treatment was being provided than was available in adult jails, it seems unfair to expose a child to prison conditions without the finding that he had committed a crime. Thus perhaps the Court's intervention in this domain was prudential rather than principled.

These facts establish children's rights to broad due process protections less firmly and clearly than some child advocates would hope. Moreover, to the extent that the children are increasingly seen as dependents needing both connections and room for experimentation rather than as autonomous individuals deserving liberty and accountability, the claims for broad due process protections also seem weakened.

This does not mean that children's due process rights are wholly extinguished, however. Indeed, one can begin to see the form that such rights should take by exploring two areas: (a) why it is wrong to think about due process protections for children against the standard of due process protections for adults accused of a crime and (b) what value due process protections might have in a juvenile court proceeding that is not a criminal proceeding.

A criminal court proceeding is predicated on several assumptions. A criminal offense has occurred. A particular person has been identified as the likely culprit. And there is reason to believe that the person *intended* to commit the act. Indeed, the intention to commit the act is a key feature that makes the act a *crime* rather than an accident.

This situation necessarily creates an adversarial relationship between the community and the alleged offender. Indeed, the relationship verges on outright hostility, for the community has been offended not only by the act of the alleged offender, but also by the *intention* to commit the act. In regarding the act as a crime, the community is implicitly assuming that the act is a reliable expression of the intentions and values—perhaps even the character—of the criminal offender.[74] And if that is true, then the community can be particularly indignant, for it suggests that the offender is hostile to the rules and values of the society and is a future threat. Thus, on the basis of act and intention, it seems reasonable to view the offender as an "enemy of the people."

The hostility of the society toward the alleged offender creates a problem for a liberal society, for it creates the potential for injustice to the alleged offender. Passion and a thirst for vengeance may lead to punishment that is vastly disproportionate to a crime. Or the wrong person may be singled out as the culprit. Or prejudice may overwhelm evidence as the basis for conviction and punishment.

To prevent these results, due process protections are established and rigorously maintained. In fact, due process protections symbolize the sort of relationship that a decent, rational, egalitarian society would have with citizens suspected of willfully attacking some of the society's basic rules. The society would want to act on its indignation (lest it lose its respect for its own rules), but it would do so in a way that respected the alleged offender as an equal until proven guilty. Moreover, it would allow time to pass so that passions could cool, and would encourage the gathering and presentation of evidence before a trained person not a party to the offense. In this way a situation that would otherwise be hostile would be merely adversarial. That seems to be the fundamental role of due process in an adult criminal proceeding.

It should be clear that a juvenile court proceeding operates on quite different assumptions, even when the event that occasions the proceeding is an act by a juvenile that would be treated as a crime if committed by an adult. One crucial difference is that juvenile offenders are seen as less culpable than adult offenders.[75] If their characters are not yet formed, if they are unusually vulnerable to the influence of others, if they are supposed to be under the supervision of an adult, then in an important sense their actions are not quite their own and they cannot justly be held responsible for them—at least not the first time. A second crucial difference is that the society is both more hopeful about, and more interested in, the future development of children. Since children are still malleable, there is not only less culpability for given offenses but also more opportunity for rehabilitation.[76]

The fact that a child's intentions are not obviously hostile to the society profoundly changes the nature of the proceeding against him or her. The society cannot be as angry, for there is less reason to assume that the society's and the child's interests are fundamentally opposed. Similarly, since the aim of the proceeding is not only to establish culpability but also to find effective means of rehabilitation, and since the immediate circumstances of the crime and the background conditions under which the child is living are both judged relevant in making these determinations, it seems perfectly appropriate that these issues should become the focus of the proceeding just as much as the question of guilt or innocence.

In sum, one might say that there are two models of a court process focused on criminal offenses. In the first model, the "hard court" model, the society is dealing with someone who it believes is hostile to the norms of the society. To make sure that its own hostility toward the offender does not overwhelm its better judgment, the society sets up rigid procedures to protect the suspected offender from its hostility until a dispassionate, accurate judgment can be made about culpability.

In the second model, the "soft court" model, the society assumes it is dealing with someone whose intentions are not necessarily bad and who might well reform if given a chance. In this situation, rigid protections for the suspected offender are less necessary (for there is less hostility to ward off), and it is more important that the society find ways to rehabilitate the offender. The aim of the process is to negotiate a new, more appropriate relationship between the suspected offender and the rest of the society.

It is natural to see the hard court model as appropriate to adult criminal court proceedings and the soft court one as appropriate to juvenile court proceedings. The crucial thing that separates the appropriateness of the hard court proceedings from those of the soft court, however, is the assumption that is made about the character and intentions of the offender. If it seems the offense was intended and that it is an accurate expression of the offender's character and values, then the hard court seems appropriate. If, on the other hand, the offense reveals less about the character and intentions of the offender and more about the immediate circumstances of the offense, about chronic environmental conditions influencing the offender, or about someone else's neglect or provocation, then the soft court seems more appropriate.

The society generally assumes that there is some correlation between the age of the offender and the intention behind his or her actions. The older the offender, the more likely it is that the actions accurately reflect personal intentions and not someone else's intentions or the exigencies of the moment. This is partly the reason the society has divided court jurisdictions by age, reserving hard court proceedings for those over age 18.[77]

The difficulty, however, is that age correlates only imperfectly with the development of character, and therefore provides a poor basis for reading character and intentions from observed actions. The offenses of some adult offenders seem more accidental than intended. And those of some juvenile offenders seem like the acts of hardened adult offenders.

Thus, both adult and juvenile courts have tended to innovate in their procedures. The adult court has adopted some soft court procedures in the form of dispute resolution mechanisms and diversion programs. The juvenile court has adopted some hard court procedures for dealing with repeat juvenile offenders, or it waives children to adult court. Table 3.1 illustrates these movements. Obviously it would be better for the society if it distinguished among criminal cases not on the basis of the age of the offender, but instead on his or her maturation and determination. Then it would have to operate only two court procedures, whereas now it is trying to operate four.

The point, however, is that the court procedures that seem just and

TABLE 3.1. Innovations in court processing: from "soft" to "hard" in juvenile court; from "hard" to "soft" in criminal court.

	Maturity/culpability of offender		
Age of offender	Immature		Mature
Youths	Juvenile court processing		Criminalization of juvenile court
	Coincidence of interest		Due process protections
	Informal proceedings	To "hard court" →	Waivers to adult court
	Therapeutic dispositions		Punitive dispositions
Adults	Court diversion		Criminal court processing
	Dispute resolution		Adversarial proceedings
	Informal adjustment	To "soft court" ←	Due process protection
	Diversion to treatment		Punitive dispositions

effective seem to depend crucially on what is assumed about the character of the offender. If he or she seems mature and hostile to the society, the correct procedures are those that protect the offender from the society's hostility and that focus attention narrowly on the question of guilt. If the person in question seems immature or the offense accidental, and the person therefore is less obviously hostile to the society, court procedures need not provide quite as much protection for the offender and instead might focus more on how the society might intervene to minimize the chance of future offenses.

This framework explains why the due process protections associated with adult criminal proceedings might be inappropriate in a juvenile court proceeding even in the case of a criminal offense. It also suggests what kinds of due process protections might be appropriate within juvenile courts. If the aims of the due process protections are to symbolize the nature of the relationship between the society and the offender and to accomplish practical purposes such as the development of high-quality information to support reasonable decisions, and if the assumptions about juveniles are as they have been described here, then due process in the juvenile court should be designed to do the following:

1. It should show juvenile offenders that, while the society intends to hold them accountable for their actions, it is not hostile to them. Nor does it assume that the act was solely theirs. The society is interested in the child as an individual, interested in the immediate circumstances of the

crime, and interested in the conditions under which the child is being reared. Far from distancing and blinding itself from the complicated, particular contexts from which juvenile crimes and juvenile offenders emerge, the court should be embroiled in these issues. This is the way the society seems to understand its relationship to children who commit crimes.[78]

2. It should include recognition of the emerging autonomy of the child.[79] The most obvious way to do this is to take the child's action seriously and hold the child accountable for his or her own conduct. Anything less would be undignified and patronizing. A second way to recognize the child's emerging autonomy is to grant the child counsel so that his or her voice may be effectively heard in the courtroom. This does not mean that the child's voice should prevail, of course. The society has some short-run interests in security that deserve respect. Moreover, it is possible that the child's current view of his or her interests may not accurately reflect long-run interests. But it does mean that there should be someone in the court who stands for the emerging autonomy and responsibility of the child.

3. To the extent that parents, legal guardians, and other caretakers are seen as sharing some of the culpability for the crime of the young offender, and to the extent that they can be seen as exacerbating or diminishing the criminal conduct of the child, it might be both just and wise to include them as parties to the court process.[80] In an important sense, the process is not just against or for the child; it is also concerned about whether those who are responsible for the child are now doing, or could be helped (or even forced) to do, a better job.

4. It should promote the collection and presentation of high-quality, relevant information both for judging culpability and for deciding on an appropriate disposition.[81] This means explicit statements about the information that would be relevant in different kinds of court proceedings, as well as adversarial proceedings to test the accuracy and completeness of the relevant information.

Thus, appropriate due process protections in a juvenile court are likely to be quite different from those in an adult criminal court, because the relationship of the society to the offender and the issues to be resolved are quite different in the two situations. It is inappropriate, then, to judge the quality of juvenile court procedures against the backdrop of criminal court due process protections. The challenge is to develop special procedures that will exploit the special potential of the juvenile court.

The Jurisdiction of the Juvenile Court

The third area of legal controversy concerns the proper jurisdiction of the juvenile court. In most states, the jurisdiction includes crimes committed by children, abuse and neglect of children by their parents or other caretakers, and so-called status offenses. Issues arise with respect to each of these. The central issue with respect to juvenile crimes is when these cases should be referred to adult courts.[82] The key issue with respect to abuse and neglect is how to define these offenses so that one can minimize state intrusions into family life and still achieve the goal of protecting children from serious harm in the short and long run.[83] The key issue with respect to status offenses is whether they should remain within the court's jurisdiction or be excluded as an inappropriate extension of state power over children.[84]

CRIMES COMMITTED BY CHILDREN

Crimes committed by children pose issues of justice and practicality. The issue of justice is whether the state can justly hold a child criminally responsible for acts that would be crimes if committed by adults. The practical issue is whether there is a more effective way to intervene with juvenile offenders to reduce recidivism than through standard adult court procedures and sentences.

For the first two centuries of American history, crimes committed by children were handled principally as a matter of justice. Children under the age of 7 were considered constitutionally innocent because they lacked the necessary mental state to commit a crime.[85] Children between 7 and 14 benefited from a rebuttable presumption of innocence, but no special institutions or procedures were available to them. They stood their chances in the adult criminal court.

As noted in chapter 2, these institutional arrangements seemed insufficient to progressive era reformers. They saw a greater opportunity to do justice and help children, and seized it. Through state legislation, they created a special juvenile court to have original (and sometimes exclusive) jurisdiction over crimes committed by children under the ages of 18 or 16, depending on the state.

There are two ways to view this invention. From one point of view, the juvenile court further decriminalized crimes committed by children. Juvenile offenders aged 7 to 16 who had previously faced adjudications and dispositions in adult courts now faced the special presumptions and procedures of the juvenile court. The issue of whether a child was guilty or innocent of a crime yielded to a much different question: whether the child was "delinquent" in social development. Investigations were conducted not only to determine whether a child committed an offense, but also to illuminate the underlying causes of the crime. The reputations of the children were protected by private procedures and sealed records. Dispositions would be based on needs more than on culpability.

Viewed from another perspective, the juvenile court extended state power over children. It did this by extending the liabilities of children to cover conduct such as incorrigibility and truancy, by denying accused children some due process protections they would have had in the adult criminal court, and by lengthening maximum periods under state supervision for some offenses beyond the limits allowed in the adult court. Of course, children had always had some liabilities for acts such as vagrancy, waywardness, incorrigibility, and so on. But codification of these liabilities in specific new legislation and creation of an administrative apparatus enthusiastic about applying the laws meant that the effective liabilities (as opposed to the theoretical ones) became much greater.[86] Although the state power was cloaked as a civil power rather than a criminal power, and was justified as therapy and assistance to the child rather than control on behalf of the community, the juvenile court nonetheless increased the vulnerability of children to state control.

These changes in the institutional arrangements for dealing with juvenile crimes created tensions that continue to this day. As we have seen, those who think that it is wrong and demoralizing to fail to hold children responsible for criminal conduct object to the relaxation of criminal liability associated with the creation of the juvenile court. They urge that the jurisdiction of the juvenile court be narrowed, and that crimes committed by children be returned to the adult criminal court.[87] Those who believe that it is unjust, ineffective, and wasteful for the state to be concerned about any conduct of children other than acts that would be crimes if committed by adults also want to narrow the jurisdiction of the court. But they want to do it by excluding status offenses from court jurisdiction. The issue of whether the court's jurisdiction over status offenses should be trimmed will be discussed a little later. Here we will concentrate on the question of whether crimes committed by children should now, as a *philosophical* matter, be "recriminalized" and, as a *practical* matter, be returned to the adult criminal court for prosecution.

Three different arguments are made in favor of returning juvenile offenses to the adult criminal court. The first is rooted in a conception of justice. The other two are based on practical arguments about the best way to accomplish particular objectives.

Many argue that justice would be enhanced if juvenile crimes were referred to adult court. The focus of the court proceeding could return to the question of guilt or innocence. Children would have access to the ordinary due process protections. If found guilty, they would become accountable for their crimes. Victims would be assured that the society cared about their losses. The rest of the society would be reassured that the society intended to uphold its laws. In general, then, the structure of mutual obligations and duties of people in the society to one another would be upheld. Justice would be done.[88]

A second argument for referring cases to the adult court is a practical (or utilitarian) argument. Some argue that the child's development would be enhanced by this referral. The child would learn that actions have serious consequences and that the society viewed his or her actions as a personal responsibility. And the child would be frightened into behaving better in the future.[89] In short, holding children accountable for their actions contributes positively rather than negatively to their future development.

A third argument is a practical argument guided by concern for community security rather than for the child's individual development. The assumptions are that sentences in the adult court would be longer and that dispositions would more effectively incapacitate youthful offenders.[90] Thus, the society would be protected longer and more reliably from juvenile crimes through criminal court processing of cases involving juvenile offenders.

Those who believe that the juvenile court should retain jurisdiction over criminal offenses committed by children argue in the same terms, but come to opposite conclusions. With respect to the issue of justice for juveniles, those who advocate continued juvenile court jurisdiction over criminal cases probably make their strongest arguments. They argue that it is unjust to treat most children who commit crimes against others as criminals. Doing so assumes that children are independent and accountable, which is inconsistent with the view of children as dependents. If the society views children as people whose characters are not yet formed and whose intentions are importantly influenced by external, transient factors, it is only just to reflect this view in the court procedures that confront children when they commit offenses. Since the juvenile court is a better vehicle for this than the overburdened adult criminal court, it is more just to deal with crimes committed by children through the juvenile institution than through the adult criminal court.[91]

With respect to practical concerns focused on the child's future development, those in favor of continuing juvenile court jurisdiction agree that it is important to view children as at least partly responsible for their conduct and to hold them accountable to the society. But they argue that this is already a feature of juvenile court processing and merely needs to be made more important by focusing more strongly on the issue of whether a child did or did not commit an offense.[92] Moreover, they do not disagree with the potential virtues of punishment. They argue, however, that for punishment to teach the lessons the society means to teach, there has to be a reasonably powerful relationship between the society and the child. Otherwise, the punishment will be rejected as unjust and illegitimate and will lose its ability to teach or command respect.[93] In their view, the juvenile court context is more likely to symbolize or establish the relationships that will make the punishment effective.

With respect to the question of community security, those who advocate the retention of juvenile court jurisdiction over criminal offenses make three different arguments. The first is that community security should, as a matter of both justice and practicality, be a less important goal than justice for the child or advancement of the child's future development. In short, community security should have less priority than other goals.[94] The second line of defense is the argument that the society's long-run interests in security are met better by juvenile court dispositions than by criminal court dispositions. In this argument, the short-run incapacitation of children in adult jails and prisons may yield a short-run security benefit but will produce a problem in the future, because it hardens the children's commitment to crime and equips them with new skills and colleagues. The third line of defense is that the transfer of children to the adult criminal court will not necessarily lead to more security through more effective incapacitation. The reason is that, in the context of the population within the adult criminal court, the children who commit crimes will look relatively innocent and therefore be treated more leniently than they would in the juvenile court.[95]

Among these competing arguments, the recent trend seems to be more in favor of those who think the juvenile court excuses too much and delivers too little in the way of either individual development or community security. This trend is evident in the fact that state legislatures are chipping away at the juvenile court's jurisdiction over criminal offenses committed by children. The jurisdiction has fallen away in great hunks in states that have lowered their age of jurisdiction and thereby exposed 17- and 18-year-olds to the rigors of the adult court.[96] Other states have passed laws requiring the juvenile court to refer cases involving serious offenses to the adult court.[97] Still others have broadened the opportunities for judges to waive cases to the adult court and have begun reviewing the extent to which they do.[98] This trend seems likely to continue.

In thinking about how far this trend *will* go, however, it is worth noting that the juvenile court retains a large portion of the jurisdiction. Discussion goes on about the edges of the jurisdiction, not about the center. Apparently the juvenile court does solve the problem of the just and effective handling of juvenile crimes, a problem that is at least two centuries old.

In thinking about how far the trend *should* go, it is worth thinking through a principled notion of what kinds of juvenile offenders might justly and usefully be referred to the adult court for prosecution and disposition. This is essentially the question of how dangerous juvenile offenders might be distinguished from others.[99]

The society currently draws the line between "dangerous" juvenile offenders (those who might justly and usefully be exposed to the rigors of the adult court) and offenders who are not dangerous on two different bases: their age and the seriousness of their crime. To a degree, these reflect different philosophical justifications for transferring the cases. The *age* of offenders is related to the issue of criminal responsibility, which is in turn linked to maturity. The seriousness of the offense, on the other hand, is related to the community's interests in security. The balance between interests in community security and the future development of the child is struck in the interests of the future development of the child when the crimes are minor. It is struck in the opposite way when the crimes become serious.

In our view, there is logic in these approaches. But we think there is a better, more principled way to draw the line that reflects both the interest in the maturity of the offender and the interest in community security.

As noted previously, one key issue in deciding whether a case should be transferred concerns the maturity of the individual. To the extent that an offender is sufficiently mature that his or her actions can be taken as a reliable expression of intentions, the society can feel justified in punishing the person in the adult court. He or she deserves both the special due process protections and the special hostility of an adult criminal court. On the other hand, to the extent that the person is young, impressionable, and immature, it is harder to view his or her actions as accurate reflections of intentions. Therefore, it is also more problematic to hold him or her justly accountable for the actions. This person deserves the softer embrace of the juvenile court.

The problem, of course, is that it is hard to judge the maturity of offenders. One can establish the standard relatively objectively by tying it to age. But that risks unfairness both to those who mature relatively early and to those who mature relatively late. One can tie the standard to the seriousness of the crime. But that seems to be motivated more by a concern for future community security than by an interest in doing justice to the individual offender: Some of the worst and most violent crimes are those in which circumstance and transient passions play the largest role.[100]

A better way of judging the maturity of juvenile offenders is to observe the persistence and rate of criminal offending as well as the seriousness.[101] Persistence and high rates of offending indicate that the crimes are neither accidents nor transient impulses. They may be the products of *accumulated* neglect and rage. The point, however, is that the crimes cannot be seen as the product of external or transient forces. They are expressions of something relatively settled and durable in the offender's temperament, something that must be treated as either a criminal intent or an illness but cannot be ignored. Repeated crimes cannot be seen as the result of youthful exuberance or indiscretion.

It also seems prudent to retain the practical notion that the balance to be struck between society's interests in community security on the one hand and individual development of the offender on the other should shift as the seriousness of the offender's crimes increases. The implication is that in deciding which offenders should be transferred to adult courts, one might retain the notion that only those who commit serious offenses should be considered. Otherwise, justice and prudence would counsel juvenile court jurisdiction.

Thus, the standard we would propose for shifting juveniles to adult criminal court would be based on persistent, serious criminal offending. Persistence is necessary to rebut the presumption of youthful indiscretion. Seriousness is necessary to shift the balance from a dominant interest in the child's development to a greater concern for community security. In all likelihood, the application of this standard would result in only a small fraction of cases being transferred to the adult court.[102] Moreover, it would allow the age of jurisdiction of the juvenile court to be widened without worry that dangerous juveniles would be insulated from effective state action.

Abuse and Neglect of Children

A second part of the court's jurisdiction focuses on the abuse and neglect of children. In settling on the boundaries of that jurisdiction, three issues must be resolved. One is the question of what specific acts or circumstances could justify a public intervention into family life. A second is why that intervention should be by a court rather than a social work agency. A third is why this court should be the *juvenile* court rather than the *adult* court.

The principal justification for intruding into the private affairs of families in this domain is the desire to protect children from specific harms inflicted on them by their parents (or other caretakers).[103] Inevitably, this limits parental rights and imposes new duties. As one commentator observed, "[L]aws against child abuse and neglect are an implicit recognition that parental rights are not absolute, and that society, through its courts and social service agencies, should intervene into private family matters to protect endangered children."[104]

The social history of limiting parental authority to allow public protection of children has a mixed pedigree. On the one hand it is seen as a bold and humane social commitment to extend the society's protection to those who, in the short run, are most vulnerable and, over the long run, are most important to the life of the society.[105] On the other hand it is seen as overreaching by public agencies that intrudes on private affairs, destroys families, discriminates against cultural minorities and the poor, and exposes children to greater hazards in the hands of public substitutes for families than they faced in their own families.[106]

Moreover, the operations of the child protection system are paradoxically seen as simultaneously underprotecting and overprotecting children at risk.[107] The problem of *underprotection* arises for three different reasons: (a) Not all cases of abuse and neglect come to light. Very small children cannot report, and older children may be too afraid or too tied to their abusive parents by bonds of dependence and love to do so.[108] (b) The ambiguity of many child abuse and neglect situations often leads to caution on the part of public officials. There is a natural reluctance to intervene too quickly lest parents be stigmatized, children demoralized, and the state assume too much responsibility. Consequently, if a situation deteriorates rapidly, the consequences for the child cannot always be prevented, even if authorities are aware of the situation. (c) Because the jurisdiction for child abuse and neglect cases is divided among social service agencies, the police, and the courts, the difficulties of bureaucratic coordination often lead to irresolution and inaction rather than to prompt, decisive intervention.[109] The consequences of underprotection occasionally appear in dramatic and tragic form: children dead, maimed, or psychologically disabled as a result of abuses inflicted on them by their own parents.[110]

The problem of *overprotection* arises from different factors, many designed explicitly to deal with the problem of underprotection. Perhaps the most important is the vague wording of the laws establishing jurisdiction. As one commentator reported,

> Most state laws authorize child protective intervention with conclusory phrases such as when the child's "environment is injurious to his welfare," when the child "lacks proper parental care," or when the parents are "unfit to properly care for such child."[111]

Such vagueness allows many situations that are not really threatening to the child to be included within the jurisdiction of the court. A second factor is the existence of laws requiring the reporting of potential cases of abuse and neglect observed by third parties such as doctors, teachers, welfare workers, and others.[112] The effect of such laws is further exaggerated by civil liability rules that motivate public officials to err on the side of reporting rather than failing to report, and from the general public enthusiasm for protecting children from parents who seem neglectful or abusive.[113]

Overprotection would not be a problem were it not for the fact that the false identification of someone as a neglectful or abusive parent and the intrusion into that family to establish the truth of the charge can be enormously destructive to family relations. The parents may be stigmatized, and the stigma may become a self-fulfilling prophecy.[114] The delicate fabric of family relations may be shredded by the jagged suspicions created during the process of investigation.[115] The parents may become demoralized by all the public attention and cease feeling responsible for the family. And, finally, public money and authority are spent needlessly.

The recent goal of public policy has been to reduce these problems of underprotecting and overprotecting children at risk. The principal device has been to limit public intervention to cases where the risks are concrete, imminent, and serious. As one commentator recommended, "Neglect statutes should be drafted in terms of *specific harms* that a child must be suffering, or extremely likely to suffer, not in terms of desired parental behavior."[116]

This approach is perhaps best exemplified by the *Standards Relating to Abuse and Neglect* published by the Institute of Judicial Administration and the American Bar Association's Project on Juvenile Justice Standards. To establish the boundaries of this jurisdiction, these proposed standards include the following items:

Statutory guidelines. The statutory grounds for coercive intervention on behalf of endangered children: A) Should be defined as specifically as possible; B) Should authorize intervention only where the child is suffering, or there is a substantial likelihood that the child will imminently suffer serious harm; C) Should permit coercive intervention only for categories of harm where intervention will, in most cases, do more good than harm.

Protecting cultural differences. Standards for coercive intervention should take into account cultural differences in childrearing. All decisionmakers should examine the child's needs in light of the child's cultural background and values.

Child's interests paramount. State intervention should promote family autonomy and strengthen family life whenever possible. However, in cases where a child's needs as defined in these standards conflict with his/her parents' interests, the child's needs should have priority.

Continuity and stability. When state intervention is necessary, the entire system of intervention should be designed to promote a child's need for a continuous stable living environment.

Recognizing developmental differences. Laws aimed at protecting children should reflect developmental differences among children of different ages.

Accountability. The system of coercive state intervention should be designed to insure that all agencies, including courts, participating in the intervention process are held accountable for all of their actions.[117]

Although these standards represent a heroic effort to give precision and clarity to this domain, one cannot help but note that substantial ambiguities remain. The most obvious is that the standards allow judgments about future risks of various kinds of harm as well as about the past actuality, and they do not address the conditions observed within a family that would support the judgments. In addition, the standards are reluctant to exclude the intangible risks associated with psychological damage.[118] They include these harms and thereby open a broad discretionary domain. Thus, even the IJA–ABA standards are fairly broad and discretionary.

Moreover, even though these standards are quite broad, they may exclude important pieces of the abuse and neglect problem. For example, they may exclude some emergency situations in which family conditions create a substantial risk of injury but there has been no prior act of abuse or neglect by the parents. Perhaps more important, they may exclude situations in which the behavior of parents is "cumulatively harmful" rather than "immediately harmful."[119] "Cumulatively harmful behavior" by parents is defined as

> Parental behavior which will cause . . . serious harm to the child if continued for a sufficient length of time. For example, a parent provides a nutritionally inadequate diet for the child which, over time, will cause serious health problems; a parent inflicts repeated, but otherwise minor, assaults on the child which, over time, will make him into an easily frustrated, violence prone individual; or a parent provides grossly inadequate emotional support and cognitive stimulation which, over time, will lead to severe developmental disabilities.[120]

Such parental conduct may be missed if standards are focused on serious, imminent, material risks to the child, because at no particular moment is the child unusually threatened. It is the cumulative pattern that creates the problem, and this pattern can be discovered only through a rather searching investigation of conditions within the family.

One other problem of trying to narrow and focus public intervention in this dimension is that the standards eventually lose contact with the prevailing community standards governing child rearing. This may be an advantage if the prevailing standards are insensitive to cultural differences in the community, or if they impose duties that some members of the community cannot meet by virtue of poverty rather than indifference to their children. But the disadvantages of reaching for language that offers precision and focus at the expense of common, communal understandings is that the language will cause the standards to lose their ability to attract support from and to instruct the community. The language will become lawyer's language rather than political or community language, and the price paid will be that the juvenile court becomes a lawyers' institution rather than the community's.

In the end, it seems unlikely that the ambiguities in this jurisdiction can be cleared up. Inevitably, the language will be ambiguous. Inevitably, mistakes of overprotection and underprotection will be made. Inevitably, the jurisdiction will tend to widen, as a necessary result of the society's strong desire to protect its children and to articulate and live by norms that impose on parents substantive responsibilities for the task of caring for and protecting children. Thus, the public will inevitably be involved in the area of child protection.

This inevitable public engagement (and the inevitable errors) in cases of child abuse and neglect raise the second key question: Why should public intervention come from a court rather than from a social work agency? Arguably, social work interventions would be more economical and effective than court interventions, particularly given the inevitability of errors. It seems reasonable to assume that most parents are well motivated toward their children and to take advantage of that fact, rather than to assume the opposite and try to construct a parental substitute through public auspices. It may also be true that the principal problem in caring for the children is not a lack of desire but rather insufficient resources or knowledge. In such cases it would be wiser to provide resources and advice to buttress the natural family, rather than to attack the parents for civil or criminal offenses.

All of this adds up to a strong social preference for dealing with abuse and neglect cases through social work agencies rather than the courts. Consequently, it is reassuring to note that, for the most part, these cases are handled in this context. Only a tiny fraction of the cases that involve potential or actual cases of abuse and neglect are handled in the context of the juvenile court.[121] But the question remains, why should any cases end up in the juvenile court?

There are essentially four answers. The first is that sometimes parents do not acknowledge their need for improved performance with respect to caring for their children, and the public must intervene forcibly to make sure that they accept the resources necessary to achieve this goal.[122] Such cases are usually nominated to the court by social workers, not the police. As one observer explained:

> As a society, we have adopted a predominantly therapeutic or "social work" response to . . . child abuse and child neglect. Almost all reports of suspected child maltreatment are made to "child protective agencies" rather than to the police. However, there is a fundamental difference between classic social work and child protective practice. Social work, in its purest form, is built upon the client's willing participation in the therapeutic process. If the client refuses to participate, the case is closed.
>
> In child protective practice, however, if the parent declines services, or refuses to cooperate altogether, then the worker must decide whether the danger to the child is so great that treatment must be imposed.[123]

Thus, the need to use state authority to coerce treatment is one reason for court involvement in some cases of abuse and neglect.

A second reason for court involvement in at least some cases of abuse and neglect is that sometimes these cases will involve the more or less temporary transfer of responsibility for the child from natural parents to someone else.[124] Occasionally, they will even involve the termination of parental rights.[125] Such actions, which concern themselves with the creation and dissolution of particular rights and responsibilities recognized by the society, are quintessentially legal work. Judgments may be guided by concerns about the best interests of a child and other kinds of practical calculations, but they involve a change in the structure of rights and responsibilities in the society. This is necessarily legal work rather than social work, though social work may be necessary to realize the goals of the restructured relationships.

A third reason to involve the courts in cases of abuse and neglect is to protect the child's interests even when the child is a ward of the state.[126] After all, the public's interest in making sure that the child is protected does not end once the child is taken from a dangerous home. It shifts to an interest in making sure that the child is well protected in his or her new condition of foster care, public custody, or adoption.[127] If the child is at risk in any of these socially constructed circumstances, this is of equal concern to the court: The child may sometimes need the court's protection in an arrangement the court helped to construct. Thus, the court must assume responsibility for holding not only parents accountable but also any other who is granted responsibility for the child.

A fourth reason for involving the courts has less to do with the requirements of the immediate case at hand than with use of the courts to articulate, establish, or reinforce community norms governing the care and protection of children. After all, when a court acts, it acts not only on behalf of an individual child but on behalf of all children. In making general representations, it creates laws and social norms as well as reflects them.[128] To the extent that parents, caseworkers, police, and others take guidance from the court on the general standards of care that prevail in the society, and to the extent that these general standards exert force not only in deciding which cases fall outside the boundaries of tolerance but also in shaping general behavior in the community, it may be necessary and desirable to involve the court in cases of abuse and neglect so that it may instruct the community about the community's responsibilities. (This point is developed more fully in the concluding section of this chapter, "The coherence of the juvenile court.")

Thus, some court involvement is probably a necessary complement to a predominantly social work approach to child abuse and neglect. But this does not answer the question of why the court should be the juvenile court. Indeed, to the extent that this jurisdiction is limited to parental acts that actually harm children, and to the extent that one focuses on the court's role in establishing and enforcing community norms, dealing with these cases in adult criminal court might be more appropriate. To the extent that the court is involved in restructuring responsibilities inside a family, the court should perhaps be one that specializes in this, such as a probate court. In fact, given that the other jurisdictions of the juvenile court seem to focus on the child as an offender, while in cases of abuse and neglect the child is a victim, the juvenile court seems singularly inappropriate as a forum for dealing with abuse and neglect.

There seem to be three reasons that cases of abuse and neglect are dealt with in the context of the juvenile court. The first is historical. This jurisdiction was specifically created at the time the juvenile court was created; the court was seen as an institution that could make a special contribution to this problem.[129]

The second has to do with the fact that the society seems to have more at stake in the handling of cases of abuse and neglect than the desire to maintain community norms by criminally prosecuting the offending parents.[130] In the individual case, it has a continuing interest in the development of the child. All other things being equal, society would prefer that the parents take and discharge that responsibility. Making arrangements that allow this to occur seems better than jailing the parents and leaving the children in the custody of the state. This does not mean that criminal prosecution is never appropriate. It just means that, as a matter of social policy, it is better for everyone if the parents can be restored to effective functioning on behalf of their responsibilities to their children and the society.

The third reason for including abuse and neglect in the juvenile court has to do with the style and the distinctive competence of the juvenile court. Its nonadversarial style fits the relationship the society would like to have with parents who are apparently not fulfilling their responsibility to their children.[131] Its willingness to investigate conditions that lie behind offenses fits the necessity of searching for patterns of abuse and neglect and making accurate judgments about future risks. Its desire to construct creative alternatives that advance the society's interests in the future development of the child and the respect for family autonomy and responsibility make it more useful than the adult criminal court, which has a more limited set of possible dispositions. In short, the juvenile court seems more expert in investigating cases, creating relationships, supplying resources, and monitoring ongoing conditions than any other kind of court.

In sum, the juvenile court is likely to continue to be stuck with the jurisdiction for cases of child abuse and neglect. For those who value the institution, that fact is unfortunate, for the court is certain to continue to fail in this area. It will fail in performance terms by producing dramatic instances of both underprotection and overprotection of children. And it will fail in terms of its ability to be accountable, because its policies and procedures in this domain will never be precise and clear.

If there is a solution to the continuing public controversy about this jurisdiction, it probably lies in four distinct areas. First, it seems important that the society recognize the magnitude of its interest in child protection and the difficulties created by that interest. Much commentary seems to assume that the society can perform perfectly in this area, that is, that it will neither overprotect nor underprotect, that its interventions will be effective, that there will be no taint of class or race bias in its operations, and so on. This does not seem possible. Any policy that makes a serious effort to protect children will necessarily require the society to take losses in each of these areas. Nonetheless, the society seems to think that child protection is a sufficiently important goal to be worth these losses. If not, the jurisdiction should be abandoned.

The second is a corollary of the first: If the society continues this interest in protecting children, it must become more tolerant of errors. It cannot be as indignant as it now is about individual cases. It cannot insist on certainty and perfection in areas that are inherently uncertain and imperfect. It must learn how to look at its average performance rather than the exceptional cases.

The third observation is more substantive. It seems that the greatest area of potential improvement in the society's response to cases of child abuse and neglect is greater reliance on interventions that continue the responsibility of the parents but equip them with the resources and training they need to do the job well and subject them to the continuing supervision of the court to make sure that they live up to their responsibilities.[132] This ongoing supervision is important both to protect the child's interests and to provide a continuing incentive to the parents. One expert observed:

The need for foster care often can be obviated through in-home, child-oriented services that "compensate" for parental deficiencies. ("Compensatory" services include infant stimulation programs, Head Start, therapeutic day care, homemaker care, early childhood or child development programs, nutritional services, and youth counseling programs.)[133]

Similarly, the IJA–ABA Standards make room for precisely such interventions in the interest of preserving families and minimizing public intervention:

Available dispositions

A. A court should have at least the following dispositional alternatives and resources: 1) dismissal of the case; 2) wardship with informal supervision; 3) ordering the parents to accept social work supervision; 4) ordering the parents and/or the child to accept individual or family therapy or medical treatment; 5) ordering the state or parents to employ a homemaker in the home; 6) placement of the child in a day care program; 7) placement of the child with a relative, in a foster family or group home, or in a residential treatment center.

B. A court should have authority to order that the parent accept, and that the state provide, any of the above services.

C. It should be the state's responsibility to provide an adequate level of services.[134]

In short, the proper form of public intervention in these cases may be to shore up families through support and supervision rather than attempting to substitute for them.

Fourth, the court should feel as responsible for holding public agencies (including itself) accountable for the abuse and neglect of children as it does for holding parents accountable. The thing that justifies public intervention is an interest in protecting children. That interest is at least as strong, and probably stronger, when the society has taken the child from the natural home as it is when the child is in the natural home.

Status Offenses

The third and most controversial part of the juvenile court's jurisdiction is status offenses, such as incorrigibility, truancy, waywardness, promiscuity, disorderly conduct, and curfew violations. The crucial issue is whether these offenses should continue as liabilities for children within the purview of the juvenile court or should be eliminated.

To those who have been concerned with the development of children's rights and have viewed the interventions of the juvenile court as essentially punitive, the statutory existence of status offenses seems an indefensible extension of state power over children.[135] Indeed, the statutes creating these offenses seem to fail in all the ways that statutes creating liabilities for citizens can fail.[136] They focus on behavior and conduct that are not particularly threatening to the community. They are written in vague language that invites abuses of discretion. And they single out a special group of people and make the laws applicable only to them. Thus, the laws seem little more than the larger society discriminating against children and, in all likelihood, against disadvantaged children rather than wealthy children. The pretense that the laws help children adds the sin of hypocrisy to an already long list of offensive features.

This perspective on status offenses is powerful, both politically and jurisprudentially. Indeed, the fact that the concept of status offenses has become part of the standard terms for discussing juvenile issues reveals the power of this perspective. Originally these offenses were not separated from the other elements of the juvenile court jurisdiction.[137] They were grouped together and distinguished from criminal conduct of children by those who thought the juvenile court's jurisdiction over children was far too broad. Moreover, in describing them as status offenses, a strong bias against their continued inclusion was created, for the very name suggests the injustice of such laws. Nonetheless, status offenses survive in the laws governing the conduct of children. They existed long before passage of the juvenile court acts of the progressive era.[138] They were reiterated (and perhaps expanded) in those special enabling statutes. And they continue in the statutes of virtually all of the states despite a decade of strong political efforts to remove them.[139] This suggests that the laws creating status offenses solve a problem for the society. Consequently, it is worth considering what that problem might be.

One view of status offenses is that they are devices to give the community power over children who annoy adults. In this view, it is the adult's anxiety about disruptive children that is the problem. The children pose no real threat to others or to themselves. Since it is wrong to impose harsh and stigmatizing penalties on children for nothing more than childhood exuberance, and since it is unseemly for adult citizens in a liberal society to be so easily frightened and offended, it is wrong to enshrine adult needs for decorum in laws.

One could attack this view directly by pointing to evidence that citizens' fears are kindled more by disorder on the streets than by actual experience with violent crime, and that heightened judicial concern for civility on the streets might well increase the sense of security of people in cities.[140] Moreover, one can argue that it is a fundamental duty of citizens—including children—to avoid giving offense, and that police and court interest in disorderly conduct might help obstreperous children (and their parents) learn this lesson. And, finally, one can observe that these protections might be particularly valuable to segments of the population that are particularly vulnerable, such as single women, mothers with children, and the elderly.[141]

Still, these arguments seem insufficient against the general principle that a free society depends on sturdy citizens who do not need the law to make community life conform to their particular ideas of decorum. Indeed, this use of the law seems especially inappropriate when its application will inevitably result in disadvantaged groups—in this case, disadvantaged children—being affected more than others. Further, there is some reason to believe that the intervention of the law will not solve the problem but will make it worse, either by escalating the struggle between children and society or by stigmatizing children so that their disadvantage deepens. It would be important, then, not to yield to these concerns about disorderly children even when the concerns are voiced by the elderly and by mothers of infants who might deserve special protection.

A second kind of argument that makes status offenses seem a justifiable focus of the law is that these offenses help the society to identify children who are particularly likely to become youthful criminal offenders. In this view, incorrigibility, truancy, and disorderly conduct are seen as precursors of real criminal offenses such as larceny, burglary, robbery, and assault. This position gains support from empirical evidence indicating an overlap between those who have committed status offenses and those who commit criminal offenses.[142] In addition, it seems clear that many incidents involving children that could be treated as criminal offenses are treated as status offenses.[143] In sum, while the line between status offenses and criminal offenses seems clear in the law, it is blurred in the lives of the children who appear before the juvenile court.

From a legal perspective, the only feature that makes this argument any more respectable than the first is that some link is established between status offenses and real criminal offenses. The law is not imposing a particular conception of decorum, but is trying to prevent offenses that really do threaten life and property in the society. The difficulty, however, is that the link is made via a prediction that the status offenders will become criminal offenders in the future. Whether the criminal justice system should condition its actions on predictions of criminal conduct is a hotly contested issue—particularly because our capacity to predict is so imperfect.[144] Moreover, there is reason to worry that the predictions become self-fulfilling prophecies through the mechanism of labeling.[145] Since it seems unjust to predicate social control on predictions of future conduct, since the ability to predict is quite imperfect, and since the predictions do more harm than good, it seems wrong to use status offenses as a device for preventing future juvenile crime.

If these are the only arguments that can be mustered for laws focused on status offenses, the laws probably should be abandoned. Even though citizens are frightened by children, and even though there is some correlation between status offenses and criminal offending, these are not good enough reasons for use of state power against children who commit such offenses.

There is another way of looking at status offenses, however. This different view sees status offenses not as devices to protect the society from children, but instead as devices to keep children in relationships that guide them toward responsible citizenship. This view of status offenses can be derived from the jurisprudence of family and children as set out by Zimring[146] and Minow.[147]

As noted previously, Zimring argued that the society should think of children as having a learner's permit. The implication is that the society should tolerate children's errors of judgment and competence without making them pay the price that would be demanded from fully responsible, "licensed" adults. While this idea of having a learner's permit has been widely understood and accepted, another idea that goes along with it seems less widely understood. The special license to err associated with a learner's permit has a price, and that price is official recognition of the (relative) incompetence of the learner. The price may also be the acceptance of some special duties associated with being a learner. The learner may, for example, have to declare his or her status and warn others that he or she does not possess full competence. More important, the learner may have a duty to stay out of harm's way, seek out teachers, and accept guidance from others who are more competent. The last two duties resemble what Minow calls the right (and duty) of affiliation.

At the extreme, of course, the learner can become so well protected and instructed that no important learning takes place. For this reason, we understand that the learner must be allowed to experiment. A sense of autonomy and accountability must be built along with technical competence if a fully responsible person is to emerge.

Viewed from this perspective, one might view status offenses as special obligations that attach to the "office" or "status" of being a child in the society.[148] These duties include being responsive to the guidance and instruction of parents (incorrigibility), attending school (truancy), avoiding the use of alcohol and drugs, and learning that there is an age when childish tantrums and posturing become threatening to the society at large. Duties may also include accepting adult guidance with respect to sexual activity.[149]

In this view, the objection that adults in the society are not regulated in this way is not really an objection, because the obligations and duties are specific to the special status of being a child in the society. They are the price of being granted a special license. Similarly, that the offenses describe status rather than acts is not an objection, because the aim of the society is to manage the status of the child and the child's relationships with others who have responsibility for him or her. This, too, is a price of the special permission to err that the society grants to children.

In sum, status offenses are not acts that give short-term offense to the rest of the society. Nor are they acts that presage delinquency. They are violations of special obligations that attach to children in the interests of equipping them to take their place in adult society. Status offenses can also be seen as signs of breakdown in the set of relationships on which the society is relying for the socialization of children and as therefore occasioning court intervention to reestablish the proper set of relationships. Whether court interventions are in fact useful in helping to reestablish the relationships within which the child learns the way into adulthood is a crucial question. But from a legal perspective, it is not obviously wrong to have laws setting out the special duties that attach to the office of the child. Nor is it obviously wrong to have some of those duties concerned with relationships as well as acts.

The Coherence of the Juvenile Court

Each of the elements that guides the jurisprudence of the juvenile court is controversial. Whether children should be seen as autonomous and accountable or as dependent and excusable is debated. So is the question of due process protections.

Not only is each element of the court's jurisdiction controversial, but also its overall coherence. It is not obvious at first glance why the same court should have jurisdiction over crimes committed by children and against them, why it should include serious offenses as well as minor, and why it should include status offenses as well as criminal offenses. Our view, however, is that there is a coherent jurisprudence that underlies the juvenile court. That jurisprudence is concerned both with an important *set of social relationships* and with certain *purposes*.

The *set of social relationships* that are important to the court are those among child, parent, others who care for the child, and the state. These relationships are guided by social recognition of the different statuses of those involved—by the different rights, privileges, and obligations that attach to the different "offices." For example, children are considered not wholly accountable for their acts because they are partially dependent. While that status mitigates their culpability when they commit criminal offenses, it also imposes special duties and makes due process protections less essential and more harmful in court proceedings. For their part, parents have a great deal of autonomy in raising their children, but this autonomy is limited by the general responsibilities that they have to their children. These duties to protect, guide, and develop their children are not owed only to the children as a matter of children's rights. They are also owed to the state as one of the duties of the office of parent. Since the parents have duties to supervise and care for their children, and since the children are in a partially dependent (or semiautonomous) status, parents generally should be parties to court action involving the child. The state's role in this context is to oversee the relationships, settle disputes that arise within them, and generally try to keep most of the work of raising children in the hands of the parents and children.

The *purposes* that guide the juvenile court are (a) to do what can be done to protect the society from juvenile crime (understood at least partly as youthful indiscretion and failures of parental supervision as well as evil intentions of children, (b) to protect children from the worst consequences of parental abuse and neglect, and (c) to establish favorable conditions under which children can grow to responsible and resourceful citizenship. In pursuing these purposes, the state seeks to economize on the use of public resources, both authority and money. And it seeks to maintain the private relationships and institutions that are by far the best at performing the task of child rearing. The state takes an interest in child rearing not only to protect itself from crimes or social dependence in the future, but also to enhance opportunities for children—a desired feature of a just as well as an accomplished society.

This view of the jurisprudence of the juvenile court makes much that now seems anomalous much more coherent. It also points the way toward some important improvements within the court. Probably the most important change is in seeing that the juvenile court's relationship to children is always partially mediated, never direct. There is always a parent, legal guardian, or public agency that is acting for the state's interests in raising children. Thus, these agents should always be part of the court's proceeding.

A second important change is in seeing that the court holds juveniles (and those who care for them) accountable, as well as excuses them (or replaces their caretakers.) The difference in the juvenile court is that the children (and their private and public caretakers) are not being held accountable for crimes. They are being held accountable for living up to the duties attached to the process of growing up. The juveniles' task is to learn, and the caretakers' task is to teach how to be citizens.

A third important change is in seeing the relevance and importance of accurate information about and diagnoses of the conditions under which children are being raised. This, far more significant than the guilt or innocence of parents and children, is the central piece of information that the court needs. The process of the court should be designed to produce this information reliably.

If this coherence does exist—if these ideas hold out the possibility of a more just and effective juvenile court—how did we go astray? How did the legal discussion and analysis (to say nothing of juvenile court operations) stray from this guiding philosophy? How did concepts that seem straightforward and obvious become so controversial? We think there are three closely related answers to these questions.

The first concerns the failures and errors of the original juvenile court. The original court erred most obviously in the injustice of its dispositions. It sent children to institutions where the quality of care, supervision, and guidance was far less than desirable and far less than the public could tolerate. It erred only slightly less obviously in its willingness to intervene, to assume responsibility for children even when there was substantial private capacity to work with. This led the society to the view that the original aims and values of the court had to be wrong, and discredited the notion that a court could be usefully engaged in fostering the development of children.

This failure, in turn, led to a second problem. In seeking to construct a different jurisprudence for the juvenile court, the society turned to a more familiar model—the model of a criminal court. This seemed particularly appropriate, since so much of the business of the juvenile court involved crimes committed by (or against) children. Once the evaluative framework of a criminal court was fixed over the juvenile court, many anomalies appeared, for example, the coddling of youthful offenders, the lack of due process protections, the existence of status offenses, and the problem of cumulative abuse and neglect. Concepts that were important to a court concerned about family relationships and the social development of children made little sense in the framework of a criminal court.

Finally, the society seems to find it hard to acknowledge that a great deal of work must go into raising children, into helping them grow from defenseless barbarians into resourceful citizens, and that the society has an interest in having this process succeed. The problem arises because of a concern that acknowledging the state's interest seems to open the door for, on the one hand, an oppressive state domination of relationships and, on the other hand, an excessive claim on the state's financial resources. No one wants the state to assume total, direct responsibility for the raising of children. The question is how the state should pursue its interests and exercise its powers in this domain.

We believe the answer to this is not by the old juvenile court, nor by a constitutionalized and criminalized juvenile court. Instead, it is by a court that assumes some loose responsibility for holding children and those who care for children accountable for the children's growing up into good citizens. In this conception, the crucial errors of the original juvenile court were not in its values and purposes, but instead in its willingness to intervene and establish a direct relationship with the child and in its failure to operate effectively in the cases it heard. The first error can be fixed by adopting the jurisprudence proposed here as a philosophical guide to the court's operations. The second depends on the society's capabilities to organize and invest in the concrete operations of the juvenile justice system. That is the subject of the next chapter.

Notes

1. The juvenile courts in the United States handled approximately 1,465,000 cases of delinquency, status offenses, and abuse/neglect in 1982. In contrast, there were about 63,963,000 children under the age of 18 in 1982. Ellen H. Nimick, Howard N. Snyder, Dennis P. Sullivan, and Nancy J. Tierney, *Juvenile Court Statistics, 1982* (Pittsburgh: National Center for Juvenile Justice, 1984), pp. 8, 14.
2. This is the standard of justice proposed by John Rawls. See John Rawls, *A Theory of Justice* (Cambridge, MA: Harvard University Press, 1971).
3. This point was emphasized repeatedly by the members of the Executive Session who served as judges, probation officers, or corrections administrators. (See Preface to this volume.)
4. Rosemary Sarri and Yeheskel Hasenfeld, Eds., *Brought to Justice? Juveniles, the Courts and the Law* (Ann Arbor, MI: University of Michigan Press, 1976).
5. Charles E. Springer, "Justice for juveniles" (Washington, DC: U.S. Department of Justice, Office of Juvenile Justice and Delinquency Prevention, April 1986).
6. For a powerful exposition of this perspective see Charles E. Silberman, *Criminal Violence, Criminal Justice* (New York: Random House, 1978), chap. 9.
7. Sanford J. Fox argued that an analysis of the history of juvenile justice reform suggests that such "reform is a complex and highly ambivalent affair in which the goal of child welfare has been but one of many motivational elements" (p. 1188). Sanford J. Fox, "Juvenile justice reform: An historical perspective," *Stanford Law Review 22*(6) (June 1970), pp. 1187–1239.
8. We are indebted to Jeffrey Bleich for emphasizing this point and carrying out the relevant research. See Jeffrey Bleich, "An analysis of juvenile justice statutes: Philosophies and trends," unpublished mimeo, Harvard University, Cambridge, MA, 1986.
9. "An act to regulate the treatment and control of dependent, neglected and delinquent children," State of Illinois General Assembly, Apr. 21, 1899.
10. For a contemporary discussion of this statute, see Julian W. Mack, "The juvenile court," *Harvard Law Review 23* (1909), pp. 104–122.
11. Sarri and Hasenfeld, Eds., *Brought to Justice?*
12. See Anne Rankin Mahoney, "The effect of labeling on youths in the juvenile justice system: A review of the evidence," *Law and Society Review 8*(4) (Summer 1974), pp. 583–614, for a review of theoretical and empirical evidence about labeling.
13. Silberman, *Criminal Violence, Criminal Justice*, pp. 313–326.
14. This point of view was expressed consistently by James Wootton in the Executive Session. (See Preface to this volume.)
15. Ibid.
16. This perspective is widely expressed but rarely documented.
17. For evidence on the failure of rehabilitation programs see Robert Martinson, "What works: Questions and answers about prison reform," *The Public Interest*, No. 35 (Spring 1974), pp. 22–54. For evidence that some juvenile programs succeed some of the time with some kids see Peter W. Greenwood,

Ed., *The Juvenile Rehabilitation Reader* (Santa Monica, CA: Rand Corporation, 1985) and Peter W. Greenwood and Franklin E. Zimring, *One More Chance: The Pursuit of Promising Intervention Strategies for Chronic Juvenile Offenders* (Santa Monica, CA: Rand Corporation, 1985).

18. Anne Larason Schneider and Donna D. Schram, *An Assessment of Juvenile Justice System Reform in Washington State*, Vol. 10, *Executive Summary* (Eugene, OR: Institute of Policy Analysis, 1983).
19. *Washington State Revised Criminal Code*, Title 13 (1977, 1978, 1979, 1981).
20. Schneider and Schram, *Juvenile Justice System Reform*, Vol. 10.
21. Anne Larason Schneider, Jill G. McKelvy, and Donna D. Schram, *An Assessment of Juvenile Justice System Reform in Washington State*, Vol. 5, *Divestiture of Court Jurisdiction Over Status Offenders* (Eugene, OR: Institute of Policy Analysis, 1983).
22. For example see *McKinney's Consolidated Laws of New York Annotated, Criminal Procedure Law*, Sec. 725.
23. Mark M. Levin and Rosemary C. Sarri, *Juvenile Delinquency: A Comparative Analysis of Legal Codes in the United States* (Ann Arbor, MI: National assessment of juvenile corrections, University of Michigan, 1974), pp. 22–23.
24. The maximum age jurisdiction for delinquency varies for the juvenile courts of various states. Six states provide jurisdiction up to age 16 [CT, NY, NC, VT, OK (boys), NE (minor offenses)], eight states provide jurisdiction up to age 17 (GA, IL, LA, MA, MI, MO, SC, TX), one state's maximum jurisdictional age is 19 (WY), and the remainder provide jurisdiction up to age 18. Letter from Ben Koller, Director of Juvenile Justice Reform at the American Legislative Exchange Council, dated Dec. 3, 1985.
25. For a legislator's views see Don McCorkell, Jr., "The politics of juvenile justice in America," in volume 2 of this series.
26. See *Revised Code of Washington Annotated*, chap. 13.32A.
27. The American Legislative Exchange Council reported that 39 states provide a specific juvenile court jurisdiction for status offenses. See Koller letter, note 24. Also see I. Rosenberg, "Juvenile status offender statutes—New perspectives on an old problem," *University of California-Davis Law Review 16* (1983).
28. "Juvenile Justice, Runaway Youth, and Missing Children's Act Amendments of 1984." Hearing before the Subcommittee on Human Resources of the Committee on Education and Labor, House of Representatives, 98th Congress, 2nd Session, on H. R. 4971 (Washington, DC: U.S. Government Printing Office, Mar. 7, 1984).
29. PL 98-473; 98 Stat. 2107.
30. Douglas J. Besharov, "Foster care reform: Two books for practitioners," *Family Law Quarterly 18*(2) (Summer 1984), pp. 247–253.
31. For a survey of permanency planning projects, see Permanency Planning for Children Project, *50 State Update* (Reno, NV: National Council of Juvenile and Family Court Judges, 1986). Examples include *McKinney's Consolidated Laws of New York Annotated*, Social Services Law, Sec. 358-a (1984, 1985), and *Massachusetts General Laws Annotated*, 119 Sec. 29B (1984, 1985).
32. Travis Hirschi discussed the relationship between crime and child rearing in

"Crime and the family," in James Q. Wilson, Ed., *Crime and Public Policy* (San Francisco: ICS Press, 1983), pp. 53–68.

33. Glenn C. Loury, "The family as a context for delinquency prevention: Demographic trends and political realities," in volume 3 of this series.
34. *Illinois Statutes Annotated,* Sec. 701–702.
35. Richard Farsons, "The children's rights movement," in LaMar T. Empey, Ed., *The Future of Childhood and Juvenile Justice* (Charlottesville, VA: University Press of Virginia, 1979), pp. 35–65.
36. For an excellent discussion of the parallels and differences in the status of these different groups of dependents see Franklin E. Zimring, *The Changing Legal World of Adolescence* (New York: Free Press, 1982), pp. 22–28.
37. For an eloquent defense of the importance of due process protections for children see Janet Fink, "Actors on the juvenile court stage," in volume 2 of this series.
38. Martha Minow, "The public duties of families and children," in volume 2 of this series.
39. These other cases were (a) *Tinker v. Des Moines Independent School District,* 393 U.S. 503 (1969) and (b) *Planned Parenthood of Central Missouri v. Danforth,* 428 U.S. 52 (1976).
40. *McKeiver v. Pennsylvania,* 403 U.S. 528 (1971).
41. *Schall v. Martin,* 467 U.S. 253, 104 S.Ct. 2403 (1984).
42. Minow, "The public duties of families and children."
43. In reaching this conclusion we are relying heavily on the views of Franklin E. Zimring and Martha Minow.
44. Zimring, *The Changing Legal World of Adolescence,* pp. 27–28.
45. Ibid., pp. x–xi.
46. Ibid.
47. Ibid., chaps. 7, 8, pp. 89–116.
48. Ibid., p. 91.
49. Ibid., chap. 4.
50. Ibid., p. 91.
51. Ibid., p. 89.
52. Ibid., p. 91.
53. Ibid., p. 96.
54. Minow, "The public duties of families and children."
55. Ibid., p. 15.
56. Ibid.
57. Ibid.
58. Ibid., p. 16
59. Ibid., p. 17.
60. Ibid.
61. Ibid.
62. Ibid., pp. 18–19.
63. Monrad G. Paulsen, "The constitutional domestication of the juvenile court," *The Supreme Court Review* (1967), pp. 233–237; Barry C. Feld, "Criminalizing juvenile justice: Rules of procedure for the juvenile court," *Minnesota Law Review* 69(2) (Dec. 1984), pp. 141–276.
64. *In re Gault,* 387 U.S. 1 (1967).
65. Justice Fortas, *In re Gault,* 387 U.S. 1 (1967), at 28.

66. Feld, "Criminalizing juvenile justice," pp. 154–157.
67. Ibid., p. 157.
68. Zimring, *The Changing Legal World of Adolescence,* chap. 6.
69. Feld, "Criminalizing juvenile justice," pp. 154–155, 158.
70. *McKeiver v. Pennsylvania,* 403 U.S. 528 (1971), at 541.
71. Feld, "Criminalizing juvenile justice," pp. 158–159.
72. *In re Gault,* 387 U.S. 1 (1967), at 13.
73. Ibid., at 27–28.
74. This analysis is developed in Mark H. Moore, "Purblind justice: Normative issues in the use of prediction in the criminal justice system," in Alfred Blumstein, Jacqueline Cohen, Jeffrey A. Roth, and Christy A. Visher, Eds., *Criminal Careers and "Career Criminals",* Vol. 2 (Washington, DC: National Academy Press, 1986), pp. 314–355.
75. James C. Weissman, "Towards an integrated theory of delinquent responsibility," *Denver Law Journal 60*(3) (1983), pp. 485–518.
76. Thomas R. Bearrows, "Status offenses and offenders," in volume 2 of this series.
77. See note 24.
78. This is the notion of "individualized" justice. See Janet Fink, "Actors on the juvenile court stage."
79. We are indebted to Janet Fink for emphasizing this point.
80. We are indebted to George L. Kelling in this connection; he observed that parents were given no role in court proceedings he observed in Hennepin County, Minnesota.
81. Fink, "Actors on the juvenile court stage."
82. Donna M. Hamparian, Richard Schuster, Simon Dinitz, and John P. Conrad, *The Violent Few: A Study of Dangerous Juvenile Offenders* (Lexington, MA: Lexington Books, 1978).
83. Institute of Judicial Administration–American Bar Association (henceforth IJA–ABA) Joint Commission on Juvenile Justice Standards, *Standards Relating to Abuse and Neglect* (Cambridge, MA: Ballinger, 1981).
84. R. Hale Andrews, Jr., and Andrew H. Cohn, "Ungovernability: The unjustifiable jurisdiction," *Yale Law Journal 83*(7) (June 1974), pp. 1382–1408.
85. *In re Gault,* 387 U.S. 1 (1967), at 16.
86. For the difference between law as a set of words and law as a social process see Donald Black, *The Behavior of Law* (New York: Academic Press, 1976).
87. Springer, "Justice for juveniles."
88. For discussions of this view of justice in the adult system see Ernst Van den Haag, *Punishing Criminals* (New York: Basic Books, 1975) and Andrew von Hirsch, *Doing Justice: Report of the Committee for the Study of Incarceration* (New York: Hill and Wang, 1976).
89. On the role of punishment in child development see Richard Barnum, "Concepts of responsibility: Development, failures, and responses," in volume 2 of this series. See also James Q. Wilson, "Raising kids," *Atlantic Monthly* (Oct. 1983), pp. 45–56.
90. These assumptions are not necessarily warranted. See Mark H. Moore, James Q. Wilson, and Ralph Gants, "Violent attacks and chronic offenders," unpublished mimeo prepared for the New York State Assembly Commission on Manpower and Productivity, 1978.

91. These views were expressed repeatedly and eloquently by Barbara Flicker and Janet Fink during our meetings. (See Preface to this volume.)
92. Ibid.
93. We are indebted to Dr. Richard W. Barnum for emphasizing this point. (See Preface to this volume.)
94. This is clearly Zimring's view of the priority to be given to competing objectives (Zimring, *The Changing Legal World of Adolescence*, pp. 91–92). "Above almost all else we seek a legal policy that preserves the life chances for those who make serious mistakes, as well as preserving choices for their more fortunate (and more virtuous) contemporaries."
95. Moore, Wilson, and Gants, "Violent attacks and chronic offenders."
96. See note 24.
97. New York State is an extreme case; it provides automatic shift of serious juvenile offenders to adult court. The adult court may "remove" the case to family court. *McKinney's Consolidated Laws of New York Annotated, Criminal Procedure Law*, Sec. 725.
98. According to the American Legislative Exchange Council, 44 states have provisions for waiving youths to adult court, though the waiver depends on the youth's age and offense. See Koller letter, note 24.
99. Jeffrey Bleich, "Juvenile court transfers: Philosophical issues," in volume 2 of this series; also Donna Hamparian, "The serious juvenile offender," also in volume 2.
100. Approximately half of all assaults and homicides are committed by acquaintances or relatives. U.S. Department of Justice, Bureau of Justice Statistics, *Report to the Nation on Crime and Justice: The Data*, NIJ-87068 (Washington, DC: U.S. Department of Justice, 1983), p. 15.
101. This follows a line of analysis developed in talking about the issue of adult criminal offenders. See Mark H. Moore, Susan R. Estrich, Daniel McGillis, and William Spelman, *Dangerous Offenders: The Elusive Target of Justice* (Cambridge, MA: Harvard University Press, 1984), chap. 2.
102. Hamparian et al., *The Violent Few*.
103. IJA–ABA Joint Commission, *Standards Relating to Abuse and Neglect*.
104. Douglas J. Besharov, " 'Doing something' about child abuse: The need to narrow the grounds for state intervention," *Harvard Journal of Law and Public Policy 8*(3) (Summer 1985), p. 554.
105. LaMar T. Empey, "The progressive legacy and the concept of childhood," in LaMar T. Empey, Ed., *Juvenile Justice: The Progressive Legacy and Current Reforms* (Charlottesville, VA: University Press of Virginia, 1979), pp. 3–33.
106. Ibid.
107. Besharov, " 'Doing something'," p. 540.
108. This is one of a category of offenses. See Mark H. Moore, "Invisible offenses: A challenge to minimally intrusive law enforcement," in Gerald M. Caplan, Ed., *ABSCAM Ethics: Moral Issues and Deception in Law Enforcement* (Washington, DC: Police Foundation, 1983), pp. 17–42.
109. Besharov, " 'Doing something'," p. 546.
110. Besharov, in " 'Doing something'," p. 541, cites a tragic example that was reported in J. Holter and Friedman, "Child abuse: Early case finding in the Emergency Department," *Pediatrics 42*(1) (1968), p. 24.

Two-year-old Larry was brought to the hospital by his mother for treatment of a broken arm. According to the hospital record, Larry's body was marked and scarred. But no report of suspected abuse was made and there is no record that anyone in the hospital questioned Larry's mother about these injuries.

A week later, Larry's parents again brought him to the hospital. This time, he had multiple bruises over many parts of his body, scars on his buttocks, and healing lesions on his upper and lower legs. Less than an hour after Larry arrived at the hospital, he died.

The medical examiner reported the cause of death to be internal injuries caused by numerous beatings.

111. Besharov, " 'Doing something'," pp. 567–568.
112. Ibid., p. 545.
113. Douglas J. Besharov, "The legal aspects of reporting known and suspected child abuse and neglect," *Villanova Law Review 23* (1977–1978), pp. 458–546.
114. Besharov, " 'Doing something'," p. 557.
115. Ibid.
116. Michael Wald, "State intervention on behalf of 'neglected' children: A search for realistic standards," *Stanford Law Review 27* (1975), p. 1004.
117. IJA–ABA Joint Commission, *Standards Relating to Abuse and Neglect*, pp. 15–16.
118. Ibid., pp. 16–17, 67–70.
119. Besharov, " 'Doing something'," pp. 580–584.
120. Ibid., p. 581.
121. "*No more than* one in four serious A/N [abuse and neglect] cases known to some public agency are referred to the court." Philip J. Cook and John H. Laub, "Trends in child abuse and juvenile delinquency," in volume 2 of this series.
122. Besharov, " 'Doing something'," p. 555.
123. Ibid.
124. IJA–ABA Joint Commission, *Standards Relating to Abuse and Neglect*. Also see Kenneth Keniston and the Carnegie Council on Children, *All Our Children: The American Family Under Pressure* (New York: Harcourt, Brace, Jovanovich, 1977), pp. 186–192.
125. IJA–ABA Joint Commission, *Standards Relating to Abuse and Neglect*.
126. Keniston and Carnegie Council on Children, *All Our Children*, pp. 196–198.
127. Permanency Planning for Children Project, *50 State Update*.
128. For a general discussion of the relationship between laws and normative practices in society, see Eugen Ehrlich, "Law and the inner order of social associations," reprinted in M. P. Golding, Ed., *The Nature of Law: Readings in Legal Philosophy* (New York: Random House, 1966), pp. 200–212.
129. Barbara Flicker, "A short history of jurisdiction over juvenile and family matters," in volume 2 of this series.
130. There is a certain tension between maintaining general community standards through punishment and helping to resolve a particular problem. This is particularly acute in all situations of domestic violence, because the state and the individuals often have an interest in maintaining the particular relationships. Recently, the trend is to emphasize arrests and general deterrence.

Attorney General's Task Force on Family Violence, *Final Report* (Washington, DC: U.S. Department of Justice, 1984).

131. The assumption is that the interests are identical. Besharov reported that most Americans think abuse and neglect is an illness rather than a crime. Besharov, " 'Doing something'," p. 553.
132. See volume 3 of this series for proposals about how to do this.
133. Besharov, " 'Doing something'," p. 585.
134. IJA–ABA Joint Commission, *Standards Relating to Abuse and Neglect*, p. 33.
135. Andrews and Cohn, "Ungovernability: The unjustifiable jurisdiction."
136. See Thomas R. Bearrows, "Status offenses and offenders," in volume 2 of this series, for an analysis and critique of the arguments against continued juvenile court jurisdiction over status offenses.
137. John Direen, *Juvenile Court Organization and Status Offenses: A Statutory Profile* (Pittsburgh: National Center for Juvenile Justice, 1974), pp. 33–45.
138. Thomas R. Bearrows points out that one of the oldest status offender laws is found in the Bible.

> If a man have a stubborn and rebellious son, that will not hearken to the voice of his father, or the voice of his mother, and though they chasten him, will not hearken unto them; then shall his father and his mother lay hold on him, and bring him out unto the elders of the city, and unto the gate of his place. . . .And all the men of his city shall stone him with stones, that he die; so shalt thou put away the evil from the midst of thee; and all Israel shall hear, and fear.
>
> From Deuteronomy 21:18–21, cited in Bearrows, "Status offenses and offenders."

139. Thirty-nine states specifically provide court jurisdiction for status offenses. See Koller letter, note 24.
140. James Q. Wilson and George L. Kelling, "Broken windows: The police and neighborhood safety," *Atlantic Monthly 249*(3) (Mar. 1982), pp. 29–38.
141. For a thoughtful discussion of the basis for fear of vulnerable populations, see Robert C. Trojanowicz, "Fear of crime: A critical issue in community policing," prepared for the Executive Session on Community Policing, Harvard University, Cambridge, MA, Apr. 10–12, 1986, pp. 19–24.
142. Frank R. Hellum and John Peterson, "Offense patterns of status offenders," chap. 4 in David Shichor and Delos H. Kelly, Eds., *Critical Issues in Juvenile Delinquency* (Lexington, MA: Lexington Books, D.C. Heath, 1980), and Joseph G. Weis, *Jurisdiction and the Elusive Status Offender: A Comparison of Involvement in Delinquent Behavior and Status Offenses* (Washington, DC: U.S. Government Printing Office, 1980).
143. Smith and colleagues have documented the enormous discretion of decision makers within the juvenile justice system regarding the label assigned to a particular case and the processing disposition that follows the initial juvenile referral. Charles P. Smith, T. Edwin Black, and Fred R. Campbell, *A National Assessment of Case Disposition and Classification in the Juvenile Justice System: Inconsistent Labeling*, Vol. 1, *Process Description and Summary* (Washington, DC: U.S. Government Printing Office, 1979).
144. For a discussion of the difficulty of prediction related to delinquency and crime control, and related cost issues, see Lyle W. Shannon, "The prediction problem as it applies to delinquency and crime control," paper prepared

for the National Institute for Juvenile Justice and Delinquency Prevention, Iowa Urban Community Research Center, University of Iowa, Jan. 1983.
145. Mahoney, "The effect of labeling."
146. Zimring, *The Changing Legal World of Adolescence.*
147. Minow, "The public duties of families and children."
148. Michael Oshima, "Towards a jurisprudence of children," in volume 2 of this series.
149. Ibid.

4
The Current System: Structure and Operations

With FRANCIS X. HARTMANN

A century of social innovation has produced a complex juvenile justice system. At its center are the juvenile court and youth corrections agencies. Farther out, but still within the boundaries of the system, are juvenile detention programs, halfway houses, probation agencies, and the police. Nearer the edges of the system are such things as youth guidance centers, family counseling programs, welfare agencies, youth athletic leagues, foster parents, and perhaps the family itself. All of these institutions can be seen as parts of the juvenile justice system for two reasons.

First, each of these institutions can nominate cases for juvenile court attention. A police department can file a delinquency petition. A probation officer may bring a case back to court. A foster parent may ask to be relieved of the duty of caring for a particular child. Parents can claim that their child is incorrigible.

Second, these institutions furnish some or all of the society's response to nominated cases. Often, cases that begin as delinquency or neglect cases wind up back in the family for continued handling. Others may end up in foster case, or with access to special recreational programs or group homes. Still others end up in the family but under close and continuing review by the welfare department or probation agency or by the court itself. A few end up in locked institutions operated by youth corrections agencies.

These institutions are linked to one another through the activities of nominating cases for attention, developing facts about the conduct and condition of the children, making decisions about how the case should be handled in the future, and then reviewing the situation as conditions change. These activities determine the ultimate consequences of the juvenile justice system: how intrusive it is; how fairly it distributes its burdens and opportunities; whether it strengthens, undermines, or replaces families; and whether it makes the lives of children safer or more dangerous. Moreover, it is only through changes in the character or relative sizes of these activities that the system can be improved. For example, by increasing the size of the family counseling system relative to the welfare department, or by experimenting with group homes at the expense of the probation department one can make important changes in the character and performance of the system. Consequently, it is important to understand how the system now operates and how its activities are distributed across its different parts.

Our analysis of the current structure and operations of the system reaches the following conclusions. (a) Viewing the juvenile justice system as consisting of law enforcement agencies concerned about crimes by or against children is less accurate and useful than seeing it as a far larger and more complex system that superintends or actually participates in the raising of children. (b) The system of nominating and escalating cases for public attention and review is not based solely on the urgency of the particular threat to the society or the child, but also on how public agencies evaluate existing private capacities to deal with the problem. (c) The enthusiasm for due process in the handling of cases involving children has some attractive features but often leaves unrepresented in court proceedings two parties with vital interests at stake in the outcome of the proceedings, namely, the parents or legal guardians of the child and an abstract person who will soon be real, called "the future child." (d) The society is greatly underinvested in experimental programs that supervise children in community settings and thereby increase society's risk of minor crimes now but possibly reduce future crime and dependence through the establishment of close connections between the child and the community.

The Boundaries of the System

In analyzing the current operations of the juvenile justice system, the first question is: Which institutions fall within its purview? One's answer is significantly influenced by one's position on what the concern of the juvenile justice system should be, whether it should be restricted to crimes committed by (or against) juveniles or whether it should be broader and focused on establishing relatively safe and compelling relationships within which children can learn to be responsible adults.

The current fashion in thinking about the juvenile justice system is to depend heavily on an analogy with the adult criminal justice system.[1] In this conception, the central focus of the juvenile justice system is on crimes committed by children. The principal institutions are, therefore, those concerned with law enforcement and crime control: the police, the probation department, the courts, and the corrections agencies. Moreover, the process is viewed as primarily a criminal proceeding in which evidence of crimes is developed and nondiscretionary judgments are made according to the applicable laws.

Figure 4.1 presents a typical effort to describe the operations of the juvenile justice system in these terms. In this picture no private institu-

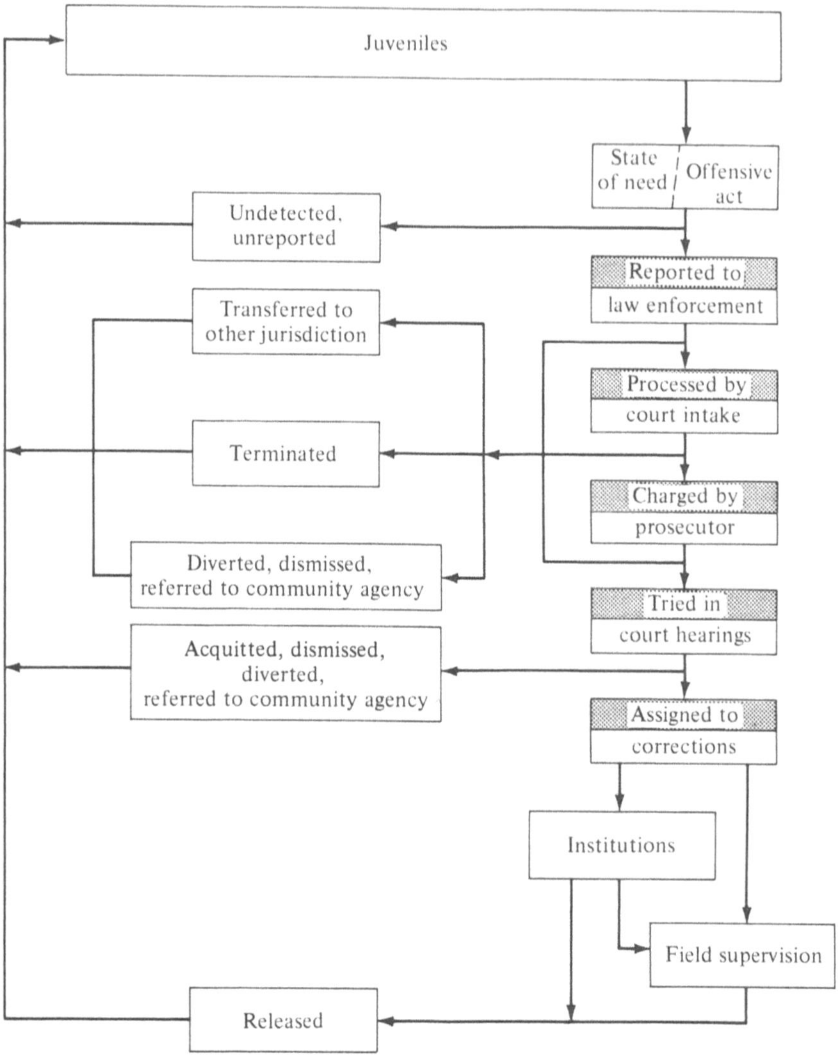

FIGURE 4.1. Generalized flowchart of the juvenile justice system. From Charles P. Smith, T. Edwin Black, and Fred R. Campbell, *Inconsistent Labeling*, Vol. 1, *Process Description and Summary* (Washington, DC: U.S. Department of Justice, 1979), p. 27.

tions such as family, church, or volunteer community groups appear. Social service institutions such as schools and welfare agencies are also ignored as a mutually exclusive (and often preferred) alternative to the handling of cases in the juvenile justice/criminal enforcement system.[2] The focus of this system is on individual children who have committed offenses. The central questions are whether the children will be treated justly and effectively with respect to their past crimes and what threat they present to the society for the future.

There is a second conception of the juvenile justice system that begins with a quite different premise. In this conception, the central purpose of the juvenile justice system is to hold children, parents, and other caretakers responsible to the society for the task of becoming or of teaching children to become responsible citizens. In this conception, crimes by children and against children are viewed not only as failures of the particular individuals involved, but also as signs of breakdown in the set of institutional relationships the society is relying on to accomplish this task. The problem is to restore these institutions to proper functioning, partly through aid but also by reminding those involved of their individual responsibilities to the broader society. In this conception, the body of family law governing such things as divorce, child custody, foster care, and so on is central to the system's concerns, as are statutes that define delinquent acts and abuse and neglect by caretakers.[3]

Figure 4.2 captures this view of the juvenile justice system. The system incorporates many more institutions than does the first conception. Parents figure prominently. So do community institutions such as schools and local businesses, and public social service agencies such as schools, welfare departments, and recreation programs. In this conception, the juvenile court's job of handling individual cases becomes less important than the job of backing up other institutions in their jobs by establishing the values that guide them and acting as the forum of last resort for difficult cases. Although difficult cases eventually may wind up in the juvenile court, they wind up there only to be pushed right back to the other institutions for continued handling. In this conception, the social service institutions are not perceived as mutually exclusive alternatives to criminal justice system handling, but as partners to police departments, probation departments, the youth corrections agencies, and the juvenile court in seeking to improve the conditions under which children are being raised.

A third way to think about which institutions constitute the juvenile justice system is empirically based: Any institution that nominates cases involving children to juvenile court for adjudication, or any institution that furnishes any part of the community's response to children who are at risk or causing risks, can be considered part of the system. For the most part, we will adopt this empirical approach. We will be interested in the question of what actually happens in the system rather than in what we think should happen. In particular, we will resist the temptation to see the system exclusively in terms of criminal justice and crime control except where that seems to be the most satisfactory explanation of what is occurring. What we will discover is an important paradox: that while the juvenile justice system involves many law enforcement agencies, it is not obviously a crime control system. Indeed, its purpose more fundamen-

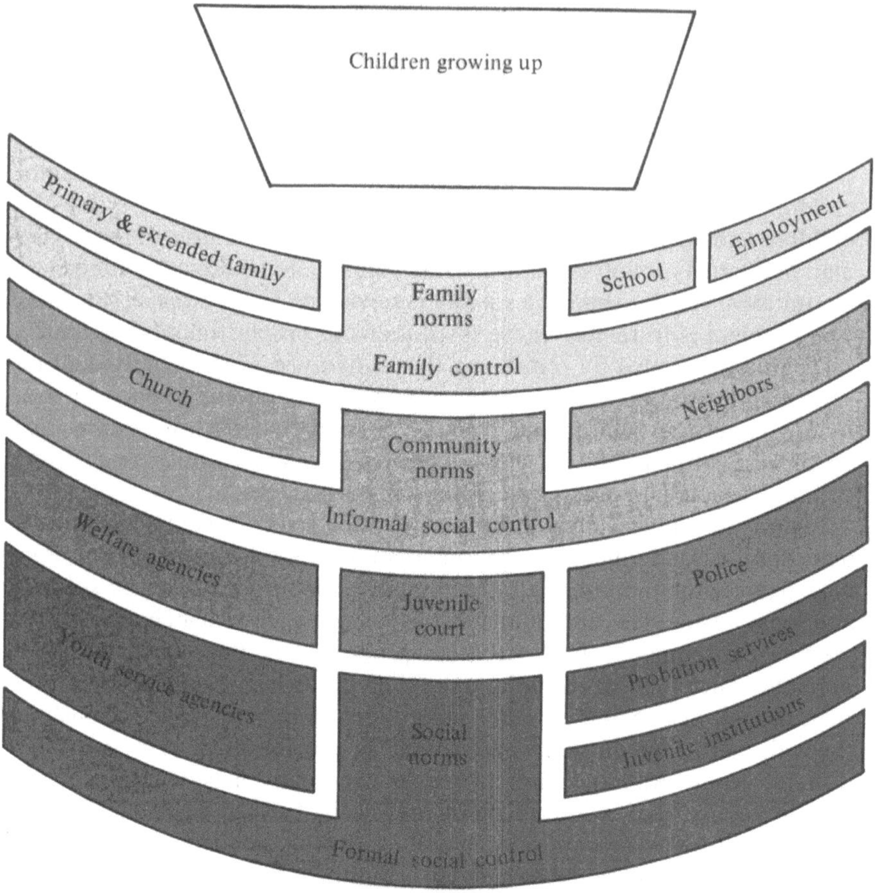

FIGURE 4.2. The court as backstop and linebacker: An alternative view of the juvenile justice system.

tally is to guarantee minimal conditions for child rearing by responding to situations in which those arrangements seem ineffective.

A Hierarchy of Private and Public Institutions

One way to think concretely about the institutional structure of the juvenile justice system is to ask who notices problems in the conduct or condition of children, and who shows up at a family's door when some event occurs (or some condition is revealed) that indicates a breakdown in a family's capacity to supervise or care for its children. Typically, intervention begins informally among those people closest to the family or caretaker—members of the nuclear family, members of the extended family, perhaps friends and neighbors who are intimate enough to notice the problem and concerned enough to intervene. In a slightly haphazard process, the intervention might gradually escalate to include relative strangers representing community institutions such as churches or neighborhood associations or, more typically, government agencies such as welfare departments, health departments, and sometimes the police. Eventually, the problem might reach the courts.

While a social theorist might formulate idealized views of the ordering of these institutions in terms of the strength of their relationship to the children and caretakers who are the focus of the intervention, in any real community, and for any specific member of that community, the order may be quite different from what the theorists expect.[4] Some communities might feel much more closely attached to their schools than their churches. Some individuals within the community might have a closer, more supportive relationship with a social worker than with a nosy neighbor or a pompous minister.

Still, from the vantage point of minimizing the intervention of public institutions in this delicate area of family affairs, one can reasonably order different levels of intervention in terms of their subtlety and legitimacy. The ordering within the private, informal sector might look like this:

Family members who live together (nuclear family)
Extended family of relatives
Local friends
Neighbors (whether friendly or not)
Parents of children's friends
Members of the same community who are acquaintances
Members of the same church
Fellow employees
Pastor
Members of the community who are unknown
Informal voluntary organization
Schoolteacher
Employer

Informal, Private Interventions

Typically, informal interventions will be offers of help: babysitting for the child while the parent works, advice about how to deal with a problem, or simply moral support and friendship. Moreover, because of the close relationship and the informal auspices of such interventions, the gestures will be interpreted by the caretaker and child as help.

Often, however, there is also implied criticism and some future demands and expectations associated with the help. The intervention includes a desire to have the child or the child's caretaker face up to a problem. If the criticism is strong enough and the initial relationship weak enough, the intervention may shatter the relationship and lead to no important improvement in the situation. If, however, the relationship is intimate and strong, there is a reasonable amount of help forthcoming, and the implied criticism is muted but nonetheless clearly signaled, the intervention has the best chance of success in restoring functioning within the family.

Generally we assume that the character of the informal, intimate relationships just described are relatively strong, otherwise they would not be activated. And it is this assumption (along with the society's general desire to avoid public or state coercion) that makes us prefer that these informal situations and relationships do much of the work of keeping families to the task of socializing children.[5]

There are three problems, however, with relying exclusively on these informal, private interventions. First, although they are generally quite effective, they are not perfectly effective. In some situations the aid offered may not be large enough, sustained enough, or skillful enough to help the family reach tolerable levels of performance. It is significant that this need not occur very often for the situations to become major social problems. If 99% of children were being raised in tolerably satisfactory conditions, several hundred thousand children would still be headed for careers of crime or social dependence.

Second, these informal institutions seem to be weakening. Society today is quite different from that of Illinois in 1899. The primary institutions are in the process of significant change, and intervenors are far less likely to be instrumental in the socialization process. An assessment of the trends affecting these institutions would reveal the following.

Nuclear family: weakened
Extended family: more widespread, weaker influence
Friends: less likely to know about problems or to intervene
Neighbors: more likely to be strangers
Parents of children's friends: less likely to intervene
Members of the same community who are acquaintances: less likely to intervene
Members of church: less likely to be a significant community
Fellow employees: less likely to know about problems or to intervene
Pastor: significant, but to fewer persons
Members of the same community who are unknown: unlikely to intervene
Informal voluntary organization: may be helpful, but less likely to be aware of specific problems

Schoolteacher: may be helpful
Employer: unlikely to intervene

Third, the strength of these private, informal systems is not evenly distributed over the population. Just as the capacities and resources of families to raise their children are unevenly distributed, so are the capacities and resources of the informal community networks that surround and buttress the families. Of course, in discussing this issue one immediately enters an ideological thicket. Some argue for the ultimate equality and goodness of human beings in terms of their capacities to form families, raise children, and create communities.[6] Others argue that some people seem incapable or disinclined to handle such responsibilities.[7] One does not have to go to either extreme to insist on three important points: (a) Yes, even in the poorest families and communities there are strong relationships of love and responsibility. (b) Yes, among wealthier citizens the relationships are sometimes impoverished. (c) Nonetheless, there are important differences in terms of the size and capacity of the social networks that can be brought into play to help families meet their responsibilities to the community. A family in the South Bronx finds fewer shreds of community support (and these bring fewer resources) than a troubled family in an ethnic area of Queens can find (or must accept).

Public Social Service Agencies

When the network of private, informal agencies fails to handle the problem, or is simply nonexistent, a different set of agencies becomes involved. These are mostly public agencies: public schools, welfare agencies, private social service agencies, the police, probation departments, the courts, or youth corrections agencies. Sometimes special youth advocacy agencies have been established to fill some important gap between the social work agencies on the one hand and the police and courts on the other.

Such agencies need not be radically separated from the communities in which they operate, but as a practical matter they usually are. Over the last half century, these institutions have sought to legitimate themselves through professional expertise and independence rather than through close political ties to the communities they serve.[8] As a result, they now find themselves strangers to the individuals of their communities when they intervene in their lives.

Consider the differences in a situation in which a teacher notices that a child is coming to school hungry or behaving badly with respect to his peers a century ago compared with today. Typically, the modern teacher would be:

Less likely	More likely
- to live in the same community	- to be wary of rejection for intervening
- to know the parents	- to be constrained by school rules and procedures
- to be personally familiar with the home situation	- to know of formal helping organizations
- to know of helpers in the child's neighborhood	- to utilize formal processes
- to know of informal neighborhood helping organizations	

Thus, interventions by public social service agencies are assumed to lack the organic relationship to children and their caretakers that used to characterize interventions from the informal institutions just described. When we say that the intervention is *formal* rather than *informal* we mean that the justification for the intervention lies in a more distant, impersonal relationship between the family and the state.[9] In some sense, this means that the power of the family—its ability to mold the intervention to its needs and interpretation of the situation—is lessened, and with that, some of the legitimacy and effectiveness of the intervention. On the other hand, the total quantity of help available to the family may be increased dramatically.

Moreover, as in the case of the informal interventions, the interventions from social work agencies are likely to be seen as help rather than obligations. But the help will carry expectations and obligations with it. The teacher will expect the parent to do a better job feeding the child, or will expect the parent to become a partner in helping to control the child's bad conduct with explanations and more effective discipline at home.

Public Legal Institutions

Police, probation departments, courts, and corrections agencies are viewed as the most formal and distant intervenors. Indeed, because they are law enforcement agencies, this distance is deemed a virtue rather than a liability.[10] Moreover, the interventions which these organizations make are rarely considered help. They are recognized both by the organizations and by those who are the object of intervention as an imposition of obligations rather than as the provision of material assistance. Since we often assume that effective interventions into the lives of children at risk or causing risks require sensitivity, intimate relationships, and assistance rather than impersonality, distance, and obligations, we assume that interventions from public legal institutions are less desirable than interventions by public social service agencies.

There are several difficulties with these commonplace assumptions, however. The first is that the line between helping agencies and obliging agencies is far less sharp than is ordinarily assumed. As noted previously, help from informal and public agencies often comes with implied obligations. It is also true that the obliging agencies often deliver assistance of some kind along with obligations. Indeed, the irony is that many valuable services are available only to children who get into enough trouble to wind up in the juvenile court.[11] So, while the distinction between helping and obliging organizations is useful, it is also potentially misleading. It would be far better to see that most interventions involve elements of both obligation and assistance, though admittedly in varying proportions.

Second, it is not always true that legal institutions have exclusively formal relationships with client families, and that social service institutions have informal relations. Often the legal institutions handle cases quite informally. Even when the police are called in, they are likely to handle the case informally in the field.[12] Of the approximately 2 million juveniles whom the police arrest annually, about half of the cases are handled informally within the police department rather than nominated to the court for continued processing.[13] Similarly, effective supervision by a probation department inevitably involves a great deal of informal negotiation and bargaining between the caseworker and the client.[14] Even the court will often seek an informal resolution of a case through family mediation, or the diversion of a juvenile case to community agencies before any formal fact-finding proceeding.[15] Such acts are informal in the sense that they do not involve the simple application of a fixed rule to an individual case. There is room for the child, the caretaker, and the representative of a public agency to work out an arrangement that serves all of their interests and maintains their relationship more effectively than does formal application of the existing rules.

On the other hand, the social service agencies increasingly rely on formal proceedings. This is most evident when social work agencies, or much less frequently schools, bring cases to the juvenile court for formal handling in the court.[16] But it is also true that these agencies themselves, in the pursuit of fairness and due process, have often created formal processes of fact-finding and adjudication within their own auspices to deal with matters such as the suspension of welfare benefits or the discipline of children in schools.[17] Again, there are important differences among agencies, with legal agencies having a stronger commitment to formality than the social service agencies. But the differences are in degree rather than kind, and there is a great deal of overlap in the actual behavior of the agencies, if not in their underlying ideology.

Third, related to this notion that legal agencies can be informal as well as formal, it is possible that legal institutions could have close and personal relationships with communities and individuals. Of course, the idea that equates justice with equity (i.e., the equal treatment of similarly situated individuals) makes distance and impersonality a virtue of the system by creating conditions in which differences among individual cases that should be irrelevant or corrupting in applying the law are most likely to be blotted out. But a different idea of justice, one that emphasized the importance of dealing with each case as a particular problem to be sorted out and that promised to be responsive to important differences between a particular case and others—that is, an idea of individualized justice—would make detailed knowledge of particular circumstances a virtue rather than a potential corruption.

Similarly, while it is customary to think of courts as relatively autonomous agencies whose legitimacy rests on their technical knowledge of the law and who must occasionally stand against legislatures and executives when they attack fundamental individual rights, it is also possible to see courts as agencies that not only do but should reflect widespread social norms and aspirations. This goal is reflected in the fact that some judges are still elected, that judicial appointments are made and confirmed by elected political representatives, and that judges may be removed by recall petitions.[18] So there is room in our conceptions of legal institutions to see them as intimate and connected to the community as well as impersonal and distant. Indeed, one can argue that the most interesting aspect of the juvenile court is that it tries to establish a court that differs from other courts in precisely these dimensions.[19]

Fourth, it is well to remember that people, including children and their caretakers, may be aided by challenges and demands as well as by assistance. In this case a certain distance and impersonality may be an advantage rather than a disadvantage. We have all seen instances in which consistent challenges and demands placed on individuals and agencies have resulted in improved performance without the need for additional resources. Apparently, reserves of capacity and skill can sometimes be mobilized by exhortation to accomplish particular tasks.

But it is also clear under what circumstances such challenges can be effective. The challenge must be legitimate—one that children and caretakers can accept as compelling on their own terms. This acceptance, in turn, depends on both their view of what is being demanded of them and on their relationship to the agency or person making the challenge. Their response also depends on their perception of their ability to meet the challenge. The closer the challenge is to their own view of their obligations, the stronger their relationship to those making the challenge, and the more able they feel to meet the challenge, the more effective the challenge will be.

On the other hand, the more distance there is between the substantive demands of the challenge and the family's current activities, the more potential benefit there is if the family successfully meets the challenge. This suggests that there is an optimal degree of distance in challenging a relationship—one that strains the relationship but does not break it. Finding that balance may be what good court processing as well as good social work is all about. In this sense, obligations and distance may be therapeutic to the client families and children as well as protective of a social norm that generally establishes duties and obligations within the society.

In sum, one can view the institutions of the juvenile justice system arranged in a hierarchy that runs from informal private interventions at one end to relatively formal state interventions at the other. This ordering is produced by a simple conception that makes one distinction between private and public responses and a second distinction between service and enforcement agencies, and that makes a judgment that private responses are lighter and easier to bear than public and that service responses are easier to justify than enforcement or legal responses. As we have seen, this simple ordering runs the risk of exaggerating the differences among kinds of interventions, since all interventions involve combinations of private and public, assistance and obligation, understanding and challenge. But this hierarchy does seem to reflect common understandings about the ordering of these agencies in terms of the society's preferences for using them, and the expectations for success.

The Process of Nomination, Escalation, and Intake

Since agencies of intervention can be ordered in this neat hierarchy, it is tempting to believe that the process of escalating a case will follow it, that cases will be handled at the lowest possible level of public intervention and only the most serious will rise to the highest levels of public intervention. To a large degree, the system does seem to work this way: The vast majority of potential cases stay at informal, private levels,[20] while the most serious cases eventually do end up in court.[21] This seems to occur naturally as the result of a shared social understanding of what is private and what public, and what can be dealt with through assistance and what requires stiff obligations and supervision along with the assistance.

Some features of the process of nomination and escalation, however, do depart from this simple view. Special features of the process of nomination, for example, lead to some relatively minor cases reaching high levels of the system fairly quickly. In effect, they preempt the system. Some features of the escalation process also hold potential for introducing the appearance (or the reality) of racial or class discrimination into the system. Thus, when the actual operation of the system is compared with the expectation that cases will be escalated in this hierarchy of institutions according to their seriousness, some significant anomalies appear. These anomalies, in turn, undermine the overall legitimacy of the system.

The Police as Nominators

The first troublesome feature is that the current arrangement of public policies and public agencies has made the process of nomination quite different from that first pictured. Specifically, nominations for public attention are *unlikely* to come from members of community institutions. They are much more likely to come from the police, from the parents themselves, or from public service providers.

The most recent data on sources of referral to the juvenile justice system indicate that the police are overwhelmingly the most important sources.[22] No doubt, this observation is partly an artifact of reporting: There is no systematic way to observe the informal nominations and handling of juvenile cases wholly within private or community institutions, and therefore the number of such events is wildly underestimated. But the importance of the police in making nominations to the juvenile justice system cannot be ignored.

Since we commonly assume that the police are generally concerned about crime, we imagine that the large number of police nominations indicates a large underlying problem of youth crime. The fact of the matter is, however, that many of these nominations do not involve criminal offenses by children. They involve curfew violations, minor disturbances, drunkenness, even truancy.[23] Why, if the cases do not involve crime, do the police make such nominations?

There are two different answers to this question that correspond to two different functions of the police. These have been deemphasized in the society's understanding of what the police are about, but have not been eliminated from police operations.[24] The first is that the police take these cases as part of their "order maintenance" function.[25] In this conception, children appearing at times and places where they are not supposed to be unsettles a community's sense of order and decorum. The police respond to particular or generalized community demands that the conduct of children be regulated not so much to reduce violent crime as to make people feel safe and secure. Obviously, in this conception, the community's interests are being advanced at the expense of children's freedom.

The second idea is that the police respond to these situations as part of their "emergency social service" function.[26] In this conception, police encounter a situation in which a child seems to be in danger, and no one else is around who can offer protection and assistance. Therefore, the police bring the case into the juvenile justice system. What qualifies the police to nominate the case is not any special knowledge or skill, nor is it their interest in crime control or order maintenance, but instead the fact that they are on the street 24 hours a day representing a public responsibility that is broader than crime control. In effect, they are the only government representatives who are so available to the public. If social workers, nurses, or doctors were prepared to work on the streets 24 hours a day, these cases would properly be theirs. The police see the children who are cold, who are alone on the streets at 2:00 in the morning. They respond as any responsible member of the society would. In this conception, both the child and the community are being aided by police nominations.

The point of these observations is to emphasize that the police involvement does not mean a crime has been committed. The police have important functions to perform in the society that go well beyond crime control.[27] In short, just as it may be important to see the juvenile court as involved in structuring relationships among children, caretakers, and the broader society rather than in simply adjudicating criminal offenses, it may be important to see the police as performing the same role, because they deal with cases in which caretaking relationships between children and caretakers have more or less temporarily, and more or less disastrously, fallen apart. The police substitute for a vigilant, informal community response to crises in relationships between children and their caretakers.

Parents As Nominators

The second important feature of the nomination process that is unexpected is the role that parents or caretakers play in nominating cases for public attention. This is particularly obvious if we include all the cases involving custody, care, and protection that appear in probate courts throughout the country.[28] But even if we restrict our attention to the cases that appear in juvenile courts, parents and caretakers are seen to play an important role: Approximately 2% of all cases in the juvenile justice system are nominated by relatives and 6.5% of status offense referrals are from parents and relatives.[29]

This fact is important for two reasons. First, in these cases the nomination is not made by an outsider; it comes directly from the nexus of child and caretaker. Thus, to the extent that this relationship is important to the society, the appeal has to be taken seriously. Even if the specific complaint turns out to be inaccurate in important ways, that a complaint is made at all signals trouble.

Second, the only thing that is at stake in such cases is the relationship between the child and caretaker. There is no criminal offense by the child, no community disorder that has been created, and no obvious abuse or neglect of the child. The only problem is that the relationship between the caretaker and the child has been exhausted and has lost its efficacy as a device for socializing the child.[30] Despite this, such a case will escalate rather quickly through the machinery of private interventions and perhaps even public service intervention. In effect, if a parent declares the relationship with his or her child bankrupt, the society must pay attention through its most formal intervention mechanism. This raises important questions about the process of escalation of cases as well as the process of nomination. For now, however, it is sufficient to see the anomaly of parental nominations within the standard notion that most cases will be nominated by people in the community who have been victimized or offended or have otherwise become concerned.

Ferreting Out Abuse and Neglect

A third interesting feature of the nomination process is that the society seems to be concerned that, left to its own operations, the system will not work effectively in cases of abuse and neglect. This seems like a reasonable worry, for the voices of the victims in such cases may well be muted. The children may be unaware of being treated worse than others. Even if they are aware, they may be afraid to report the treatment lest it worsen or they lose the love of their parent. To deal with this problem, many states have passed mandatory reporting laws that impose the duty on physicians, teachers, and other citizens who are in a position to observe abuse and neglect to report such instances when they see them.[31] In our terms, these laws are devices for changing the process of nomination by mobilizing heretofore passive actors, or devices for escalating these cases from informal, private handling to more formal, public levels of the system. These laws have increased the number of abuse and neglect cases being handled at all levels of the system, and have therefore increased the number of abuse and neglect cases in the overall operations of the juvenile justice system.[32]

These observations about the process of nomination show how the system of nomination, review, and escalation can be preempted by special features of the system. To a degree, the system is preempted by the immediate availability and broad interests of the police. To a degree, it is also preempted by the power given to parents to nominate their own children as problems for them and the society. And it is preempted by the society's current concern for abuse and neglect of children and the worry that such treatment will be underreported due to the disadvantaged position of children. Of course, cases nominated through these routes will not necessarily stay in the formal public institutions dealing with children at risk. Most of them, having been nominated within institutions that are already at high levels in the hierarchy of the community's response, will be pushed back into institutions that are lower in the hierarchy. The point is that these features of the nomination process will inevitably result in some cases that do not seem particularly serious being handled at a level in the system that looks inappropriate, that looks to be too heavy-handed for the problem as it is ultimately viewed or even as it is defined at the outset.

Private Capacity and the Process of Escalation

The fact that these preemptions exist and result in some potentially minor cases being escalated rather quickly in the system signals something important about the process of escalation as well as the process of nomination. Our view of how cases should (or actually do) escalate to different levels of public response borrows heavily from an analogy with the adult criminal justice system. The assumption in the adult system is that cases reach higher levels of public intervention as a function of (a) the seriousness of the offense being considered and (b) the criminality of the offender as revealed by prior criminal offenses. The more serious the offense, and the longer the past record, the more appropriate and likely is heavy state intervention. A similar model applied in the juvenile justice context would suggest that the more serious the delinquent offense, and the more serious the prior record of offending, the more likely a heavy state intervention. To a great degree, this is what happens: The probability that a case will be handled informally is inversely related to the seriousness of the offense, and the probability that a child will end up in an institution is positively correlated with the seriousness of the offense and the number of previous contacts the child has had with the juvenile justice system.[33]

But there is an additional factor that seems to receive more consideration in the juvenile justice system than in the adult system and often plays a decisive role in determining both the escalation of the case and the nature of the ultimate disposition. That factor is the adequacy of the existing private and community arrangements to supervise and make investments in the child. The stronger these agencies—the more available and effective a parent, guardian, or relative to deal with a child's misconduct—the greater the likelihood that the case will be deescalated and returned to the family and the community for a private, informal resolution.

To a degree, this tendency can be seen as an expression of the general view that private handling of cases is better than public. In this respect, it would be as applicable in the adult system as it is in the juvenile system. But it can also be seen as reflecting the dependent status of children, and the superordinate status of parents and caretakers. In effect, parents are seen at least partly as agents of the community in helping to socialize children, and they are not only expected to fulfill this role, but are given the room to do so even if things do not seem to be going well.[34] Keeping as many cases as possible within private informal networks also makes sense as a device for economizing on the use of both public funds and public authority.

However sensible, there is a potential danger in relying on private and community capabilities to supervise, care for, and discipline the child when these agencies seem adequate to the task. The danger comes from the fact or the appearance of racial or class discrimination in the operations of the juvenile justice system.

If the adequacy of private or community institutions dedicated to caring for children is an issue in decision making within the juvenile justice system, then someone in the system must make an investigation and a judgment about this matter. Inevitably, the judgment must be subjective, because describing objectively what constitutes sufficient competence in supervising and caring for children is extremely difficult. It is even harder to guarantee that the conditions are reliably met.[35] In this subjective process, class or racial biases can (or appear to) enter in.

This suspicion is raised, of course, when poor children or minority children end up deeper in the juvenile justice system than do rich children or white children charged with comparable offenses. This result can be explained in three different ways with significantly different moral and practical implications for the operations of the juvenile justice system.

One explanation is that individuals in the juvenile justice system who nominate and escalate cases are, in fact, biased against poor people and minorities. It is sufficient for them to know that a child is poor or belongs to a minority group and is in trouble to decide that the family or community is too weak to be trusted with the child. This, obviously, is intolerable.

The second possibility is that the bias creeps in in an un-self-conscious way. Officials make a conscientious effort to evaluate the situation and genuinely believe that they are doing so in an unbiased way. It just happens that when they interpret the data, they are unconsciously influenced by the economic status or race of the child. This is equally intolerable but probably easier to fix than the first problem, since the second starts with good motivations among officials.

The third possibility is that the real capacity to care for children at risk is, in fact, correlated with economic status or race. This is the most troubling possibility, for it implies that a perfectly conscientious and accurate effort to assess the capacity of private or community institutions to care for children would nonetheless produce decisions in which poor and minority children penetrated the system more deeply than others. Indeed, it is possible to interpret the overrepresentation of poor and minority children and families in the juvenile justice system in precisely this light: not as an expression of discrimination, but instead as the result of real differences in family and community capacity.[36] In this sense, public interventions are being sucked into a vacuum rather than being applied where they don't belong.

Which view one takes depends on one's judgment about two issues—whether it is reasonable to look at private capacities to supervise and guide children as a factor to be considered in escalating cases in the system and whether the system is making reasonable judgments about this issue. Both of these issues are controversial, but there seems to be more agreement about the appropriateness of examining background conditions than there is confidence in our ability to do this well.

The Process of Adjudication

A few cases of children at risk or creating risks reach the dockets of the juvenile court. Just as the society's image of the juvenile justice system is dominated by an analogy to the adult criminal justice system, so the image of proper adjudication of cases that reach the juvenile court is also dominated by the analogy with the adult criminal court. In this conception, there are two parties at interest: the defendant (represented by defense counsel) and the state (represented by the prosecutor). The issue to be decided is whether the defendant did or did not commit a criminal offense against the community. The task of the judge is to make sure that the proceedings are consistent with rules of evidence and other aspects of courtroom procedure. The aim of the court proceeding is to produce justice, both in the sense of fairness to the accused and suitable punishment for an accused found to be guilty. It is assumed that this aim is best pursued by an adversary process that tests the strength of the evidence alleging that the defendant committed a crime.[37]

In recent years there has been a sustained effort to add much of this spirit and some specific trappings to juvenile court proceedings. Those interested in the rights of children have attacked the discretionary powers of the juvenile court and sought to introduce such rights as the right to counsel, the right to a jury trial, and the right to know the specific charges against the child.[38] Those concerned about the threat that juvenile offenders pose to the community have urged that some notion of accountability and sternness be added to the juvenile court.[39] As a philosophical matter, this implies that the concept of guilt be introduced in the juvenile court. As a practical matter, it means tougher sentences. And there have also been voices urging the opening up of the juvenile court, particularly to victims who want their victimization taken seriously.

These trends, if developed further, would gradually produce a miniature version of the adult criminal court. The only difference would be a slightly greater concern for the particular circumstances of the case, including the strengths of the family and community from which the child came. And even these differences would erode as the court focused increasingly on the characteristics of specific offenses committed by or against the child.

The virtues of an adult criminal court establish one standard for measuring the performance of the juvenile court. The question is whether there is any different standard. Our answer is yes. If the issue before the juvenile court is how to create a structure of obligations around the child and those who care for the child that is sufficient in the short run to protect the community from the child or the child from the caretakers, and that over the long run promises to facilitate the child's development, then, to do this job well, the juvenile court would have to differ from the adult criminal court in three crucial areas: (a) the recognition of the parties at interest in the court proceeding, (b) the focus of the evidence that is gathered and reviewed, and (c) the overall style and purpose of the proceeding.

Generally, criminal court proceedings revolve around a familiar trio: a victim, a defendant, and the state. This common trio also exists in the juvenile court. In the case of crimes committed by children, the child occupies the role of defendant. In the case of crimes committed against children, the child is in the role of victim. It is tempting to imagine that the defendant, the victim, and the state are the only parties to be represented in juvenile court processing.

From our particular vantage point, we see two additional parties lurking in the shadow of the court. The most important additional party is the parents or caretakers of the child. Admittedly, they may be more or less central to the case. They are obviously central in cases involving abuse and neglect of the child. They are much farther from the scene in cases involving older juvenile offenders who have repeatedly committed violent crimes. Although their centrality may vary, in cases involving juveniles they are necessarily involved for several reasons.

First, from their own point of view, they are involved because their reputation as responsible caretakers is at stake. Unfortunately, their interests in this situation are by no means obvious. Probably they would like to avoid the embarrassment and loss of privacy and control to which their child's behavior exposes them. But they might choose to deal with this by blaming everything on the incorrigibility of their child rather than by using the occasion to reaffirm their commitment to the child and bringing additional resources to the tasks of supervision and guidance. Alternatively, parents or caretakers may be grateful for some social affirmation of their responsibility to the child and the child's responsibility to them, since this may strengthen their own resolve and capacity in dealing with the child. Or the parents might be interested in having the court help them to secure or organize services from public agencies to which they are entitled. Finally, in the most ironic and tragic cases, the parents may be willing to shift the responsibility for the child to the state, not because they want to wash their hands of a child who has become a burden, but simply because they judge that the state can provide a flow of services to the child that are substantially greater than the parents can provide as private citizens.[40]

From the society's point of view, the parents or caretakers are involved for two slightly different reasons. One is that, in the case of offenses committed by children, the parents share some of the responsibility for the crime, since it is their duty to supervise and guide their children. That is consistent with the view that children are subordinate to their parents or caretakers and therefore cannot quite be seen as independent moral agents.

The second is that the parents' interests and capabilities will affect the dispositional decisions of the court. Indeed, for all but the most serious crimes and the most persistent young offenders, the parents are likely to provide most of the effective postdisposition supervision of the child. Generally speaking, the child will be returned to their care and custody, perhaps under the guidance of a probation officer or with the assistance of special programs made available by the court. If the parents seem adequate to the task of managing the risks the child is creating for the community or for himself or herself, the court may well decide to keep the parents in that important role. Interests in economy, family autonomy, and generally maintaining responsibility for child rearing within private institutions will all line up on the side of keeping the child under the supervision of the parents. If, on the other hand, the parents seem disinclined or unable to furnish the necessary level of care, and if their efforts cannot be supplemented by other private or public agencies, then the court's disposition will be quite different because its interests in future problems will overwhelm its interest in staying uninvolved.

For these reasons, the parents, caretakers, or others in private and public agencies who are supposed to care for the child can be seen as parties at interest in juvenile court proceedings. It is worth noting that except in the case of child custody proceedings, there is no explicit place given in formal adjudications to parents and caretakers.[41] They are often there informally pleading for some disposition of the case that accommodates their interests. The judge may make use of them in a variety of informal ways. But there is no explicit role granted to parents or public caretakers of the child.

The second party lurking in the shadows of the juvenile court whose presence should be acknowledged is someone called "the future child." We use this awkward phrase to signal an important problem, namely, the difference between the expressed interests of the child who appears before the court and the interests that child might express several years later looking back. The basic notion is that children are not always good judges of what they need to equip themselves for the future. In particular, they may be unwilling to make painful investments in schooling, and may be particularly resistant to effective supervision of their conduct and instruction about their obligations to others. Yet these things may be very important not only for the immediate security of the community, but also for the long-run success of the child. In this respect, then, the interests of the future child may be quite different from the expressed interests of "the current child."

This difference creates difficulties for the effective representation of the child's interests. It is tempting for the child's defense counsel to think in traditional lawyer–client terms: the lawyer's job is to protect the client's liberty, secure whatever privileges and services are available, and ward off any liabilities.[42] In this, the lawyer generally finds a willing partner in the current child. Whether this is in the client's long-run interest, however, is more problematic. But defense counsel may feel ill-equipped to ask questions about the client's long-run interests. It is much easier to feel responsible to a real current child than to an abstract future child.

Yet somehow this future child's interests must be represented, for they are importantly at stake in the court's decisions. The child cannot reliably represent these interests because his or her judgments are likely to be flawed. The child's own counsel may also find it difficult to represent the child's long-run interests for the same reason. The prosecutor cannot represent these interests because his or her responsibilities are more toward short-run community security than toward the future development of the child. The parents cannot reliably represent these interests for they have no official standing and have been at least partly discredited by the time the child comes to the court. It seems that it must be up to the judge to protect the interests of the future child. But that gives the judge a more substantive role in the court proceeding than is usual, and it draws on expertise that the judge does not necessarily possess. In the end, the interests of the future child must be represented by the conscientiousness of all those party to the court proceeding. They must find a way to represent that interest as at least one element of their deliberations and decisions. And this conclusion has important implications for other features of juvenile court processing.

In addition to incorporating parents and the future child in juvenile court proceedings, the juvenile court must open itself up to the presentation of different material facts about the case at hand. In traditional criminal court processing, the focus of the proceeding is on the evidence related to a criminal offense. Under special circumstances, evidence about the background and character of the defendant may be introduced.[43] And when it comes to making a disposition, the criminal court may consider not only the crime, but also the background of the offender.[44] Generally speaking, however, the question of the defendant's current relationships in the community, and the existence of someone who can vouch for his or her continued good conduct and future development, are not taken seriously.

In contrast, in the juvenile court proceeding attention is focused much less on the evidence of a crime committed by or against the child. The crime is what brings the case to the court's attention, but the issue of guilt or innocence is not the central one. What have more importance are two other features of the case: the background and character of the offender and the capacity of the parents and other caretakers to keep the child safe and to provide for his or her moral and social development. These are relevant in the juvenile court in terms of both justice and practicality. They are related to justice because they involve the question of whether the child is a relatively independent moral agent, and therefore justly vulnerable to criminal punishment, or is so young, so ill, or so disadvantaged that he or she cannot justly be held responsible. They are related to practicality because they might shed light on the question of what kind of intervention or disposition would be in the interests of community security, the child's future development, and economy in the use of public authority and money.

The third feature of juvenile court proceedings that might properly differ from criminal court proceedings is the general aim and style of the proceedings. In the criminal court the aim is to do justice by establishing the guilt or innocence of the accused through a formal adversary proceeding. The concept of justice is quite well defined, and the procedures are well suited to protecting it. In a juvenile or family court the aim is far more complex, and the process that supports it is quite different. The substantive question should be what arrangement of institutions and responsibilities will be sufficient to assure the community that the child will be supervised well enough to avoid future offenses, cared for adequately to prevent immediate harm to the child, and invested in sufficiently to minimize the chance that the child will end up as a criminal or social dependent. These can be understood as the aims of justice insofar as a child is entitled to such services. These can also be understood as justice insofar as they represent an integration of the interests of the competing parties (e.g., the child, the parents, the victims, or the community). Or this can be understood as a useful way for the court to behave even if it is not quite consistent with notions of justice. This issue, however, is far different from a simple adjudication of guilt or innocence.

To support useful deliberations and wise decisions, it is probably helpful to see the juvenile court process as more like a civil than a criminal court proceeding—even when it is dealing with crimes committed by children and even when one of the possible outcomes is the placement of the child in a state institution. In the process a dispute or a problem is resolved through mediation and application of the law, rather than a judgment being made about guilt or innocence. In essence, this second view of the juvenile court sees the court as responsible for organizing and revitalizing the institutions that surround the child and as sharing responsibility for the child's effective supervision, care, and discipline. In this context it resembles a housing court that manages relationships between landlords and tenants, or a bankruptcy court that protects various interests when a corporation claims it can no longer meet its obligations.[45]

Formal Dispositions

A few of the cases that are entered on the dockets of the juvenile court result in formal dispositions, for example, a decision to commit a child to the care and custody of a state agency rather than to leave the child in the community in the care of parents or other caretakers. The vast majority of these cases involve instances of delinquency.[46]

To many, the decision to commit a delinquent child to the care and custody of a state agency for a certain length of time is closely analogous to a sentencing decision in the adult criminal court. In the criminal court decision the judge is expected to balance competing interests in doing justice (in the sense that the punishment fits the crime), in deterring both the offender and others from committing future crimes, in incapacitating the offender to promote community security, and in creating conditions under which the offender might be rehabilitated.[47] The likely result of the decision is a period of confinement in an institution. Such institutions vary in the degree of security and amenities they provide. The judge is guided principally by the gravity of the defendant's offense and secondarily by the background and history of the defendant. Current connections to the community are given scant attention. The judge's sentencing decision is seen as an important culminating event that determines much of the justice and practical impact of all that has gone before. Moreover, it is viewed as decisive with respect to representing the community's interests, and it will have a profound influence on the handling of individual offenders by the corrections agency—even in a world in which the corrections agencies can release prisoners on parole and can establish classification systems for managing the prison population committed to their care.

Obviously the analogy to formal dispositions in the juvenile court is close. It is perhaps closest in the fact that the frequent result of a juvenile court commitment of a child to a youth authority is loss of liberty. Indeed, it was that fact (plus the lack of any evidence that the interests of the child were being served by the commitment) that caused the Supreme Court to view the juvenile court process as one in which children's due process rights existed and had to be protected.[48] But there are also some important differences, particularly when the juvenile court is viewed as an institution that tries to mobilize both private and public institutions to meet their obligations in raising children.

One crucial difference is that typically a youth authority has a great deal more discretion and more variety in the dispositions it can make than does a corrections department.[49] Often this discretion is established as a statutory matter.[50] The statutes that establish the sentencing authority of judges in the adult court, and the policies, programs, and resources of adult corrections agencies, are often quite specific with respect to such issues as how long a person may be kept under state supervision, the appropriate forms of state supervision, and sometimes even the rules that determine what sort of offenders may be held in what kind of facilities.[51] Moreover, the result of these statutes over time has been to produce a relatively small number of forms of state supervision over convicted offenders. There is probation on the one hand and more or less secure facilities for 24-hour supervision on the other.[52]

In contrast, youth authorities are typically granted much broader discretion.[53] They have not always been very creative in using this discretion. The use of locked institutions remains the dominant way the states exercise their supervision over children who are placed in their charge.[54] And there have been recent efforts to narrow the discretion of youth authorities through statutes.[55] But the fact remains that the youth authorities are generally freer to decide how best to supervise the children placed in their care than are corrections agencies. This reflects a greater social tolerance of the misconduct of children and a greater willingness to run risks with them in the interest of justice. This tolerance, however, is gradually being eroded as society perceives the role of children in crime changing and as it senses a lack of accountability and performance in the youth corrections agencies.

A second crucial difference is that the mix of substantive purposes that are to be balanced and pursued by commitment of a child to a youth authority are quite different from those pursued by commitment of an adult to the adult correctional system. To the extent that youth commitments are for crimes, their purposes might be seen as similar to those in the adult court, namely, retribution, general and specific deterrence, incapacitation, and rehabilitation, the balance among these shifting depending on judicial philosophy or the particular background of the defendant. The difference in committing a youth to the state's care is that the programs to which the youth is exposed must accommodate two additional facts. First, the child is still developing, therefore still able to use investments, and therefore still entitled to them. Second, to the extent possible, the task of fostering the child's development and responsibility should be left to private institutions.

Sometimes it is assumed that the interest in the child's development is captured by the concept of "rehabilitation" or "treatment." To us, the idea of fostering a child's development as a responsible citizen seems different from the common understanding of what constitutes rehabilitation and treatment. Specifically, punishment and discipline are part of the concept of fostering responsibility and development. They are deployed to help children learn what is expected of them and that they are responsible for their acts. Of course, to be effective in fostering responsibility, the punishment must be administered by a credible source in a fair way. Otherwise, it simply breeds hostility.[56] But even with this important qualification about what constitutes punishment, punishment is generally considered inconsistent with treatment and rehabilitation.

In addition, we understand that the way children develop is through relationships to others. Consequently, how to construct the relationships, how to embed them in an instructive, compelling social environment, is an important focus of attention. In contrast, the idea of treatment and rehabilitation emphasizes pathology that can be treated on an individual basis separated from the relationships that surround the child. The image is of a doctor and patient rather than of a mobilization of relationships to protect, instruct, and make demands on the child. In these respects, the concept of fostering the child's social development seems different though not unrelated to rehabilitation and treatment.

In seeking to integrate the different (and sometimes competing) objectives of juvenile commitments, the society has latched onto various justifications. For many decades, the touchstone for making dispositions was captured by the phrase "the best interests of the child."[57] The vitality and power of this concept gradually eroded for three different reasons. One is that it was sufficiently vague as to fail to give precise guidance. This, of course, is true of all such well-meaning guidelines, but is not much noticed until the concepts begin to fail on substantive grounds. The two substantive failings of this phrase were, first, that it was used to justify many decisions that were manifestly not in the best interests of the child, and second, that it failed to accommodate community interests in short-run security and the desire to hold children and their caretakers accountable for failures to meet their responsibilities to the society.

More recently the concept guiding decisions to detain juveniles was captured in the phrase "the least restrictive placement."[58] This often stood alongside the injunction to "at least do no harm."[59] What these phrases reflected was a profound disillusionment with the fairness and efficacy of the juvenile court as an institution that could, in fact, serve the best interests of the child. In the late 1960s and early 1970s, there was a widespread sense that the juvenile court had abused its discretion and effectively imprisoned children for acts that would not be crimes if committed by adults.[60] In addition, it was judged that institutionalizing children not only failed to rehabilitate them, but stigmatized them by labeling their behavior delinquent.[61] Finally, there was a strong belief that children, left to their own devices, would gradually learn a sense of responsibility.[62] Thus, the proper juvenile dispositions were those that were the smallest.

Currently, the phrase that captures the aim of juvenile dispositions is "accountability" or "just deserts."[63] This phrase expresses frustration with the perceived ineffectiveness of the juvenile justice system in controlling youth crime, and a general sense that the juvenile court has literally allowed children to get away with murder.

There are two difficulties with all of these guidelines. The first is that none of them adequately reflects the society's special interest in fostering a child's capacity for responsibility, nor in making sure that the private and public institutions that have the responsibility for doing this meet their obligations. The second is that despite the differences in emphasis and spirit among these phrases, not much has changed in terms of the real alternatives available in youth corrections. In most areas, the programs look much like they always have: a choice between probation on the one hand and a locked institution on the other.[64] It is quite rare to find programs that renegotiate relationships among the child, his or her caretakers, and the community; that establish firm structures of accountability of the child to the caretaker and the caretaker to the community; or that provide services to buttress rather than replace the care and supervision provided by the private caretakers.[65]

These observations lead to the third important difference between adult corrections departments and youth authorities. In designing programs, creating appropriate facilities, and placing children, there should be more room for private sector involvement, experimentation, and risk than in the adult corrections agencies.[66] The role for the private sector is large for both historical and philosophical reasons. As chapter 2 indicated, private agencies such as church groups and voluntary associations have long been active in assuming responsibility for children who are at risk or creating risks. The YMCA, the boys clubs, the Boy Scouts, even police athletic leagues, are all historically rooted.[67] Today, increasingly, they are involved not only in prevention programs, but also in programs for those who have been adjudicated delinquent. The philosophical reason is that the society has always preferred that the activity of raising children remain in diversified, private hands, lest the society become too homogenized. There seems to be a great deal of room to build on these traditions.

The room for experimentation is created by three facts. First, most of the programs to which large-scale commitments were made in the past seem to have failed. Therefore, no approach or orthodoxy can now be confidently embraced. Second, how to handle children who have been adjudicated delinquent remains an important problem to be solved, and thus the society cannot simply decide to do nothing in this area. Third, a few programs have worked with some kids some of the time.[68] This demonstration of feasibility should stimulate continued investments.

The legal scope for experimentation with corrections programs—particularly those involving the private sector and relatively modest levels of supervision and control—would be useless were it not for one additional fact, namely, that the society seems to be prepared to run more risks with respect to future security when they are dealing with children than when they are dealing with adults.[69] This does not mean that the society is uninterested in its security, nor that it is willing to excuse all juvenile misconduct. The point is simply that this is not society's only concern when it comes to children and therefore, at the margin, it is willing to trade some security from future crimes against some enhanced prospects for rehabilitation and for increased responsibility among parents and caretakers. It is this fact that makes it possible to create and use a greater variety of programs than are now being used.[70]

Summary and Conclusions

The society has deployed a complex set of institutions to protect itself from the risks associated with unprotected, unsupervised, and unsocialized children. Central to this system are the family, laws mandating guardians for children when natural parents are inadequate or do not exist, the juvenile court to handle specific cases when the existing care arrangements have apparently frayed, and a variety of programs and institutions used to complement or substitute for the private child care arrangements.

While one can view the central purpose of this set of institutions as that of controlling crimes committed by or against children, it operates as though its purposes were broader: to do what can be done to create minimally acceptable conditions for raising children when natural, private arrangements seem inadequate to the task. This focus is strongly indicated by the following facts: (a) Many situations that do not involve crimes by or against children are nominated for public attention. (b) Cases in which relationships between parents and children have broken down are escalated rapidly through the system. (c) In dealing with crimes committed by children, the system investigates the family background of the child as well as the circumstances of the crime and relies on the parents to supervise the child in all cases except those involving the most threatening children. (d) The system intervenes forcefully when children are threatened but not criminally attacked by their parents.

In pursuing the objective of guaranteeing minimally attractive conditions for raising children and dealing effectively with the small number of cases in which the process of child care seems to be failing disastrously, the system should also strive to keep the costs of the intervention low. The costs are reckoned not only in terms of public expenditures, but also in terms of infringements on the principle of family autonomy and responsibility and the use of the state's coercive authority. The aim, then, is for the juvenile justice systems to deal with the fewest possible cases, and to deal with those cases with the least expensive, least coercive, least intrusive interventions.

This effort is hurt by drawing sharp lines between informal and formal, helping and obliging, and social service and law enforcement institutions. It is helped by viewing the system as an interrelated set of institutions that can be arranged in a hierarchy of cost and intrusiveness, and whose special capabilities are to be mobilized to deal with the problems presented by each case. Most of the activity will take place outside the juvenile court. The court's role is to backstop the other institutions, and to resist stepping in too early or too often.

This perspective also has implications for how the court and the juvenile corrections system should operate. With respect to the juvenile court, the implications of this perspective are that the parents or legal guardians of the child should always be a party before the court, and that someone must represent the interests of the future child as well as the current child. With respect to the juvenile corrections system, it seems important for society to run small, short-run risks of continued criminal victimization by allowing experimentation with programs that rely heavily on parental and community supervision of children. This is consistent with the aims of minimizing cost and intrusiveness, keeping responsibilities for child rearing fixed on parents and other legal guardians, and advancing the interests of the future child.

Notes

1. Charles P. Smith, T. Edwin Black, and Fred R. Campbell, *Inconsistent Labeling,* Vol. 1, *Process Description and Summary* (Washington, DC: U.S. Department of Justice, 1979).
2. Throughout the meetings of the Executive Session, the desire to construct some alternative social service-based approach to juvenile justice was frequently expressed. The aim was to avoid the coercion, stigma, and separation that are associated with juvenile court actions. (See Preface to this volume.)
3. On the body of law that is administered through the juvenile court, see Barbara Flicker, "A short history of jurisdiction over juvenile and family matters," in volume 2 of this series.
4. For a discussion of the differences between *Gemeinschaft* and *Gesellschaft* concepts of social solidarity see Talcott Parsons, *The Structure of Social Action,* Vol. 2 (New York: Free Press, 1968), pp. 686–694.
5. Kenneth Keniston and the Carnegie Council on Children, *All Our Children: The American Family Under Pressure* (New York: Harcourt, Brace, Jovanovich, 1977), chap. 9.
6. See Jane Jacobs, *The Death and Life of Great American Cities* (New York: Random House, 1961) on the cohesiveness of modest urban communities.
7. Edward C. Banfield, *The Unheavenly City Revisited* (Boston: Little, Brown, 1974).
8. This is generally true for public bureaucracies. For a discussion of the impact on policing see Mark H. Moore and George L. Kelling, "To serve and protect," *The Public Interest,* No. 70 (1983), pp. 49–65.
9. Parsons, *The Structure of Social Action,* pp. 686–694.
10. Separation from the community was often considered an aid to impartiality. Impartiality, in turn, was considered a virtue.
11. This point was made by a neighbor who works in a family guidance center. Often, poor clients cannot qualify for state financial assistance until they are before the court on a criminal matter.
12. Donald J. Black, "The social organization of arrest," *Stanford Law Review 23* (June 1971), pp. 1087–1111.
13. Edwin T. Black and Charles P. Smith, *A Preliminary National Assessment of the Numbers and Characteristics of Juveniles Processed in the Juvenile Justice System* (Washington, DC: U.S. Department of Justice, 1981).
14. George Kelling, "Caught in a crossfire of concepts: Correction and the dilemmas of social work," *Crime and Delinquency 14*(1) (Jan. 1968), pp. 26–30.
15. See for example New York State's mandatory PINS diversion legislation, chap. 813, *Laws of New York,* 1985.
16. Philip J. Cook and John H. Laub, "Trends in child abuse and juvenile delinquency," p. 111, in volume 2 of this series; Howard N. Snyder, John L. Hutzler, and Terrence A. Finnegan, *Delinquency in the United States, 1982* (Pittsburgh: National Center for Juvenile Justice, 1985), p. 2.
17. J. S. Fuerst and Roy Petty, "Due process—How much is enough?," *The Public Interest,* No. 79 (Spring 1985), pp. 96–100.
18. See generally *American Jurisprudence,* 2nd. ed., Vol. 26, Judges, Sec. 13–20 (Rochester, NY: Lawyers Cooperative Publishing, 1967), pp. 104–109.

19. Julian W. Mack, "The juvenile court," *Harvard Law Review 23* (1909), pp. 104-122.
20. Philip J. Cook and John H. Laub, "Trends in child abuse and juvenile delinquency," in volume 2 of this series.
21. Peter W. Greenwood, Allan Abrahamse, and Franklin Zimring, *Factors Affecting Sentence Severity for Young Adult Offenders* (Santa Monica, CA: Rand Corporation, 1984).
22. Seventy-seven percent of delinquency and status offense referrals in U.S. juvenile courts in 1982 were made by police. See Howard N. Snyder, John L. Hutzler, and Terrence A. Finnegan, *Delinquency in the United States 1982* (Pittsburgh: National Center for Juvenile Justice, 1985), draft, p. 3.
23. Eighty-six percent of intake referrals for status offenses in California in 1976 were made by police. See Charles P. Smith, David J. Berkman, Warren M. Fraser, and John Sutton, *A Preliminary National Assessment of the Status Offender and the Juvenile Justice System: Role Conflicts, Constraints, and Information Gaps* (Washington, DC: U.S. Department of Justice, 1980), p. 74.
24. Herman Goldstein, *Policing a Free Society* (Cambridge, MA: Ballinger, 1977).
25. James Q. Wilson, *Varieties of Police Behavior* (Cambridge, MA: Harvard University Press, 1968). See also James Q. Wilson and George L. Kelling, "Broken windows: The police and neighborhood safety," in *Atlantic Monthly 249*(3) (Mar. 1982), pp. 29–38.
26. Goldstein, *Policing a Free Society.*
27. Ibid.
28. Unfortunately, no national compilation of the volume of custody, care, and protection cases handled through probate court is available. This is partly attributable to the varying jurisdiction of probate courts from state to state.
29. Smith et al., *A Preliminary National Assessment of the Status Offender,* p. 85.
30. This can sometimes result in violence. See Paul Mones, "The relationship between child abuse and parricide: An overview," in Eli H. Newberger and Richard Bourne, Eds., *Unhappy Families: Clinical and Research Perspectives on Family Violence* (Littleton, MA: PSG, 1985).
31. Douglas J. Besharov, "Unfounded allegations—A new child abuse problem," *The Public Interest,* No. 83 (1986), pp. 18–33.
32. Ibid.
33. Greenwood et al., *Factors Affecting Sentence Severity.*
34. See Zimring's discussion of Wald's view of family autonomy, Franklin E. Zimring, *The Changing Legal World of Adolescence* (New York: Free Press, 1982), chap. 4, and Michael S. Wald, "State intervention on behalf of 'neglected' children: A search for realistic standards," in Margaret K. Rosenheim, Ed., *Pursuing Justice for the Child* (Chicago: University of Chicago Press, 1976).
35. This is one of the consequences of having imprecise definitions of abuse and neglect. See discussion in chapter 3.
36. The Executive Session faced this possibility when Ellen Schall described the population that remained in detention in New York City. She noted that the largest group of children was the children whose parents did not come to get them. (See Preface to this volume.)

37. Janet Fink, "Determining the future child: Actors on the juvenile court stage," in volume 2 of this series.
38. Ibid.
39. James Wootton articulated well this view in the Executive Session. (See Preface to this volume.)
40. See note 11.
41. We are indebted to George L. Kelling for relating his observations of juvenile court proceedings in Hennepin County, Minnesota.
42. Fink, "Determining the future child," pp. 284–291, also W. Vaughn Stapleton and Lee E. Teitelbaum, *In Defense of Youth* (New York: Russell Sage Foundation, 1972).
43. See generally *American Jurisprudence,* 2nd ed., Vol. 29, *Evidence,* Sec. 339–351, pp. 388–401.
44. Concerning the appropriateness of an individual's background in making sentencing determinations for adults, the Supreme Court found in *Williams v. New York,* 337 U.S. 241, 247 (1949), for example, that criminal sentences should be based "on the fullest information possible concerning the defendant's life and characteristics." In *Pennsylvania v. Ashe,* 302 U.S. 51, 55 (1937), the Court reasoned that "for the determination of sentences, justice generally requires consideration of more than the particular acts by which the crime was committed and that there be taken into account the circumstances of the offense together with the character and propensities of the offender."
45. Robert Jordan and William Warren, *Bankruptcy* (Mineloa, NY: Foundation Press, 1985).
46. Howard N. Snyder, John L. Hutzler, and Terrence A. Finnegan, *Delinquency in the United States, 1982* (Pittsburgh: National Center for Juvenile Justice, 1985).
47. Anne Larason Schneider and Donna D. Schram, *An Assessment of Juvenile Justice System Reform in Washington State,* Vol. 10, *Executive Summary* (Eugene, OR: Institute of Policy Analysis, 1983). For discussion in adult setting see Alfred Blumstein, Jacqueline Cohen, and Daniel Nagin, Eds., *Deterrence and Incapacitation: Estimating the Effects of Criminal Sanctions on Crime Rates* (Washington, DC: National Academy of Sciences, 1978).
48. *In re Gault,* 387 U.S. 1 (1967).
49. Edward M. Murphy, "Managing risk in juvenile corrections," in volume 2 of this series. Also see John M. Pettibone, Robert G. Swisher, Kurt H. Weiland, Christine E. Wolf, and Joseph L. White, *Services to Children in Juvenile Courts: The Judicial-Executive Controversy* (Columbus, OH: Academy for Contemporary Problems, 1981).
50. Pettibone et al., *Services to Children.*
51. Alfred Blumstein, Jacqueline Cohen, Susan E. Martin, and Michael H. Tonry, Eds., *Research on Sentencing: The Search for Reform,* Summary Report (Washington, DC: U.S. Government Printing Office, 1983), and Leslie T. Wilkins, *The Principles of Guidelines for Sentencing: Methodological and Philosophical Issues in Their Development* (Washington, DC: U.S. Government Printing Office, 1981).
52. Michael Sherman and Gordon Hawkins, *Imprisonment in America: Choosing the Future* (Chicago: University of Chicago Press, 1981), and National Institute of Justice, *NIJ Reports/SNI* (July 1984).

53. Pettibone et al., *Services to Children.*
54. "[T]he average number of residents in public juvenile facilities in the United States was slightly over 50,000" in 1982, higher than the figure in both 1977 and 1979, according to the Office of Juvenile Justice and Delinquency Prevention, *Children in Custody: Advance Report on the 1982 Census of Public Juvenile Facilities* (Washington, DC: U.S. Government Printing Office, 1983).
55. For example, the New York State Juvenile Offender Act (chap. 478, Laws of 1978) severely restricted the discretion of the state Division for Youth regarding the length of stay and security level of juvenile offender placements.
56. Richard W. Barnum, "Concepts of responsibility: Development, failures and responses," in volume 2 of this series.
57. For a critique of the best interests of the child standard in the context of foster care placement see Robert H. Mnookin, "Foster care—In whose best interest?," *Harvard Educational Review 43*(4) (Nov. 1973), pp. 599–638.
58. Institute of Judicial Administration–American Bar Association Joint Commission on Juvenile Justice Standards, *Standards Relating to Dispositions* (Cambridge, MA: Ballinger, 1980), pp. 34–38.
59. Zimring, *The Changing Legal World of Adolescence,* chap. 5.
60. Charles E. Silberman, *Criminal Violence, Criminal Justice* (New York: Random House, 1978).
61. Anne Rankin Mahoney, "The effect of labeling upon youths in the juvenile justice system: A review of the evidence," *Law and Society Review 8*(4) (Summer 1974), pp. 583–614.
62. The view expressed in Edwin M. Schur, *Radical Non-Intervention: Rethinking the Delinquency Problem* (Englewood Cliffs, NJ: Prentice-Hall, 1973), reflects the idea that society should define away much of the problem of delinquency by accepting a wider array of appropriate youthful behaviors. Often writers, notably Jean Jacques Rousseau, *The Social Contract* (Chicago: Henry Regnery, 1954), argue for a natural, self-regulating propensity of humans to develop properly. For a more contemporary treatment see Emmy E. Werner and Ruth S. Smith, *Vulnerable But Invincible: A Longitudinal Study of Resilient Children and Youth* (New York: McGraw-Hill, 1982).
63. Schneider and Schram, *Juvenile Justice System Reform in Washington State,* Vol. 10.
64. Black and Smith reported that of 508,910 juvenile case dispositions made by the courts nationally in 1977, 49% were to probation; 13% to training schools and secure facilities; 6% to camp or ranch; and the remainder to foster home, group home, social service agency, or other miscellaneous categories. Black and Smith, *A Preliminary National Assessment.*
65. J. David Hawkins, R. F. Catalano, G. Jones, and D. Fine, "Delinquency prevention through parent training: Results and issues from work in progress," and Brigitte Berger, "Multiproblem families and the community," both in volume 3 of this series. See also Kenniston, *All Our Children,* chap. 9.
66. Noreen Blonein from California made this point in Executive Session meetings. (See Preface to this volume.)
67. George L. Kelling, "The end of the nightstick," in volume 2 of this series.
68. Peter W. Greenwood and Franklin E. Zimring, *One More Chance: The Pursuit of Promising Intervention Strategies for Chronic Juvenile Offenders* (Santa Monica, CA: Rand Corporation, 1985).

69. A comparison of the cases of Jerome Miller and John Boone in Massachusetts is quite instructive. See *Jerome Miller and the Department of Youth Services* (A), (B), and (B: Sequel), John F. Kennedy School of Government, Case Program Distribution Office, Harvard University, C14-76-101.0, C14-76-102.0, and C14-76-102.1 (1976), and *Massachusetts Department of Corrections* (I), (II), and (III), John F. Kennedy School of Government, Case Program Distribution Office, Harvard University, C14-77-165.0, C14-77-166.0, and C14-77-167.0 (1977).
70. Edward M. Murphy, "Managing risk in juvenile corrections," in volume 2 of this series.

5
Emergent Problems

With Saul Weingart

To position the juvenile justice system to contribute most effectively, stewards of the system should consider the problems the society will face with its youth in the near future.[1] This issue seems straightforward: It is a matter of estimating the number of children creating risks or at risk in the society over the next decade.

Yet this question, like every other question we have considered, turns not only on the objective conditions in the society, but also crucially on what the society authorizes the juvenile justice system to do.[2] If the society thinks it is unjust or ineffective for the juvenile justice system to handle dangerous juvenile offenders (preferring that this problem be handled in the adult criminal court), then dangerous juvenile offenders cease to be a problem for the juvenile justice system. Similarly, if the society deems it unjust or ineffective for the juvenile justice system to intrude in family life to protect children from anything but the most imminent and serious threats, then cases involving smaller or more uncertain risks will disappear. Finally, if the society views breakdowns in the relationship between parents and caretakers, impermanent foster care arrangements, or disputes over child custody as beneath the dignity of the court, then these problems, too, will be irrelevant. One cannot estimate the potential demands (or opportunities) for the juvenile justice system without knowing for what purposes it will be used.

On the other hand, the society might not want to determine purposes solely on principle. It might prefer a more pragmatic approach in which the decision about purposes was based on reasonably objective estimates of the sorts of problems it faces in the future. If it seemed likely that dangerous, youthful offenders were a minor and diminishing threat, the society might be content to leave this problem within the nation's juvenile courts even though it might more justly and effectively be dealt with in the adult criminal justice system. If it seemed that problems of abuse and neglect were growing, and if no other institutions seemed capable of handling them or inclined to do so, the society might place that responsibility within the juvenile justice system, even though, as a matter of principle, it would prefer not to. And if it seemed that the society was increasingly confused about who was responsible for caring for children, and thus exposed children to the future risks associated with inadequate care-taking arrangements, the society might decide that this was an important job for the nation's juvenile courts. Thus, the society might not be able to decide on the best use of the institutions of the juvenile justice system without objective estimates of the seriousness of the varied problems that will arise for the nation's youth.

Unfortunately, objective estimates are hard to make. The society knows about the magnitude and character of these problems only through its past efforts to handle them.[3] Since current observations of youth crime, child abuse and neglect, and status offenses are the product of both the objective conditions affecting children and the public's past actions with respect to these problems, any current effort to estimate the size of the problems is hopelessly contaminated by past authorizations and investments.

To overcome these difficulties in estimating the future demands and opportunities for the juvenile justice system, we will rely on the following approach. Instead of looking at only one kind of problem, we will look at each of the three classes of problems that define the areas within which the juvenile justice system might plausibly make a contribution, and from which the work load of the system is now drawn. Thus, we will examine trends affecting crimes committed by children, the problem of abuse and neglect of children, and situations indicating a breakdown in the relationship between children and caretakers. With respect to each, we will consider how important each has been in the work load of the juvenile court and juvenile justice system. In addition, we will try to look behind the current work load of the system and see what can be determined about trends in objective conditions that are contributing to that work load and in the development of systems that are nominating the cases for attention by the juvenile court or other public agencies. The aim is to determine how the level and mix of cases handled by the system will, could, or should change in the future.

Perhaps not surprisingly, the conclusion is that the most important challenges facing the system lie in the areas of abuse and neglect and in situations in which the relationship between child and caretaker has eroded badly. These areas, rather than crimes committed by children, are the ones that contain the greatest potential for explosive growth, and therefore are the proper focus of prudent experiments and investments. The issues with respect to crimes committed by children are much more straightforward and better understood. Moreover, the society's approach to crimes committed by children is likely to be improved by taking the problems of abuse, neglect, and status offenses more seriously. The reason is that these problems will be solved through programs that strengthen the family rather than replace it. And, as the society makes progress in these areas, it is apt to discover that these approaches represent potentially attractive solutions to some juvenile crime problems as well.

Trends in Juvenile Crime and Delinquency

One problem at or near the center of the juvenile justice system is crimes committed by children. As a historical fact, crimes committed by children have always accounted for the largest portion of the cases handled by the juvenile court. Figure 5.1 presents data on juvenile court adjudications for delinquency (including status offenses) on the one hand and on abuse and neglect of children on the other. One can see that the historical trend is for delinquency dispositions to increase. Figure 5.2 divides delinquency into criminal offenses and status offenses. One can see from this figure that juvenile crimes have always constituted the bulk of the workload.

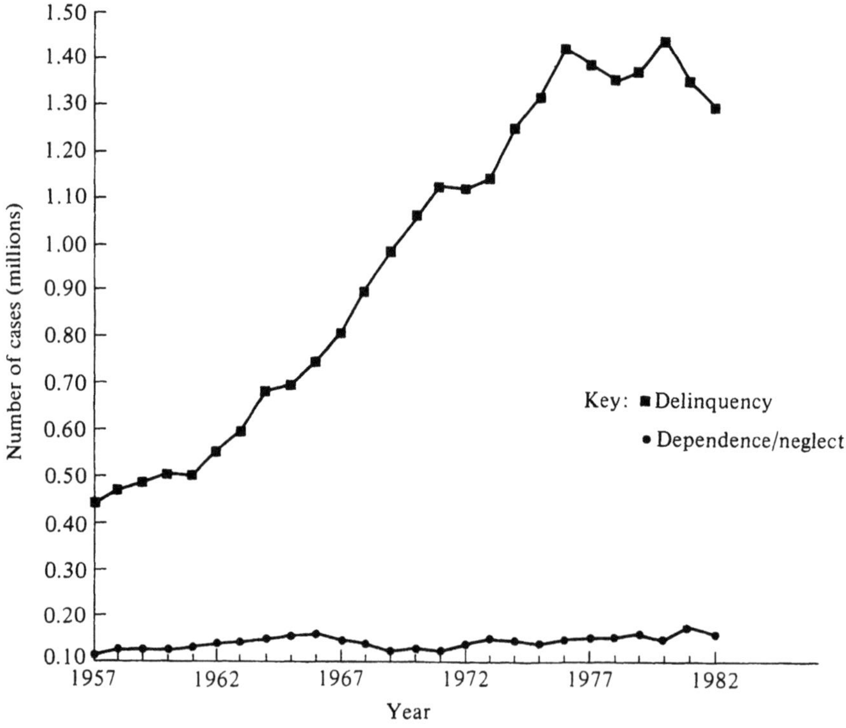

FIGURE 5.1. Number of juvenile court adjudications for delinquency and neglect, 1957 to 1982. From E. H. Nimick, H. N. Snyder, D. P. Sullivan, and N. J. Tierney, *Juvenile Court Statistics, 1982* (Pittsburgh: National Center for Juvenile Justice, 1985), pp. 8, 14.

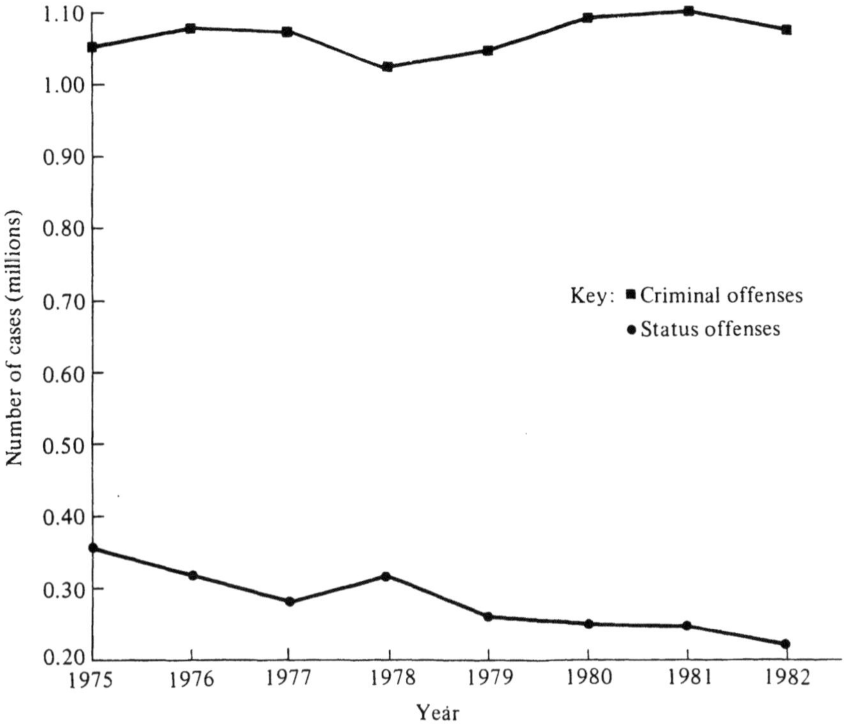

FIGURE 5.2. Number of juvenile court adjudications for criminal and status offenses, 1975 to 1982. From H. N. Snyder, J. L. Hutzler, and T. A. Finnegan, *Delinquency in the United States, 1982* (Pittsburgh: National Center for Juvenile Justice, 1985), p. 9.

Many assume that the trends shown in these figures will continue, for it is a common perception that levels of juvenile crime and victimization have been increasing over the last several decades.[4] Surprisingly, the available data on victimization by juveniles (as distinct from delinquency cases handled by the juvenile court) provide little support for the view that juvenile crime is increasing. The general population does not seem to be increasingly at risk from juvenile offenders. Nor does it seem that the juvenile population is increasingly criminal.

Figure 5.3 presents data on the number of incidents in which juveniles (those aged 12 through 17) attacked their fellow citizens. These data were gathered from general surveys of the U.S. population.[5] The figure indicates that the number of victimizations was stable or declined slightly over the period 1973 to 1981. Figure 5.3 also indicates that the number of victimizations by offenders older than age 17 increased over this period; hence, the contribution of juvenile offenders to the overall crime problem has declined relative to that of older offenders.

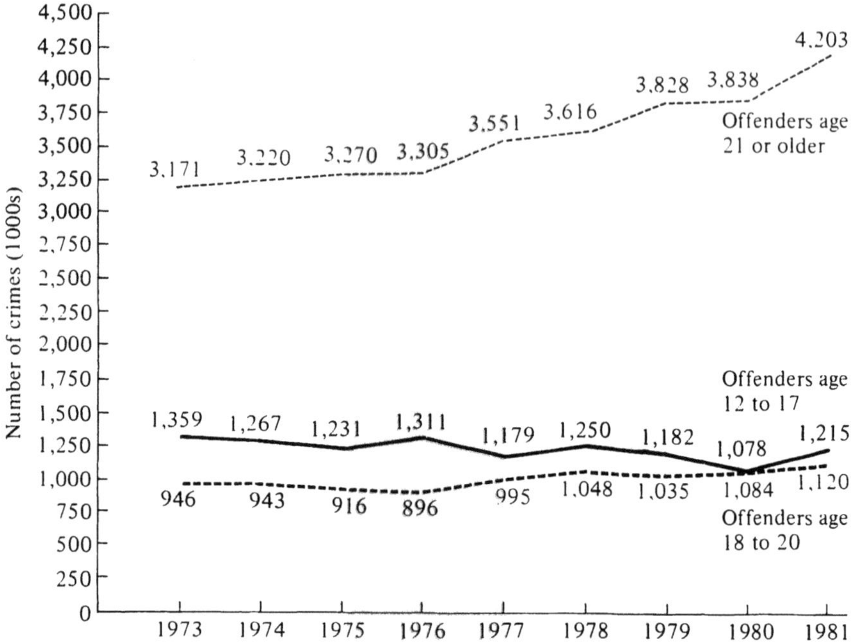

FIGURE 5.3. Total estimated raw number of personal crimes, by year and age of offender, National Crime Survey national data, 1973–1981. Age group figures include perceived ages of alone or of oldest multiple offender. Excluded are incidents (about 6% of total) in which the victim did not know whether there was more than one offender, and victimizations (about 1% of total) committed by children perceived to be under 12 years of age. From John H. Laub, *Trends in Juvenile Criminal Behavior in the United States: 1973–1981* (Albany, NY: Hindelang Criminal Justice Research Center, State University of New York, 1983), p. 15.

Figure 5.4 takes these same data and calculates the rate at which the youthful population of the United States committed personal offenses over this same period. This figure indicates that the offending rate was stable or declined slightly, like the victimization rate.

A broadly similar picture emerges when one examines data on the rate at which the nation's police arrest juveniles for relatively serious crimes. Figure 5.5 presents data on arrest rates for youths aged 13 through 17 for different categories of crime.[6] The period portrayed in this figure is longer than that portrayed in the previous two figures. The victimization data begin in 1973 and continue only until 1981, while the arrest data start in 1965 and continue to 1983. Figure 5.5 shows the same stability in arrest rates from 1975 to the present that Figures 5.3 and 5.4 show for the victimization rate. However, Figure 5.5 reveals a substantial increase in arrest rates from 1965 to the mid 1970s. Thus, the level rate of offending in the last decade represents a high plateau that was reached only after rapid growth in the late 1960s.

Given this stability in levels of victimization and arrest, it is hard to understand why there is a common perception that youth crime is on the rise. One possible explanation is that the seriousness of the offenses has increased over this period, even though the overall rate has not changed very much. Four pieces of evidence provide some support for this view.

First, the disposition rate has increased in recent years.[7] We know that the severity of the disposition is influenced by the seriousness of the charge and the offense record of the juvenile.[8] Hence, one interpretation of the increased proportion of cases resulting in dispositions is that the cases and records are more serious. (The other interpretation, of course, is that the courts have become more aggressive and now treat minor cases more seriously.)

The hypothesis that juvenile offenses have become more serious gains additional support from a second important piece of evidence: that arrests for violent offenses now constitute a larger portion of total juvenile arrests. This fact can be inferred from the trends revealed in Figure 5.5. Arrests for violent offenses have remained stable, while arrests for property crimes have declined.

A third piece of evidence supporting the hypothesis of increased seriousness is drawn from a comparative analysis of two cohorts of children growing up in Philadelphia.[9] Those boys who reached the age of 16 in 1974 committed about the same number of crimes as those who became 16 in 1961, but the seriousness of the crimes they committed was much greater. Table 5.1 presents data comparing these two cohorts in terms of the seriousness of the offenses they committed.

The fourth piece of evidence is that, while the overall pattern of juvenile offending has been relatively stable, in very large cities juvenile offense rates—particularly rates for violent offenses—have been increasing. Figure 5.6 presents data showing increases in personal victimizations by youthful offenders in cities with populations of more than a million.

Thus, it is possible that the nation's cities are experiencing increases in the seriousness of juvenile offenses, a phenomenon that may be magnified by widespread coverage of a small number of particularly outrageous crimes. It is this view that has spawned a great many special policies and procedures to deal with unusually dangerous, persistent, or active juvenile offenders.[10]

There are two other hypotheses that could explain the common view that youth crime has been increasing. One is that citizens base their fears about crime not on rare experience with real criminal victimization, but instead on the much more common experience with disorderly conduct and incivilities that seem threatening but are not crimes. There is a great deal of empirical support for this hypothesis.[11] An increase in teenaged disorderliness might translate into higher levels of fear of teenaged crime.

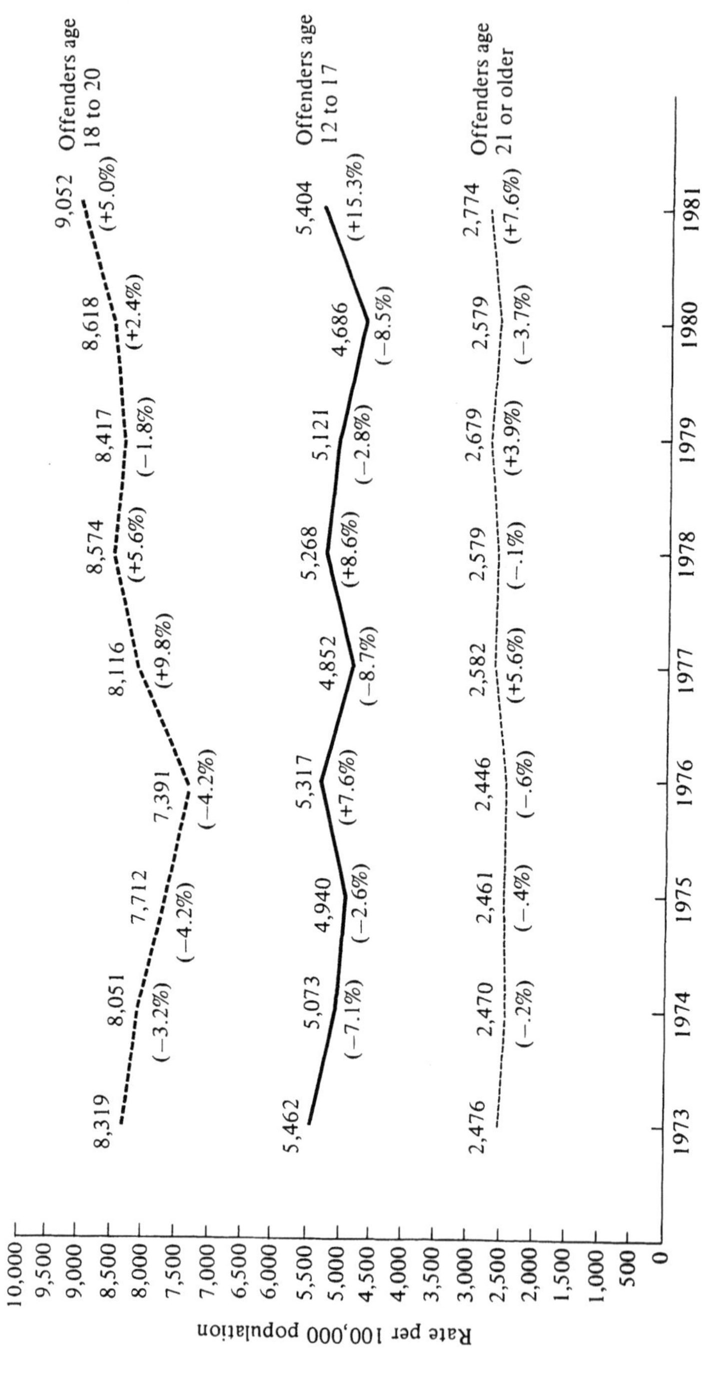

Population base:

Year	1973	1974	1975	1976	1977	1978	1979	1980	1981
12 to 17	24,881,521	24,962,923	24,910,271	24,661,508	24,291,303	23,737,816	23,077,501	23,009,841	22,491,837
18 to 20	11,369,132	11,712,785	11,879,746	12,119,575	12,264,007	12,225,692	12,296,111	12,572,180	12,374,537
21 or older	128,079,370	130,371,553	132,868,762	135,107,961	137,507,165	140,217,230	142,869,393	114,797,676	151,545,119

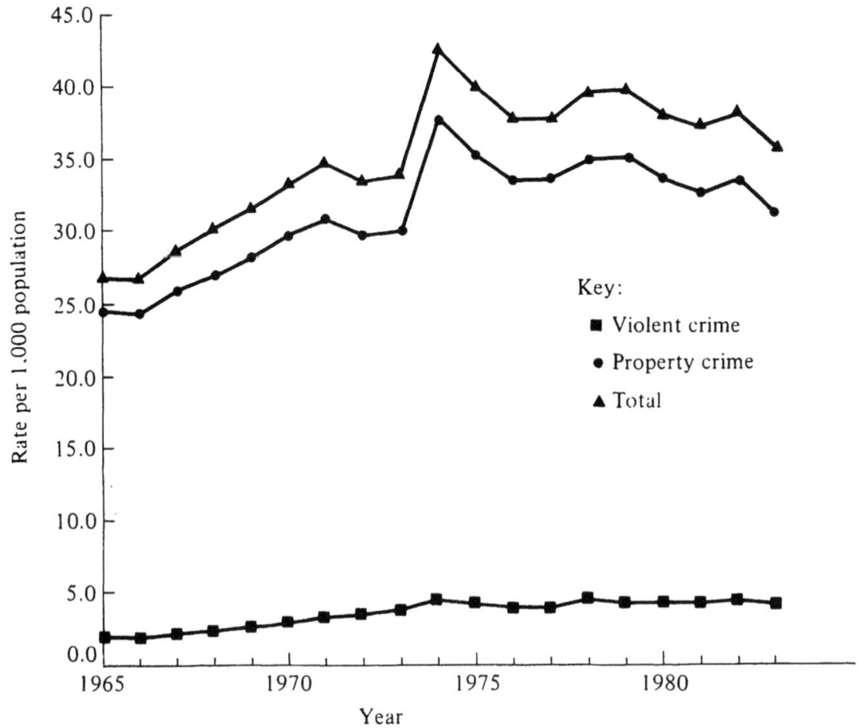

FIGURE 5.5. Arrest rates for youths aged 13 to 17 per 1,000 population, 1965 to 1983. From Philip J. Cook and John H. Laub, "Trends in child abuse and juvenile delinquency," in volume 2 of this series, Table 7.2.

Perhaps sales of "boom boxes" are more highly correlated with the society's fears than are real levels of muggings.

The third hypothesis that explains the public's view that juvenile crime has been increasing is that the population's tolerance for youthful exuberance and violence has declined. A more conservative mood transforms the same objective facts about youthful offending into a serious social

---

FIGURE 5.4. Estimated rates of offending in total personal crimes (per 100,000 persons in each population subgroup) by year and age of offender, National Crime Survey data, 1973–1981. Age group figures include perceived age of alone or of oldest multiple offender. Excluded are incidents (about 6% of total) in which the victim did not know whether there was more than one offender, and victimizations (about 1% of total) committed by children perceived to be under 12 years of age. Percentage in parentheses is percent change from the previous year. From John H. Laub, *Trends in Juvenile Criminal Behavior in the United States: 1973–1981* (Albany, NY: Hindelang Criminal Justice Research Center, State University of New York, 1983), p. 17.

TABLE 5.1. Offense seriousness score.

	Cohort I		Cohort II males	
Offense seriousness score	N	%	N	%
less than 20	4,330	42.38	330	2.08
20–29	449	4.40	2083	13.11
30–39	470	4.60	5	0.03
40–49	335	3.28	—	—
50–59	31	0.30	3	0.02
60–69	229	2.24	—	—
70–79	156	1.53	5	0.03
80–89	67	0.66	1068	6.72
90–99	12	0.12	2	0.01
100–199	1,516	14.84	3446	21.69
200–299	1,337	13.09	1106	6.96
300–399	605	5.92	880	5.54
400–499	367	3.59	578	3.64
500–599	59	0.58	318	2.00
600–699	61	0.60	544	3.42
700–799	67	0.66	395	2.49
800–899	25	0.24	554	3.49
900–999	8	0.08	856	5.39
1000–1999	66	0.65	3279	20.63
2000–2999	20	0.20	260	1.64
3000–3999	3	0.03	83	0.52
4000+	1	0.01	96	0.60
Total	10,214	100.00	15891	100.00

Source: Marvin E. Wolfgang and Paul E. Tracy, "The 1945 and 1958 birth cohorts: A comparison of the prevalence, incidence, and severity of delinquent behavior," in Daniel McGillis et al., Eds., *Dealing with Dangerous Offenders*, Vol. 2, *Selected Papers* (Cambridge, MA: Harvard University, 1983).

problem. One small fact that might support such a hypothesis is that the population is, in fact, aging. Figure 5.7 presents data on the past, current, and (projected) future age distribution of the population. It shows that youth (age 17 and under) now constitute a historically very small proportion of the population. If age breeds less tolerance for youthful excesses, and if the dominant mood of the society is shaped by the age groups that are relatively large, it is possible that simple demographics are producing a society that is now less tolerant of adolescents.[12]

Predicting future levels of juvenile crime and delinquency is difficult due only to uncertainty about future rates of offending by the juvenile population. The demographic situation is pretty well determined. There will be an absolute and relative decline in the population aged 13 through 17 from now until the early 1990s. The youth population will then begin to grow and will reach high absolute levels in 1995 as a result of the "echo baby boom." Even then, however, the youth population will be smaller in absolute terms, especially as a proportion of the overall population, than it was in the mid- and late 1960s.

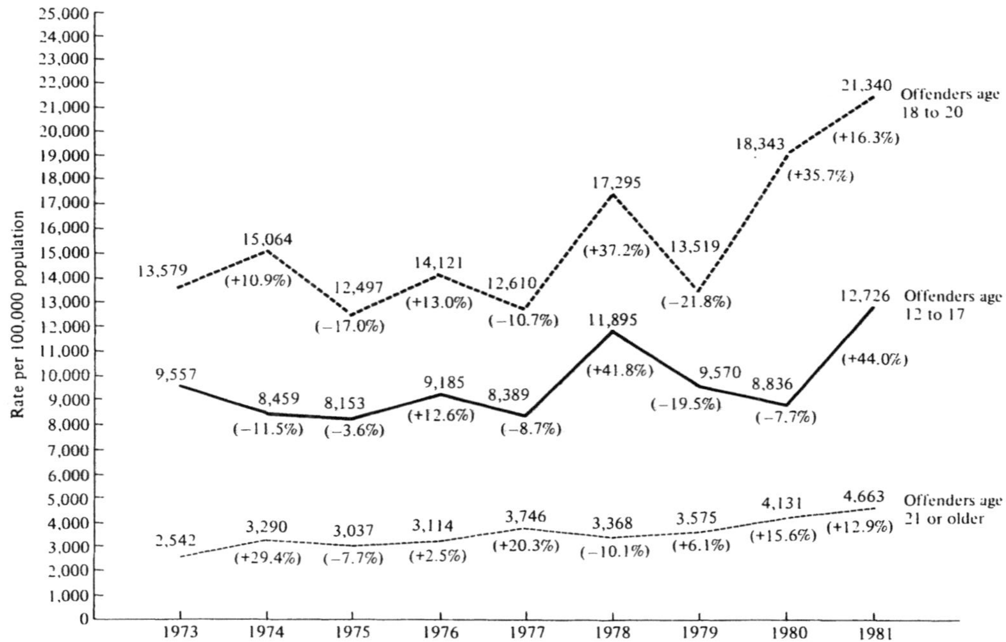

Population base:

Year	1973	1974	1975	1976	1977	1978	1979	1980	1981
12 to 17	1,759,879	1,753,583	1,754,892	1,737,916	1,692,930	1,634,922	1,591,241	1,620,790	1,562,815
18 to 20	868,239	846,176	844,241	841,749	869,510	931,336	877,719	892,313	858,368
21 or older	11,503,217	11,348,001	11,404,849	11,248,702	11,218,043	11,373,427	11,224,858	11,676,765	11,577,568

FIGURE 5.6. Estimated rates of offending in total personal crimes (per 100,000 persons in each population subgroup) in cities of 1 million or more persons, by year and age of offender, National Crime Survey national data, 1973–1981. Age group figures include perceived age of alone or of oldest multiple offender. Excluded are incidents (about 6% of total) in which the victim did not know whether there was more than one offender, and victimizations (about 1% of total) committed by children perceived to be under 12 years of age. Percentage in parentheses is percent change from the previous year. From John H. Laub, *Trends in Juvenile Criminal Behavior in the United States: 1973–1981* (Albany, NY: Hindelang Criminal Justice Research Center, State University of New York, 1983), p. 21.

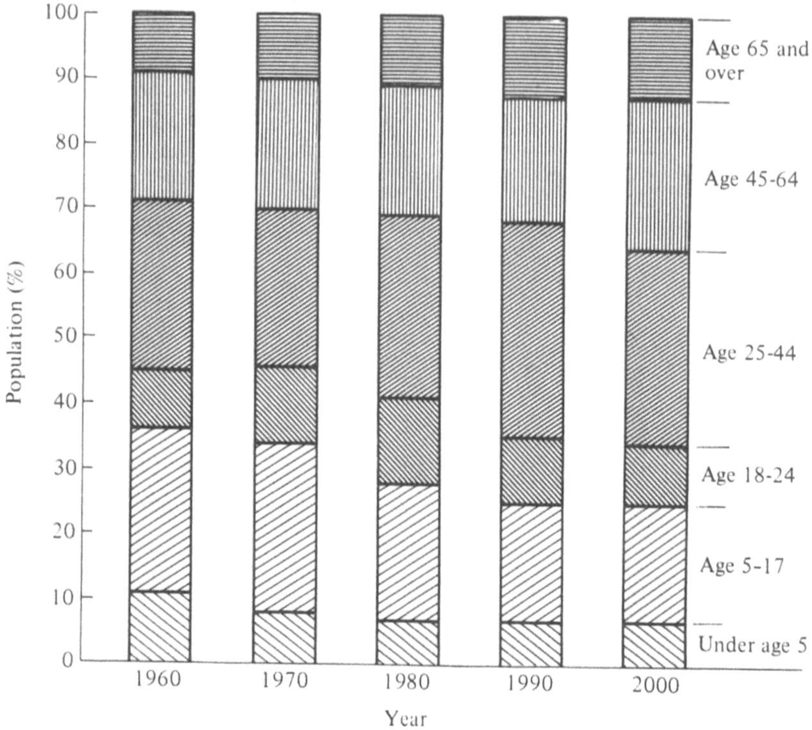

FIGURE 5.7. U.S. population by age, 1960 to 2000. From *Statistical Abstract of the United States 1986,* 106th ed. (Washington, DC: U.S. Department of Commerce, 1986), pp. 24–25.

What remains uncertain is how much criminal conduct these future youth cohorts will generate. One can approach this question historically by examining the range of variation in offending rates for the juvenile population. When one uses this approach, one observes that current levels of juvenile offending are relatively high by historical standards of the last several decades, but the levels have remained constant. Thus, one does not know whether to treat current rates of offending as unusually high and likely to fall, or as a new norm.

Alternatively, one can consider the factors that are correlated with or that theoretically influence crime rates to see whether they are increasing or decreasing.[13] This approach suggests that current offense rates should not drop, for few factors that are empirically or theoretically related to criminal offending are likely to improve. Demographic factors are against reductions in rates of offending. Indeed, the youth population will shift in the direction of becoming increasingly urbanized—a factor associated with higher rather than lower levels of criminal conduct.[14]

Similarly, the institutions that might contain and shape youthful conduct along productive paths seem likely to deteriorate rather than improve.[15] Family structure is weakening. While this does not necessarily imply a loss in family functioning, the odds favor that result. Schools are now moving in the direction of excellence and higher standards.[16] This may well carry many children who would otherwise not be challenged to greater levels of performance than is possible in today's schools. But it also carries the risk that more children will drop out rather than continue to fail. Youth employment remains high.[17] The service economy may well end up providing more opportunities for youth employment than did the manufacturing economy, which might improve the employment status of children, but this trend is not yet evident in employment statistics.

If one had to guess, then, it seems reasonable to bet that the juvenile offending rate would remain at today's current high but stable level. The likelihood that the offending rate would increase seems slightly greater than that it would decrease, largely because the factors that influence levels of juvenile crime are all moving in the wrong direction. Indeed, the only factors pointing toward a *decrease* in the rate of juvenile offending are that the current level is high by historical standards, and that there are now far more adults per adolescent than a generation ago.[18]

In sum, the situation with regard to juvenile crime seems to be the following: For the next several years, the society will enjoy a decrease in the overall level of juvenile crime due to a continued decline in the absolute size of the youth population, and a constant or only slightly increasing juvenile offending rate. Starting in the 1990s, the rate of juvenile crime is likely to increase in both absolute and relative terms, reaching its peak in 1995. In that year, the society will face about 10% to 25% more juvenile crime than it had in 1980.[19] Within this overall pattern, it is possible that the society will experience an increase in the violence of juvenile crime, particularly in large metropolitan areas. It also seems likely that the society's tolerance for juvenile crimes and general juvenile misconduct will decline.

This sets the stage for a prolonged crackdown on juvenile crime. An important question is how disciplined and selective that response will be in choosing its targets. An equally important question is how the society will deal with juvenile offenders who are not particularly dangerous. A worrisome scenario is one in which the society's fears, kindled by general adolescent misconduct and given point by a very small number of dangerous youthful offenders, fuel a broad effort to incapacitate juvenile offenders at enormous public expense and with a substantial risk of injustice to young offenders. A more optimistic scenario would be one in which the society's ability to distinguish the rare dangerous youthful offender from all the others improved. Such offenders would be successfully incapacitated, and all other youthful offenders would be made to feel responsible for their own criminal misconduct and supervised in programs that drew heavily on private and community resources, thereby preserving the society's interests in the child's future development as well as in effective, current incapacitation. This seems to be a more just and effective response to the challenge of juvenile crime in the future. Thus, positioning the juvenile justice system for the second rather than the first scenario should be high-priority business.

Trends in Child Abuse and Neglect

The second problem included within the jurisdiction of the juvenile court and juvenile justice system is that of abuse and neglect of children. From the vantage point of the nation's juvenile courts, from 1950 to 1975 this problem remained remarkably stable. Over this period the court handled an average of 2.0 cases of abuse and neglect per 1,000 children under the age of 18 (+ 0.3 cases per thousand, *Juvenile Court Statistics*[20]). Recently the problem seems to have increased: In 1981 the rate was 2.9 per 1,000 and in 1982 2.7 per 1,000.[21] The important questions are, does this trend reflect real changes in underlying rates of abuse and neglect, increased nominations from a large pool of previously invisible offenses, or some combination of both; and in any case, is the trend likely to continue?

Such questions are hard to answer for several reasons. First, despite heroic efforts to clarify and standardize the concepts of abuse and neglect, the legal definitions remain frustratingly imprecise.[22] Second, because the victims of such offenses are often intimidated or inarticulate, the offenses are generally hidden from public view.[23] Third, the systems for identifying and nominating the cases are still developing and therefore operate inconsistently.[24] For all of these reasons, estimates of the universe of cases to be handled are quite imprecise.

The best estimates of the prevalence of abuse and neglect come from the *National Study of the Incidence and Severity of Child Abuse and Neglect*—a study based on data collected from 26 counties in 10 states during the period May 1979 to April 1980.[25] The study used a very strict definition of abuse and neglect: There had to be evidence of "clearcut and serious maltreatment causing avoidable injury, illness, or emotional/behavioral impairment, resulting from purposive acts or extreme inattention by a parent or other adult caretaker."[26] (Interestingly, the study included cases of repeated truancy or delinquency if the child's guardian knew about the situation but refused to take any action.) Table 5.2 presents the resulting estimates of the rates of abuse and neglect in the general population. These rates, projected nationally, indicate some 625,000 cases of serious abuse and neglect in the year studied.[27] In the same year about 160,000 cases were disposed of in the juvenile court.[28] Thus it seems fairly clear that the juvenile court is handling no more than one quarter of the serious cases of abuse and neglect in the society.

TABLE 5.2. Estimates of the rates of abuse and neglect in the general population.

Abuse 5.7/1,000		Neglect 5.3/1,000	
Physical	3.4	Physical	1.7
Sexual	0.7	Educational	2.9
Emotional	2.2	Emotional	1.0

Source: Philip J. Cook and John H. Laub, "Trends in child abuse and juvenile delinquency," in volume 2 of this series, p. 113.

Given the large universe of unreported cases, it is quite possible that virtually all the changes in the juvenile court's handling of abuse and neglect cases come from changes in systems of reporting and handling rather than from changes in the underlying problem.[29] Surely there has been a great deal of social activity with respect to improving these systems.[30] Still, one would like to see more objective estimates of trends in levels of abuse and neglect.

One potentially useful indicator of these trends is the criminal homicide rate for young children. As Cook and Laub explain: "A majority of homicide victims aged four and under are killed by relatives, suggesting that these cases are the logical extreme outcome of physical abuse in the home."[31]

Table 5.3 presents data on murders of children for the years 1965 through 1982. The data for children aged 1 to 4 indicate sharp increases from 1965 to 1973 and relative stability thereafter. This contrasts oddly with the trends in the handling of abuse and neglect cases within the juvenile court, which were stable during the rapid increases and went up only later. It is as though the society's response to the problem has lagged by several years. At any rate, the underlying problem of abuse and neglect, like the problem of juvenile crime, seems now to be stable at high levels.

How cases of abuse and neglect will be handled within the juvenile justice system is another major uncertainty. There is reason to believe that these cases will accumulate first within child protection and social work agencies. Most of the new reporting laws mandate the involvement of such agencies. And a recent study by Russell and Trainor indicated the response to this mandate: The volume of cases reported to child protective services doubled from 10.1 per 1,000 children in 1976 to 20.1 per 1,000 in 1982.[32] This was in the same period when the cases adjudicated by the juvenile court moved from 2.0 to 2.7 per 1,000. Thus it seems likely that most of the work will be done within child protection agencies.

At the same time, it is clear that many cases will be handled by institutions such as police, prosecutors, and courts. This will occur partly because these institutions will see cases that the child protection agencies

TABLE 5.3. Homicide victimization rates per 100,000 for children under age 5.

	Infants		Children aged 1–4	
	Homicide	Homicide and undetermined[a]	Homicide	Homicide and undetermined
1965	5.5	—	1.1	—
1966	5.8	—	1.2	—
1967	6.4	—	1.1	—
1968	4.8	7.7	1.4	2.4
1969	4.3	7.9	1.6	2.8
1970	4.3	7.9	1.9	3.2
1971	5.1	8.2	2.1	3.4
1972	5.2	8.1	1.8	3.1
1973	5.2	8.1	2.5	3.6
1974	5.5	9.1	2.2	3.5
1975	5.8	8.9	2.5	3.6
1976	5.6	9.0	2.5	3.6
1977	5.6	8.9	2.7	3.8
1978	5.0	7.6	2.6	3.5
1979	5.2	7.8	2.5	3.3
1980	5.9	7.8	2.5	3.3
1981	6.1	8.4	2.6	3.2
1982	6.7	8.7	2.7	3.2

[a] The sum of the homicide victimization rate and the death rate due to "injury undetermined whether accidentally or purposefully inflicted."
Source: Philip J. Cook and John H. Laub, "Trends in child abuse and juvenile delinquency," in volume 2 of this series, Table 7.5.

miss. Indeed, the *National Study of the Incidence and Severity of Serious Child Abuse and Neglect* found that only one third of cases they considered relevant were known to child protection agencies.[33] The other two thirds were found in the records of police, hospitals, and schools.

But the police, prosecutors, and courts will be involved for two other reasons as well. One is that there is increasing public concern about the abuse and neglect of children and an increased willingness to respond with punitive actions against parents.[34] Some reporting laws are also now mandating prosecutorial involvement in decisions about how to handle certain cases of child abuse and neglect, particularly sexual abuse.[35] In fact, this seems to be part of a general trend to bring prosecutors and courts into domestic violence cases involving dependents within the family, whether children or spouse. The second reason that the police are involved is that there is increased recognition of the importance of police investigative skills in determining the facts surrounding some instances of abuse and neglect.[36] Thus, police, prosecutors, and courts are likely to become increasingly involved for both investigation and adjudication.

Looking ahead, one can reasonably make three predictions. First, it seems likely that the number of cases of abuse and neglect nominated will increase rather than decrease. Everything is pushing in this direction: The underlying rates of abuse and neglect seem stable or increasing, the systems of reporting are maturing, and family structure is weakening.

Second, the magnitude of the increase will be determined most fundamentally by policy decisions affecting the reporting and handling of these cases rather than changes in the underlying problems. The reasons are that there is a large pool of cases to be explored and that the system for nominating and reporting is probably changing faster than the real incidence of the problem.[37] The apparent incidence of the problem thus can increase dramatically as long-standing problems are identified as new cases.

Third, it remains unclear where in the juvenile justice system these cases will accumulate. It seems likely that it will be within child protection and social work agencies rather than with the police, prosecutors, and the juvenile court. Increasingly, however, it seems likely that cases will be handled jointly.

Trends in Status Offenses and Guardianship

The third problem potentially within the jurisdiction of the juvenile court is the situations in which children have violated special rules designed to keep them in a set of relationships that prepares them for future citizenship, or in which the relationships are nonexistent. These situations include children running away, parents giving up trying to manage children, the society failing to establish relatively permanent foster care arrangements, and parents fighting over custody of the child. The situations may even include instances in which children have stopped going to school and thereby threaten their own futures.

This issue is now commonly discussed in terms of "status offenses." The particular terminology and the typical discussion of the issue insists on an analogy between such offenses as running away, curfew violations, incorrigibility, and truancy on the one hand and criminal offenses such as robbery, burglary, and larceny on the other. The offenses are viewed as similar in that the children are regarded as responsible for their acts, and the law is brought to bear against the child for violating special responsibilities of childhood.

Treating violation of special rules connected with being a child as status offenses has two important implications for estimating the future work load of the juvenile justice system. First, since there are strong arguments against the laws that create status offenses and a strong political movement to eliminate such offenses, one must reckon with the possibility that the "offenses" will be defined out of existence. Second, to the extent that the statutes creating status offenses remain, and to the extent that the principal social concern in creating such statutes is, in fact, to achieve effective control over minor misconduct by children, it is possible that forms of criminal misconduct should be added to this category. Indeed, many analysts (and some states) view disorderly conduct and the illegal possession of alcohol and drugs in the category of status offenses as well.

Thus, one way to estimate future case loads to be handled at different levels of the system is to think of status offenses as minor forms of crime committed by children. The only interesting questions are whether the acts will remain criminal offenses, and if so, how often they will be committed and how often arrest will result.

A different way to make estimates about future case loads in this area is to see the public's concern in the issue as making sure that the child is within a relationship that provides for protection and guidance, both now and in the future. This concern seems quite explicit in the case of statutes defining incorrigibility. The only point of such statutes is to protect the relationship between the parents and child and to recognize the parents' right (and responsibility) to guide their child.[38] The concern is also present when juvenile courts are called on to make plans that establish more permanent foster care arrangements for those who have become wards of the state due to the lack (or disqualification) of natural parents.[39] Further, we believe that this concern is implicit in the focus on runaways, curfew violators, and truants.

If one takes this perspective on status offenses, then the problems of estimating the future case load are similar to the problems of estimating future levels of abuse and neglect. The quality of the relationships between parents and children becomes the focus, rather than the individual acts of the children. Thus, one might view all those instances when the court steps in to affirm the responsibility of an adult for a child as part of the case load. At its widest, this interpretation would include the establishment of legal guardians, adoption procedures, and child custody decisions in divorce cases. Somewhat more narrowly, it would include decisions about foster care placements, incorrigibility complaints, children and parents who violate court orders governing their relationships to one another, and children who have run away because of abuse or neglect at home. And it might include not only truancy and curfew violations, but also minor criminal offenses when these were understood as at least partly the consequence of insufficient parental supervision.

Obviously, any estimate of the future demands (or opportunities) for juvenile justice intervention within this amorphous area will be exceedingly uncertain. Philosophically, it is unclear what behaviors and conditions are the proper or important focus of intervention. Legally, it is uncertain whether the statutory basis for intervention will remain constant or will change. Operationally, the system of nominating and handling these cases is rapidly changing and developing. Analytically, the measurement systems that could register levels and changes in the underlying problems exist only in very rudimentary forms.

Three approaches are potentially useful in exploring the dimensions of this domain despite the difficulties. One is to rely on the existing material on status offenses as now understood. A second is to review what is known about children on the street, principally runaways and youth gangs. A third is to examine what is happening to the general state of legal guardianship of children—how many are living with natural parents and how many of these live in one-parent families, how many are now in foster care and how many of these are frequently moved and unlikely to be adopted.

Figure 5.2 indicated that adjudications for status offenses have declined in absolute terms and have diminished as a fraction of the juvenile court case load over the last several decades. These national trends obscure some important differences among states. Table 5.4 presents more refined data on the share of status offenses referred to juvenile court in five states in 1975 and 1976. This table indicates that the relative importance of status offenses varied from 11% of the petitions to 42%.

When one looks at the systems nominating status offenses for public attention, one sees a slightly different picture. The vast majority of these case are nominated by the police. Figure 5.8 presents data on the share of status offenses within the overall pattern of police arrests of juveniles.

The other principal way that status offenses come to public attention is through parental nominations. Indeed, that is generally how "incorrigible" petitions come to the juvenile court. Table 5.5 presents data on the complainants for different status offenses. One can see the overwhelming importance of the police in nominating these cases and the secondary but not negligible importance of parents and school officials as nominators.

As noted in chapter 4, there are two different ways to view the heavy police involvement in these cases. One way is to see it as a confirmation that these offenses are like other sorts of crimes and that the police intervene out of an interest in maintaining public order. The other way to see police intervention is as the inevitable result of failed private supervi-

TABLE 5.4. Referrals to intake by offense type.

State	California[a] (1976)		Utah[b] (1975)		Texas[c] (1976)		Maryland[d] (1976)		Virginia[e] (1975–1976)		Average
Offense	No.	%	No.	%	No.	%	No.	%	No.	%	%
Status	33,178	26	7,362	30	27,708	42	6,133	11	10,689	26	27
Delinquent	95,695	74	16,878	70	39,032	58	49,798	89	30,164	74	73
Total	128,873	100	24,240	100	66,740	100	55,931	100	40,853	100	

[a] Data from Bureau of Criminal Statistics Printouts.
[b] Data from report by John Howard Association, *Unified Correctional Study for State of Utah, 1976*, p. 119.
[c] Texas Judicial Council, *Texas Juvenile Probation Report, 1976*, p. 42, Table 7B.
[d] Data taken from Maryland Governor's Commission on the Administration of Justice, October 4, 1977.
[e] Data taken from Virginia, *FY 1978 Comprehensive Justice Plan*, p. 35.
Source: C. P. Smith, D. J. Berkman, W. M. Fraser, and J. Sutton, *A Preliminary National Assessment of the Status Offender and the Juvenile Justice System: Role Conflicts, Constraints, and Information Gaps* (Washington, DC: U.S. Department of Justice, 1979), p. 83.

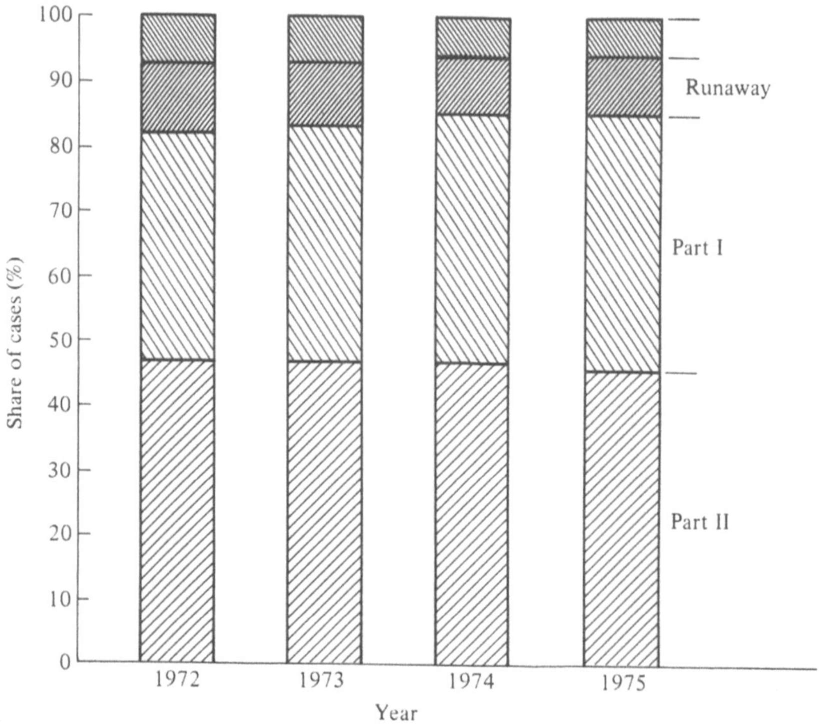

FIGURE 5.8. Juvenile status and criminal offense arrests, share of cases 1972–1975. *Note:* Part I and Part II offenses refer to categories of crime tracked in the FBI's Uniform Crime Reporting Program. Part I crimes include murder, rape, robbery, assault, burglary, larceny, motor vehicle theft, and arson. Part II crimes include the remaining offense categories. From C. P. Smith, D. J. Berkman, W. M. Fraser, and J. Sutton, *A Preliminary National Assessment of the Status Offender and the Juvenile Justice System: Role Conflicts, Constraints, and Information Gaps* (Washington, DC: U.S. Department of Justice, 1979), p. 75.

sion of children. The children are on the street because their parents have not demanded that they be home. The police step in because there is no one else who feels responsible for the society as a whole.

The widespread sense that the problem of children on the streets could be handled more effectively by non-law enforcement agencies and without the implied criminal intention that goes along with police involvement has spawned the development of a great many new programs. These include programs of youth advocates, who find temporary placement for children held by the police for status offenses; runaway shelters; and crisis counseling and hotlines for children who have nowhere else to turn. The development of these agencies provides not only an alternative means of dealing with some status offenses and offenders, but also a

TABLE 5.5. California status offense referrals to intake by source of referral, 1976

Source	Frequency No.	Frequency %
Law enforcement	27,707	83.5
School	650	2.0
Parents/relatives	2,168	6.5
Private agency	0	0
Welfare department	154	0.5
Other court	1,124	3.4
Probation department	645	1.9
Other/unknown	730	2.2
Totals	33,178	100.0

Source: C. P. Smith, D. J. Berkman, W. M. Fraser, and J. Sutton, *A Preliminary National Assessment of the Status Offender and The Juvenile Justice System: Role Conflicts, Constraints, and Information Gaps* (Washington, DC: U.S. Department of Justice, 1979), p. 85.

different mechanism for nominating cases for public attention and a different window on the problem of unsupervised youths.

Indeed, a report from an informal network of agencies dealing with runaway and missing children provides a second way of estimating the size and character of the problem of unsupervised children. Interestingly, this report describes the network's potential clients in five different categories:

"*runaways*" are children and youth who are away from home at least overnight without parental or caretaker permission.

"*homeless*" are youth who have no parental, substitute foster or institutional home. Often, these youth have left, or been urged to leave with the full knowledge or approval of legal guardians and have no alternative home.

"*system kids*" are youth who have been taken into the custody of the state due to confirmed child abuse and neglect, or other serious family problems. Often these children have been in a series of foster homes, have had few opportunities to develop lasting ties with any adult, are school drop-outs, and have few independent living skills.

"*street kids*" are long-term runaway or homeless youth who have become adept at fending for themselves "on the street," usually by illegal activities.

"*missing children*" can refer to any child whose whereabouts are unknown. It is most often used to refer to children who are believed to have been abducted and victims of foul play and/or exploitation.[40]

Estimates of the sizes of these populations and the trends affecting them are quite uncertain. A 1975 report for the Department of Health and Human Services estimated a population of 730,000 runaway and homeless children.[41] Current estimates place the number at 1.3 to 1.5 million.[42] In contrast, the National Network of Runaway and Youth Services, consisting of 210 agencies representing 312 facilities and 230 individual foster care homes, provided at least one night of shelter to about 50,000 children in a one-year period, 1983 to 1984. In addition, it turned away about 6,700 youth because facilities were filled to capacity.[43]

The immaturity of these agencies and the networks that link them prohibit more precise estimates of the character of this problem, but the rough estimates make it obvious that the problem exists, and these agencies provide an interesting alternative to police and jails as a method of dealing with it.

A third way of exploring the dimensions of the problem of ineffectively supervised children is to examine directly the status of the legal guardianship of children. Inevitably, this involves looking at the legal structures of such guardianship; the functional status of the structures remains inscrutable without much more detailed information. The trends affecting legal guardianship make the situation look serious now and ominous in the future. Data on supervision by natural parents is the most shocking. As Cook and Laub reported:

> There are various indicators of the decline of the nuclear family. First is the fraction of births that are out-of-wedlock. This fraction stood at 4.5% for the 1955 cohort, which reached its most active delinquent phase in 1970–71. The 1965–67 cohorts, which reached their most active phase in the early 1980s, included nearly twice this percentage of illegitimate births. (The non-white illegitimacy percentage is much higher than the white percentage, and increased from 20 to 30 percent between 1955 and 1967.)
>
> The period since 1970 has also been characterized by a gradual decline in the percentage of children living with two parents. For all children, this percentage dropped from 85 to 75 between 1970 and 1982; for black children, the percentage dropped from 58 to 42. During this same period the percentage of children with mothers in the labor force increased from 39 to 55.[44]

Although these trends in family structure seem quite threatening when viewed against a commonsense notion that close supervision by parents is an important bulwark against the risks of failed socialization, Cook and Laub also pointed out that, so far at least, these trends have not been accompanied by dramatic changes in the rates of juvenile offending. These, as noted previously, have been stable in the period in which they should have been rising if there were a close and powerful link between the structures of legal guardianship and rates of juvenile offending. Cook and Laub speculated that the society has not had to pay the anticipated price because the overall ratio of adults to children is changing in favor of adults. In their view, the general climate of the adult society produces an important socializing effect, even if the generally increasing capacity to supervise children is not reflected in the fine structure of the society.[45]

When natural parents are not available, the society responds by creating a substitute. The most important substitute is the foster care system. Thus, the apparent weakness in natural parenting relationships is reflected in the growth of the nation's foster care system. Over the last several decades, the number (and per capita rate) of children in foster care systems has grown tremendously.[46] Moreover, that growth occurred at the same time that the supply of adoptive parents began to decline. The result has been that many children stay in the limbo of foster care for a very long time.[47] The luckiest stay with the same foster care parents. But the usual experience is for children to be moved frequently as the limited capacity for foster care is stretched over a very large caseload.

It is difficult to know whether the trends that are devastating family structure will continue. It is also difficult to know whether the consequences will be as bad as one might expect, for there is a great deal of evidence to suggest that family function can be created even in very inauspicious structural conditions. Without being able to observe family function directly, it is hard to know whether the structural problems are, in fact, reflected in reduced functioning. Still, it is clear that there is a very large potential universe of cases in this domain, and that the volume of such cases has increased rather than decreased.

Summary: The Future Work of the Juvenile Justice System

The amount and character of the work facing the juvenile justice system in the future is only partly a matter of the objective conditions of children's conduct and condition. It is also a matter of deciding what tasks the society will authorize the juvenile justice system to perform, and of making investments in the capacity of the system to identify problems and intervene effectively. Since there is uncertainty about both the conduct and condition of the children, and what the juvenile justice system will be authorized to do, one cannot reliably estimate the future workload of the system.

Since there is no objective answer to the question of how the work load of the system might change in the future, the society must make a judgment. In making that judgment, it can usefully think in terms of several factors—the basic demographic trends affecting the number of children and the legal structures of guardianship within which children are being raised; the rate at which these demographic trends are likely to produce behaviors and conditions that register as crimes committed by children, as intolerable abuse and neglect of children, and as weakening structures of supervision and guidance of children; and the rate at which the systems that nominate cases for possible public intervention from these domains are developing and the precision with which they operate. Such estimates not only provide an estimate of the likely future work load of the juvenile justice system but also suggest how decisions to authorize certain kinds of interventions and investments in certain kinds of nominating systems will change the total volume and character of that work load.

First, both the absolute number of children and their proportion in the overall population are declining now and will continue to decline until 1995, when they will once again rise. The absolute number of children will rise to levels above those reached in the late 1960s, but the proportion of children in the population will probably never again be so large.

Second, the social structures for supervising children generally seem to be weakening. Family structure seems to be loosening, illegitimacy has increased, and the foster care system has not yet been able to fill the gap. Moreover, while these trends cut across all economic classes and ethnic groups, they seem particularly severe among poor urban populations and among blacks in the central cities.

Third, there are an increasing number of private and public agencies now positioned to observe and nominate cases to the juvenile justice system. While the police have always been important in dealing with juvenile criminal offenses and status offenses, their engagement with children and their caretakers is likely to increase as they shift their focus from "crime fighting" to "community policing." Welfare agencies, having been taken out of the case work business over the last several decades, now find themselves being drawn back in as the society becomes more interested in making fathers live up to their child support obligations, and as some knowledge is gained about simple methods for improving parental supervision. These agencies are also now joined by networks of concerned physicians mobilized to look for cases of child abuse and neglect and shelter care facilities created to provide temporary housing for runaway children.

Thus, in objective terms, what seems likely to happen is that the juvenile crime problem will continue to decline in absolute terms and as a proportion of the overall crime problem. That overall decline may go along with an *increase* in the number of relatively sustained and serious juvenile offenders. The larger problems, and the greater opportunities for explosive growth in the work load of the juvenile justice system, lie more in the domains of abuse and neglect and failed guardianship. That is both where the objective problems lie and where the old systems of intervention are reinvigorating themselves and new systems are being established. Moreover, there is a resource to be deployed in this area, and that is the increase in the proportion of adults in the overall population. Whether and how the juvenile justice system should respond to these problems and use this potential of the growing adult population is the question.

Notes

1. We are indebted to and rely heavily on discussion with Philip J. Cook and John H. Laub
2. Philip J. Cook and John H. Laub, "Trends in child abuse and juvenile delinquency," in volume 2 of this series.
3. See LaMar T. Empey's treatment of the social construction of delinquency in *American Delinquency: Its Meaning and Construction* (Homewood, IL: Dorsey Press, 1978).
4. Fred Dubow, Edward McCabe, and Gail Kaplan, *Reactions to Crime Project*, Executive Summary (Washington, DC: U.S. Department of Justice, 1980).
5. The U.S. Department of Justice's Bureau of Justice Statistics has sponsored the National Crime Survey since 1973, and publishes reports of its findings. For example, see *Criminal Victimization in the U.S.: 1973–82 trends*, NCJ-90541, 9/83.
6. The FBI sponsors the Uniform Crime Reports (UCR). See *Crime in the United States* (annual) FBI, U.S. Department of Justice (Washington, DC: U.S. Government Printing Office).
7. This inference is based on a comparison of arrest rates versus disposition rates. See Figures 5.2 and 5.5 and the increasing disposition rates listed on page 9 of Howard N. Snyder, John L. Hutzler, and Terrence A. Finnegan, *Delinquency in the United States, 1982* (Pittsburgh: National Center for Juvenile Justice, 1985).
8. Peter W. Greenwood, Allan Abrahamse, and Franklin Zimring, *Factors Affecting Sentence Severity for Young Adult Offenders* (Santa Monica, CA: Rand Corporation, 1984).
9. Marvin E. Wolfgang and Paul E. Tracy, "The 1945 and 1958 birth cohorts: A comparison of the prevalence, incidence, and severity of delinquent behavior," in Daniel McGillis et al., Eds., *Dealing with Dangerous Offenders*, Vol. 2, *Selected Papers* (Cambridge, MA: Harvard University, 1983).
10. Donna M. Hamparian, J. M. Davis, J. M. Jacobson, and L. E. McGraw, *The Young Criminal Years of the Violent Few* (Cleveland, OH: Federation for Community Planning, 1984).
11. Skogan and Maxfield observed that "neighborhood crime and disorder remain the most important predictors of fear, even when community integration and personal vulnerability are taken into account." Wesley G. Skogan and Michael G. Maxfield, *Coping with Crime* (Beverly Hills, CA: Sage Publications, 1981), p. 123. Quoted in Robert C. Trojanowicz, p. 27, "Fear of crime: A critical issue in community policing," paper prepared for the Executive Session on Community Policing, Harvard University, Cambridge, MA, Apr. 10–12, 1986.
12. Cook and Laub, "Trends in child abuse," and Barbara Boland and James Q. Wilson, "Crime and American culture," *The Public Interest*, No. 70 (1983), pp. 22–48.
13. See Saul Weingart, "Serious juvenile offenders: Projecting the caseload," unpublished mimeo, Harvard University, 1984.
14. C. Lee Athey and Charles Tremper, "Juvenile arrest trends in the United States: 1970–1981," unpublished mimeo (Sacramento, CA: American Justice Institute, 1983).

15. David P. Farrington, "Early precursors of frequent offending," and Glenn C. Loury, "The family as context for delinquency prevention: Demographic trends and political realities," both in volume 3 of this series. Also see Travis Hirschi, "Crime and the family," in James Q. Wilson, Ed., *Crime and Public Policy* (San Francisco: ICS Press, 1983), pp. 53–68.
16. National Commission on Excellence in Education, *A Nation at Risk: The Imperative for Educational Reform* (Washington, DC: U.S. Government Printing Office, 1983); Denis P. Doyle and Terry W. Hartle, *Excellence in Education: The States Take Charge* (Washington, DC: American Enterprise Institute, 1985).
17. Walter E. Williams, *Youth and Minority Unemployment* (Stanford, CA: Hoover Institution Press, 1978), and W. Kip Viscusi, "Market incentives for criminal behavior," Paper from the Center for the Study of Business Regulation (Durham, NC: Fuqua School of Business, Duke University, 1983).
18. Cook and Laub also noted that the prevalence of drug use by high school seniors is in decline. Cook and Laub, "Trends in child abuse," p. 123.
19. Cook and Laub, "Trends in child abuse," pp. 124–126.
20. Ibid., p. 118, citing data compiled by Ellen H. Nimick, Linda Dahmar, Howard Snyder, and Dennis P. Sullivan, *Juvenile Court Statistics, 1981* (Pittsburgh: National Center for Juvenile Justice, 1983).
21. Ibid., p. 118, citing data compiled by Nimick et al.
22. See discussion in chapter 3. See also Institute of Judicial Administration–American Bar Association Joint Commission on Juvenile Justice Standards, *Juvenile Justice Standards* (Cambridge, MA: Ballinger, 1980).
23. Mark H. Moore, "Invisible offenses: A challenge to minimally intrusive law enforcement," in Gerald M. Caplan, Ed., *ABSCAM Ethics: Moral Issues and Deception in Law Enforcement* (Washington, DC: Police Foundation, 1983), pp. 17–42.
24. Douglas Besharov, "The legal aspects of reporting known and suspected child abuse and neglect," *Villanova Law Review 23* (1977–1978), pp. 458–546.
25. U.S. Department of Health and Human Services, National Center on Child Abuse and Neglect, *Executive Summary: National Study of the Incidence and Severity of Child Abuse and Neglect* (Washington, DC: U.S. Government Printing Office, 1982).
26. Cook and Laub, "Trends in child abuse," p. 113.
27. Ibid.
28. Ibid.
29. Cook argued forcefully that there is an infinite amount of potential work in this area. Limits are created by the society, which sets limits on rights and responsibilities to intervene rather than objectively estimating needs.
30. Besharov, "The legal aspects of reporting."
31. Cook and Laub, "Trends in child abuse," p. 118.
32. Alene Russell and Cynthia M. Trainor, *Trends in Child Abuse and Neglect: A National Perspective* (Denver: American Humane Association, 1984). Cited in Cook and Laub, "Trends in child abuse," p. 118.
33. U.S. Department of Health and Human Services, National Center on Child Abuse and Neglect, *Executive Summary*. Cited in Cook and Laub, "Trends in child abuse," p. 113.

34. Attorney General's Task Force on Family Violence, *Final Report* (Washington, DC: U.S. Department of Justice, 1984).
35. Ibid.
36. We are indebted to Christine Nixon for emphasizing this point.
37. We are indebted to Phil Cook for emphasizing this point.
38. For an argument against this point of view see R. Hale Andrews, Jr. and Andrew H. Cohn, "Ungovernability: The unjustifiable jurisdiction," *Yale Law Journal 83*(7) (June 1974), note, pp. 1383–1409.
39. See note 31 in chapter 3.
40. The National Network of Runaway and Youth Services, *To Whom Do They Belong? A Profile of America's Runaway and Homeless Youth and the Programs That Help Them* (Washington, DC: The National Network of Runaway and Youth Services, July 1985).
41. Cited in National Network, *To Whom Do They Belong?*, p. 5.
42. Ibid.
43. Ibid., p. 11.
44. Cook and Laub, "Trends in child abuse," pp. 120–121.
45. Ibid., pp. 121–123.
46. Robert H. Mnookin, "Foster care—In whose best interest?," *Harvard Educational Review 43*(4) (Nov. 1973), pp. 599–638.
47. Douglas J. Besharov, "Foster care reform: Two books for practitioners," *Family Law Quarterly 18*(2) (Summer 1984), book review, pp. 247–253.

6
Alternative Futures

Looking backward from the present, it is not difficult to characterize the basic thrust of America's juvenile justice system. Indeed, it is all too easy to see the biases and limitations of the system, and to interpret these as expressions of the basic values guiding the society's response to children at risk or creating risks. Thus, we now recognize the grotesque overreaching of the juvenile court to address conduct and conditions that were not particularly threatening, the overreliance on public institutions to substitute for family and community in situations in which only minimal risks existed, and the complacent sentimentality that justified disastrous interventions with a serene confidence that the best interests of the child were being served.[1]

Looking ahead, it is hard to imagine that the future juvenile justice system will be as narrow and limited. For the future, we like to believe that all things are possible. Thus, we imagine a juvenile justice system that controls juvenile crime fairly and effectively and that maximizes the healthy development of youth. We imagine a court that protects children from the abuse and neglect of their parents, but avoids unnecessary intrusions into family life. We imagine a court that promotes relationships between parents and children that are just and successful in fostering resourceful citizenship, but whose vision of those relationships is broad enough to encompass the diversity of a pluralistic society. We imagine a juvenile justice system that is informal and private in handling minor affairs, but that becomes quite formal and accountable when deciding matters of importance. We imagine a juvenile justice system that experiments with new forms of supervision for disruptive children with no risk to the society, and new forms of intervention into families with no risk that families will be disrupted and demoralized by the interventions.

Yet, if anything is certain, it is that 20 or 30 years from now it will be possible to interpret the basic thrust of the juvenile court and the juvenile justice system in much narrower terms. The system will express some values at the neglect of others and will develop some capabilities more than others. It will thus come to embody one vision of the court and the system more closely than others.

To guide the society's ideas about the future of the court and the system, then, it might be useful to set out some stark, overly simplified images of the juvenile court and the juvenile justice system. In essence, these are the pictures the society might see looking backward 30 years from now. The point in developing these images is not to predict which of our prospective concepts will materialize. Indeed, given that the images will be caricatures, it seems quite unlikely that the society will actually produce any of them exactly. Instead, the purpose is to allow the society to see the alternatives more clearly, to imagine the kind of investments that if made today would carry the court and the system toward one future rather than another.

Defining Dimensions

The first step in setting out alternative images of the juvenile justice system is to identify the defining dimensions of the system and the ways in which they might vary. Seven different dimensions seem important to us in defining the character of the system.

Dimension 1: The Jurisdiction of the System

The first dimension concerns the system's jurisdiction. As we have seen, the jurisdiction can be more or less broadly defined. It can include crimes committed by children, or crimes committed against children. It can include only those offenses by children that would be crimes if committed by adults, or offenses by children that violate their special responsibilities and roles in the society. It can include only the most serious and imminent threats from parents to the well-being of the children, or threats that are less serious or more distant.

Note that the issue here is partly a matter of formal authorizations for court action. It is also a question of the operating focus and preoccupation of the system. The court might be authorized to deal with a great deal more than juvenile crimes. If, however, its work load is composed overwhelmingly of juvenile crimes, this circumstance will determine its character more than its formal authorization. Indeed, part of the reason it is difficult to see the juvenile court as anything other than a criminal court for children is that so much of the court's work load consists of crimes committed by children.

Dimension 2: The Organization of Intake

What sorts of cases the court and the system will actually handle depends on informal authorizations and the systems of nomination and intake, as well as on the formal authority of the court. The organization and character of the intake process thus become the second defining characteristic of the system. Two aspects of the intake process are particularly important: (a) the events or conditions that trigger public intervention and (b) the institutions that make the nominations. One possibility is that juvenile crimes trigger the intervention and nominations are generally made by victims and police. Another possibility is that observations of abuse and neglect trigger the intervention and nominations are made by physicians, teachers, neighbors, or police. A third possibility is that problematic relationships between parents and children trigger the intervention and the nominations are made by the parents, who accuse their children of incorrigibility, or by the children, who flee home and are taken into shelter care. The system may have all of these capabilities or only a few. It may be heavily weighted toward one kind of intervention or spread evenly over the entire spectrum.

Dimension 3: Capacity for Informal Dispositions

The third defining dimension of the system is the scale and character of the legal and institutional machinery available for informal dispositions. The issue is not only *how many* cases can be dealt with "in the anteroom" of the juvenile court, but also *how* the cases are handled. Some systems will have little capacity developed in this domain, preferring to rely on the juvenile court and its relatively formal processes. Others will rely much more heavily on informal arrangements, reserving the relative expense and formality of the court for only the most serious or most resistant cases. Among those systems that have a well-developed capability for informal dispositions, the capability can be located within different organizations: police departments, probation departments, adjuncts of the court itself, free-standing youth advocacy agencies, special case screening committees made up of representatives of welfare and law enforcement agencies. Moreover, these agencies can proceed in quite different ways. Their investigative efforts can be focused on specific offenses committed by a child or parent, or can range more broadly over the general circumstances in which the child is being raised.[3] And they may be authorized and equipped to make different kinds of dispositions. There may be more or fewer capacities for temporary placements in foster care, family counseling, drug and alcohol abuse treatment, special tutoring for children, and so on.

Dimension 4: The Process of Adjudication

The fourth defining characteristic of the system is the character of the adjudication process within the court. One important aspect of this is the information considered relevant to the court's decisions. Does the court focus on the issue of culpability for given offenses, or does it look more generally at the background circumstances to help it decide not only the issue of guilt or innocence, but also the best kind of disposition to make? A second important aspect is the character of the process. Is it formal and public, or informal and private? Is the child represented by counsel? Is there a jury? May the case be waived to criminal court? Are parents and legal guardians treated as parties at interest in the court, or excluded from the process? A third issue is the disposition or sentencing policies that guide the court. Are dispositions guided by narrow statutory or administrative guidelines, or do they leave broad discretion to the judge? Does the judge continue to supervise the case and retain the power to change the disposition, or is the case handed over to an administrative agency? What array of dispositions is potentially available to the court as a matter of formal authorization?

Dimension 5: Youth Corrections

A fifth defining dimension of the system is the character of the youth corrections agencies. The issue here is largely the question of the "portfolio" of dispositions that the organization is maintaining.[4] How many different kinds of programs are available, in what quantities? Is it a system based exclusively or largely on public institutions, or does it rely at least partly on programs that draw on private and community resources for less intensive supervision of children? What portion of the programs is frankly experimental?

A second important feature of the youth corrections process is who decides the proper form and level of supervision. Does the judge retain the power to determine exactly how a child will be supervised, or does the youth corrections agency acquire that power once the child is committed?[5] What role does the community or the victim play in that decision?

Dimension 6: Levels of Community Involvement

The sixth defining dimension of the juvenile justice system is the role of the community in the process of adjudications and dispositions. In some systems the community might play a major role in hearing cases, making dispositions, and managing the family and child. In others the community might play a minor role, with most of the work left to the experts employed by public service organizations. Or one can imagine mixed systems in which the community plays an important role in minor cases but is left out once the stakes get very large. Of particular interest in this area is what role the victim plays in cases involving juvenile crimes.

Dimension 7: Public Resources Utilized

The seventh defining dimension is a summary of the principal resources the system relies on to produce its results for the society. In general, one can think of the juvenile court and the juvenile justice system as drawing on two different kinds of resources. The most obvious is material resources used to help family and children. This comes in the form of welfare payments, family counseling services, shelter care for runaways, special tutoring for truants, medical examinations for children who are temporarily detained, wilderness experiences designed to build character and a sense of responsibility, sometimes even the institutionalization of a child whose parents seem unable to supervise or care for him or her adequately. These costs register in budgets and expenditures of public agencies.

Another kind of resource, however, is the power to coerce or oblige people within the society to do something that they are not now doing, and to administer punishment to remind the recipient of the punishment and others that they have certain responsibilities to the broader society. This kind of resource is clearly invoked when a child is jailed for committing criminal offenses, or when a parent is prosecuted for child abuse. It is also utilized when parents agree to supervise their child more closely under the threat that if they do not, the child will be placed in an institution. And it may even be utilized when a neighbor criticizes the behavior of a child and accuses the parents of being neglectful. There is no budget that records the uses of authority and obligation, but the magnitude of the expenditures registers in the resentments of those subjected to the claims. These resentments can be diminished if the obligations are justified by a purpose that commands the allegiance of the subject, by clear community support for the judgment, or by clear legal authority. The point is that there is always a price to be paid for invoking the power of the state and the community along with the potential benefits, and thus the use of such power must be considered one of the resources utilized by the court and the system. Some systems will rely heavily on this resource and save on money; others will rely more on money and less on obligation and authority to achieve the desired results.

Alternative Futures

To imagine and describe alternative futures of the juvenile court and the juvenile justice system, it is useful to start with the current system. Alternative visions can then be described in terms of changes made in one or more of its defining dimensions. The changes in the defining dimensions become the investments or innovations that must occur if the court or the system is to move in a particular direction. The particular direction, in turn, represents a new strategy for the system—one that legitimates and authorizes the court in different terms and deals with a different set of social problems than are characteristic of the current system. Six different conceptions of the court and the system are described briefly here.

The Traditional Court

The traditional juvenile court should, by now, be quite familiar. Its characteristics are set out starkly in Table 6.1. It has a somewhat diffuse jurisdiction that is centered on crimes committed by children, but also includes instances of abuse and neglect and a variety of ill-defined status offenses. The principal nominators of cases are the police, followed at some distance by social work agencies and parents. The system for handling cases informally is developing and includes a large fraction of the potential cases. For the most part, this informal handling and screening is carried out through agencies in the justice rather than the social service system, that is, within youth bureaus of police departments, probation units within the juvenile court, or through some other agencies that have close relationships with the juvenile court. The court is somewhat hostile to agencies that seek to deal with problems of children wholly outside the context of the court, largely because these agencies consistently attack the court and present themselves as superior alternatives.

TABLE 6.1. The "traditional" juvenile court.

Defining dimensions	Specific characteristics
Jurisdiction	Crimes committed by children/abuse and neglect of children/status offenses
Organization of intake	
Triggering events	Juvenile crime/evidence of abuse and neglect/ truancy, curfew violations, incorrigibility, promiscuity
Nominating institutions	Police/social work agencies/parents/neighbors
Capacity for informal dispositions	
Reliance on informal dispositions	Heavy, but large minority of cases come to court
Institutions relied upon	Probation departments/social work agencies/ parents
Process of adjudication	
Relevant information	Evidence of offense/family background
Formality of proceedings	Informal, but court-like
Disposition guidelines	Discretionary sentencing guided by "best interests of child"
Youth corrections	
Portfolio of programs	Training schools/probation/few alternatives
Decision-making procedures	Commitment to youth authority/limited judicial influence
Community involvement	Little; private proceedings to avoid stigma
Principal resources utilized	Uses both authority and money extensively

When cases reach the court for adjudication, the court carries out a rather elaborate background investigation that includes not only facts pertaining to specific offenses that give it jurisdiction, but also facts about the immediate circumstances of the crime, the history of the child, and the apparent capacity of the family to supervise and guide the child. These facts are used to apportion culpability in the particular incidents, to gauge the character of the risks the society will face in the future, and to devise an appropriate intervention. While the process is becoming a bit more formalized (with legal representation of the child now the norm), it remains largely private and informal. The judge has very wide latitude in deciding the appropriate disposition of the case. The judge's decision is supposed to be guided by the best interests of the child in the future, but inevitably it embraces concerns about protecting the society from crimes committed by children.

The judge retains a great deal of power over the case except when he or she commits the child to a youth authority. Then, the youth authority assumes the responsibility and can keep the judge from interfering in the case. Generally, in the traditional juvenile justice system youth authorities have few options for supervising children. There is typically some provision for parole or limited supervision within the community. There are also large, locked public institutions. And there may be some experimental wilderness experience or community work programs. But the overall portfolio is dominated by relatively superficial supervision within the community on the one hand and locked institutions on the other.

For the most part, in the juvenile court proceedings and in the disposition decisions neither victims nor parents nor community interests are represented. The case is seen as the society (represented by the court) confronting the child. The interests of the community in protecting itself, in ensuring that the child will become a resourceful citizen, and in relying on parents and legal guardians to take the major responsibility for that job are all abstractly represented by the judge. He or she must juggle these considerations without anyone in the courtroom other than the child and (sometimes) the child's counsel. Moreover, for the most part, the judge thinks of deploying court authority against the child, not against the parents or legal guardians of the child, even though the judge has some formal and informal powers to oblige them to change their conduct with respect to the child.

This system is a relatively expensive one. It uses a great deal of both authority and money. Moreover, its authority is justified principally on legal grounds; it rarely reaches out to the community for support by offering explanations of what it is doing or seeking to engage the community in its deliberations. The largest portion of its money goes into supporting children in the institutions. These institutions are supposed to supervise and develop children, but they always seem to end up supervising more than developing.

The Individualized Justice Court

One alternative to the current justice system is the "individualized justice" court. The basic idea is that the juvenile court is essentially a criminal court, but one that approaches the ideal of *individualized* justice far more closely than the adult system now does. It might become an idea to which the adult criminal court could aspire. Its principal characteristics relative to the traditional juvenile court are described in Table 6.2.

The jurisdiction of this court would shift decisively in the direction of criminal offending by children. Abuse and neglect cases would be eliminated from the jurisdiction, as would status offenses and issues of child custody and guardianship. The court concerns itself exclusively with juvenile crimes.

Consistent with these changes, its principal nominating mechanisms would be victims of crime and the police. Other social work agencies and parents would become less significant than they now are. The events that would trigger court intervention would be crimes exclusively. All other offenses and conditions would be ignored or referred to others. Indeed, clearing out the noncriminal offenses would be the principal task of the informal system of dispositions. This function would probably be located in the police or probation departments. Perhaps these agencies would be aided by an interagency committee including prosecutors, welfare agencies, and child protection authorities to refer noncriminal cases to appropriate agencies.

In handling the cases of juvenile crime, the court would retain the broad interests of the traditional juvenile court. It would look not only at evidence of whether a particular child did nor did not commit a crime, but

TABLE 6.2. The "individualized justice" court.

Defining dimensions	Specific characteristics
Jurisdiction	Crimes committed by children
Organization of intake	
Triggering events	Juvenile crimes
Nominating institutions	Police/victims/witnesses
Capacity for informal dispositions	
Reliance on informal dispositions	Only if evidence of criminal culpability is weak
Institutions relied upon	Police/probation
Process of adjudication	
Relevant information	Evidence of offense/family background/context of offense
Formality of proceedings	Relatively formal
Disposition guidelines	Discretionary sentencing
Youth corrections	
Portfolio of programs	Training schools/probation/restitution programs
Decision-making procedures	Extensive judicial involvement in case
Community involvement	Limited
Principal resources utilized	Authority

also at the immediate circumstances of the crime, the background of the child, and the surrounding family circumstances. It would do this in the interests of individualizing the justice to be meted out in the case, that is, in the interests of closely examining the particulars of the case to determine how culpability should be apportioned, and what would be a fair and effective disposition of the case.

This court would break from the practices of the traditional juvenile court in terms of the degree of formality and openness. Because it was a court concerned with meting out justice to criminal offenders, it would rely more heavily than the current court does on due process. The child would be entitled to counsel. The state's interests might be represented by a prosecutor. A jury would be allowed if the child requested it. Formal rules of evidence would be relied upon. The public would be invited to attend in order to ensure the accountability of the court.

In terms of dispositions, the judge would be given structured discretion.[6] Statutes would limit the kind of dispositions that could be made based on the offenses charged and the circumstances surrounding the offense. If the judge wished to impose a different sentence, he or she would have to give reasons. The corrections system would be one in which a wide variety of programs existed. Secure institutions would be a small part of the overall portfolio. They would be joined by an array of halfway houses, group homes, intensive community supervision, restitution and community work programs, and traditional probation. The aim would be principally to provide for effective but decent supervision of the child, but there would also be an interest in rehabilitation and the future development of the child.

In this court, both the victim and the community would be much more intimately involved. The victim would be involved in giving testimony, and perhaps in having his or her losses restored by the offender in restitution programs. The community would be invited in as an audience for the proceedings, and might be asked to take some role in supervising the child in the future. The parents or legal guardians of the child would not be so prominent in the case (since it would be seen largely as a criminal proceeding of the state against the child), but in less serious cases they might be viewed as part of the future arrangements for supervising the child.

Compared with the traditional juvenile court, this court would use less authority. It would jettison the cases that cause the current court its biggest problems with intrusiveness and overreaching and focus only on those situations in which everyone agrees a state interest exists. In these cases it would bring state authority to bear in a way that would be a model of justice. Indeed, such a court would challenge the adult criminal court as a court of justice by setting new standards for the society in the handling of criminal cases. In substantive terms, the challenge would be to individualize justice by looking more closely at the facts surrounding a criminal offense in the interests of fairly apportioning culpability. In procedural terms, the challenge would be to live up to the strict obligations of due process. Thus, the juvenile court would take some of the advantages of juvenile court jurisprudence and none of the disadvantages, and some of the virtues of adult court processing and none of the defects. In terms of money it might be cheaper than the current court, since its case load would be smaller and it would deal with juvenile offenders through institutions that were cheaper and drew more extensively on volunteer community resources than the old system.

Thus, the individualized justice court would be more precise in its focus, more careful in its interventions, and more effectively integrated into the community. It would leave unanswered the question of what to do with children who were abused and neglected, who were runaways, or who were generally unsupervised.

The Austere Justice Court

A second alternative to the traditional court continues the notion that the juvenile court should concentrate on crimes committed by children, but incorporates a different idea of justice. This alternative can be described as the "austere justice court." Like the individualized justice court, this court would focus on crimes committed by children and would exclude all the other concerns. It would draw its case load from victim and police nominations. It would seek a higher degree of formality and openness in the court proceedings. Because these would be understood as criminal proceedings, due process protections would be granted to the youthful defendants. All of these features would make it a justice court.

It would differ from the model of individualized justice in that it would be much less interested in the circumstances surrounding an offense. The central question would be simply whether the child did or did not commit the offense. The circumstances of the crime and the family background of the child would be regarded as irrelevant.

Consistent with this basic philosophy, initial screening of cases would be done only on the basis of the seriousness of the offense and the quality of the evidence. These would also be the focus of the courtroom proceedings. Dispositions would be strictly determined by statutes that established fixed penalties for given offenses. Any aggravating or mitigating factors would be related to the character of the offense, not to circumstances surrounding the offense or to family background that might be seen as mitigating guilt. The purpose of the disposition would be principally to impose a just punishment, to deter the current offender from future offending, and in general to deter others. Any rehabilitative effect would result from the imposition of the just punishment. The form of the punishment would be loss of freedom in an austere if not aversive setting. The punishment would be administered by the state, since the offense is against the state. Decisions about dispositions would be influenced by the

TABLE 6.3. The "austere justice" court.

Defining dimensions	Specific characteristics
Jurisdiction	Crimes committed by children
Organization of intake	
Triggering events	Juvenile crime
Nominating institutions	Police/victims/witnesses
Capacity for informal dispositions	
Reliance on informal dispositions	Only if criminal culpability is weak
Institutions relied upon	Police/probation
Process of adjudication	
Relevant information	Evidence of offense only
Formality of proceedings	Formal
Disposition guidelines	Determinant sentencing tied to offenses and prior misconduct
Youth corrections	
Portfolio of programs	Training schools/probation/restitution
Decision-making procedures	Extensive judicial involvement
Community involvement	Involvement of victims
Principal resources utilized	Authority

judge, the prosecutor, and the victim, who would all retain continuing supervision over the case. The offender would not be turned over to a youth corrections authority.

Thus, the austere justice model strips away many of the trappings of the individualized justice model. The justice meted out is stark. This has the virtue of increasing the likelihood that like cases will be treated alike in the system, but has the disadvantage that any facts that might reasonably cause a case to be treated differently will not be noticed. Table 6.3 describes this court (and its associated system) relative to the traditional court.

The Community Accountability Court

A third alternative might be described as a "community accountability court." This vision differs from the individualized and austere justice courts in that this court would assume responsibility for crimes committed against children as well as for crimes committed by children. It would resemble the justice court in that its focus would be on specific offenses involving concrete losses to victims and its intention would be to hold those who committed the offenses responsible for them. It would differ from the justice court in that it would seek to establish its authority over the conduct of children and parents through close relations to the community as well as through the application of statutes and common law. This is reflected in the establishment of informal "community boards" to deal with minor instances of criminal conduct by children and worrisome but not dangerous abuse and neglect by parents. It might also be reflected in a decision to have the judges of the courts elected or appointed for limited terms by elected politicians. Table 6.4 describes other changes in the defining dimensions of the system relative to the traditional system that are consistent with the spirit of giving the community the responsibility to hold children who attack citizens and parents who attack children accountable for their misconduct.

Relative to the traditional court, the jurisdiction would narrow due to the elimination of both status offenses and problems in relationships between parents and children that are not expressed in terms of physical attacks or sustained physical neglect. Relative to the justice court, the jurisdiction would expand to include attacks on children.

The events that would trigger court interventions in this model would primarily be criminal attacks by children or against children. The principal nominators would be victims or witnesses of the attacks. The focus of investigations would be the seriousness of past attacks (or instances of neglect) and the likelihood that the events would be repeated in the future. The less serious cases would be referred to a community board for an informal resolution. The informal resolutions include probation, restitution, and community service for minor crimes committed by children, and family counseling and advice in minor cases of abuse and neglect. The more serious cases would be sent forward to the court.

The process within the court would be a formal court proceeding, but one that encouraged the involvement of the community and emphasized that the court was acting on behalf of the community as well as in accord with abstract laws. The focus of the proceeding would be the presentation

TABLE 6.4. The "community accountability" court.

Defining dimensions	Specific characteristics
Jurisdiction	Crimes committed by children/crimes committed against children
Organization of intake	
Triggering events	Juvenile crime/serious, obvious abuse and neglect
Nominating institutions	Police/social work agencies/neighbors
Capacity for informal dispositions	
Reliance on informal dispositions	For less serious cases only
Institutions relied upon	Police/probation/community boards
Process of adjudication	
Relevant information	Evidence of offenses/prior misconduct
Formality of proceedings	Relatively formal
Disposition of guidelines	Structured discretion geared to offenses
Youth corrections	
Portfolio of programs	Heavier reliance on probation and restitution/ coerced treatment for families
Decision-making procedures	Heavy judicial involvement
Community involvement	Heavy involvement in informal dispositions/court open to public/victims' role emphasized
Principal resources utilized	Authority backed by community standards

of evidence about the offenses committed by or against the child. Victims would be invited to testify. In the case of crimes committed by children, parents might be considered partially responsible for the offense insofar as it resulted from lax supervision. Members of the community would be invited into the court as observers. Dispositions would be guided by statutes that bounded, but did not eliminate, judicial discretion.

Possible dispositions in the case of juvenile crimes would include confinement in institutions, halfway houses, and group homes; participation in restitution and community work programs; intensive probation; and strict parental supervision. Judges would retain the power (and the responsibility to the community) to adjust the sentences. Possible dispositions in the case of abuse and neglect would include criminal prosecution of the parents followed by imprisonment or probation, termination of parental rights and custody of the child, temporary placement of the child in foster care, injunctions to cease the practices of abuse and neglect, or continuing court supervision of the parents. Here, too, the judge would have power from (and be responsible to) the community for the dispositions.

In terms of the resources being utilized, this enterprise would make relatively heavy use of authority and obligations as compared with service. The idea is that a vigorous defense of community standards would lead to improved conduct not only in the cases brought to the court, but also more broadly. Establishing close links to the community would help to legitimate what might otherwise be a dangerous use of coercive authority and would add a dimension of community obligation as well as legal obligation to the enterprise.

The Children's Rights Court

A fourth alternative to the traditional juvenile court would be one that made securing children's rights and needs its central concern—a court that could advocate and insist on the interests of children with other institutions in the society. Table 6.5 describes this court and an associated system supporting it.

The court's jurisdiction would include crimes committed by children and abuse and neglect of children. Threshold conditions triggering court intervention would be more lenient than those in other courts we have considered, with the exception of the traditional court, in particular with regard to less serious forms of abuse and neglect. Nominating agencies would include police, social work agencies, teachers, and perhaps most importantly, the child.

The focus of pretrial investigations would be on the family circumstances of the child, and not only on what offenses the child had committed but also on the particular ways in which the child's care and supervision had been deficient. A formal process would be used to decide

TABLE 6.5. The "children's rights" court.

Defining dimensions	Specific characteristics
Jurisdiction	Crimes committed by children/crimes committed against children
Organization of intake	
Triggering events	Juvenile crime/instances of abuse and neglect
Nominating institutions	Police/child/defense counsel
Capacity for informal dispositions	
Reliance on informal dispositions	For juvenile crimes, heavy reliance/for crimes against juveniles, less reliance on informal dispositions
Institutions relied upon	Probation/youth advocacy groups
Process of adjudication	
Relevant information	Family background/social circumstances
Formality of proceedings	Formal in presentation of evidence
Disposition guidelines	Discretionary decision making guided by rule of "least restrictive alternative"
Youth corrections	
Portfolio of programs	Probation/restitution/additional services to children
Decision-making procedures	Heavy judicial involvement
Community involvement	Limited
Principal resources utilized	Public monies to meet needs/authority to protect child from abuse

whether the interests of the child would be served by taking the case forward to the court or by handling it at informal levels of the system. The child would have the right to be represented by counsel. Counsel could argue that the case should not go forward if such action threatened to stigmatize the child and would not deal with the background conditions affecting the child. The child, in turn, could argue that the case must go forward if he or she was threatened by parents or needed the court to impose duties on his or her parents or others who had responsibilities toward the child such as schools, welfare agencies, and so on.

Once the case was in the court, the rights of the child would be scrupulously honored: There would be extensive due process protections if the proceeding was against the child for a criminal offense; the court would protect and advance the substantive interests of the child vis-a-vis the parents or other caretakers if the child was being deprived. Indeed, it is even possible that a proceeding started as one against the child might be turned to one on behalf of the child if the child seemed more a victim than a victimizer! To ensure these results, the child's rights to counsel would be extensive and scrupulously honored. The counsel would take a leadership role in proposing appropriate dispositions for the case, which would reflect the child's rights and interests.

Dispositions would be guided by the principle of "the least restrictive placement" in cases involving offenses by the child. They would be guided by the child's interests in protection and permanency in custodial relationships in cases involving abuse and neglect.

Victims of the crime and the community would be kept distant from the court to reduce the pressures on the court to pursue short-run security interests at the expense of the child's rights and future development. In sum, the court would become an instrument for protecting and advancing children's rights to liberty, care, and protection in the society.

The Family Court

A fifth alternative to the traditional juvenile court could be called a "family" court. Its aim would be to keep families functioning with respect to raising their children at least minimally successfully; if the families were not up to the task, it would construct minimally acceptable public alternatives to natural parents and families. Table 6.6 defines the characteristics of this court relative to the traditional juvenile court.

In many ways, the family court (and its associated system) seems similar to the traditional court. Like that of the traditional court, the jurisdiction of the family court would include crimes committed by children, abuse and neglect of children, and situations in which the relationships between parents and children were eroding or nonexistent but not immediately threatening. Indeed, this is the only version of the court so far that

TABLE 6.6. The "family" court.

Defining dimensions	Specific characteristics
Jurisdiction	Crimes by children/abuse and neglect of children/status offenses
Organization of intake	
Triggering events	Juvenile crime/instances of abuse and neglect/breakdowns in family relationships
Nominating institutions	Police/social work agencies/neighbors/parents/schools
Capacity for informal dispositions	
Reliance on informal dispositions	Heavy reliance on informal dispositions
Institutions relied upon	Police/probation/family mediation/youth advocacy groups
Process of adjudication	
Relevant information	Evidence of offenses/family background
Formality of proceedings	Relatively formal
Disposition guidelines	Discretionary decision making guided by goal of maintaining family relations
Youth corrections	
Portfolio of programs	Probation/family mediation/restitution/group homes
Decision-making procedures	Judicial oversight
Community involvement	Extensive in nominations, processing, and dispositions
Principal resources utilized	Authority backed by community

includes status offenses. This court would draw cases broadly from police, social work agencies, health officials, teachers, parents, and children. The focus of pretrial investigations would be the same as those in the traditional court: not only evidence of offenses but also of the immediate circumstances surrounding the offenses, the history of the offenders, and the family relationships that surrounded the offenses and the offenders. Minor cases would be disposed of informally. Only the most serious would come to the court. As in the traditional court, however, the cases that came forward would be those in which the relationship between parent and child was badly damaged and those posing an immediate threat to life and/or property from the child or to the child. The process in the court would be structured but informal, with a premium placed on developing accurate and complete information about the situation. These all make the family court seem very much like the traditional court.

There are two crucial differences in this conception, however. The first and most important is that the parents or other legal guardians would be considered a central party at interest in the case. Their role in cases of abuse and neglect is obvious: They must be discouraged from continuing the practices that threaten their child. It is worth noting, however, that in this model the state would also have a strong interest in keeping the family together if it could. As a result, its capacity to protect the child from the parent would be somewhat compromised. In the case of crimes committed by children, lax parental supervision and training might be seen as part of the reason for the crime. In addition, more effective parental supervision might be seen as a better solution to the problem of future crimes by the child than public institutionalization or supervision. In the case of incorrigibility, the relationship between parents and children is obviously central. Thus, in all cases the problem and the solution would be seen at least partly in terms of restoring or using family relationships to accomplish public purposes, and this would place parents as well as children at the center of these cases.

Second, the overwhelming orientation of the family court would be to restore functioning within the existing family rather than to try to replace it with some more or less permanent public alternative. Given the difficulty of creating anything nearly as good as an ordinary family through public auspices, the overwhelming aim of the court would be to keep the current family together. This doctrine is not "radical nonintervention" with respect to children.[7] It is a presumption in favor of reliance on natural families as society's agents to perform the necessary social task of raising children. It is also a doctrine that countenances the court's superintending families and intervening with exhortations, obligations, and assistance if there are serious difficulties with the raising of the children and if such efforts might be successful in restoring family functioning. The aim is always to work with what is there rather than to construct a public alternative.

Summary

These visions of the future of the juvenile justice system seem to pose a stark choice. Some (such as the traditional court, the individualized justice court, and the austere justice court) are quite familiar, but contain obvious problems and limitations. Others (such as the children's rights court and the family court) seem much more exotic, maybe even ludicrous. This should not be surprising, because they were created by taking some of the values of and aspirations for the court and extending them well beyond what currently seems feasible in political, legal, or operational terms.

Inevitably, the society is always going to have a juvenile justice system. The crucial questions these stark, somewhat bizarre alternatives force us to confront are these: (a) If none of these alternatives is acceptable, what is? (b) Are there changes in the mandate and operations of the court that would move us toward a more just and effective juvenile justice system in the future? (c) If so, what are they? It is these questions we seek to answer in the next chapter.

Notes

1. This interpretation of the juvenile court owes a great deal to Anthony Platt. Anthony M. Platt, *The Child Savers/The Invention of Delinquency* (Chicago: University of Chicago Press, 1969).
2. We are indebted to Pamela Swain of the Office of Juvenile Justice and Delinquency Prevention of the U.S. Department of Justice for insisting that we go through this exercise. We learned a great deal by taking her advice.
3. For a discussion of the operations and legitimacy of "community boards" see Mark L. Sidran, "Back to the source: Diversion of juvenile offenders to the community in the State of Washington," in volume 2 of this series.
4. For a discussion of youth corrections that introduces the language of financial management as a useful metaphor see Edward M. Murphy, "Managing risk in juvenile corrections" in volume 2 of this series.
5. For a legal discussion of this issue see John M. Pettibone, Robert G. Swisher, Kurt H. Weiland, Christine E. Wolf, and Joseph L. White, *Services to Children in Juvenile Courts: The Judicial-Executive Controversy* (Columbus, OH: Academy for Contemporary Problems, 1981).
6. For a general discussion of alternative philosophies and methods of sentencing see Joseph C. Calpin, Jack M. Kress, and Arthur M. Gelman, *Sentencing Guidelines: Structuring Judicial Discretion* Vol. 2. *Analytic Basis for the Formulation of Sentencing Policy* (Washington, DC: U.S. Department of Justice, 1982).
7. For a description of radical nonintervention see Edwin M. Schur, *Radical Nonintervention: Rethinking the Delinquency Problem* (Englewood Cliffs, NJ: Prentice-Hall, 1973).

7 Toward Juvenile Justice

The strategic questions the society must face in deliberating on the future of the juvenile court and the juvenile justice system are the same as they have always been: first, whether the focus of these institutions should be on crimes committed by juveniles or on the conditions under which children are being raised; second, how public institutions, both service-oriented and legal, might be used in the context of other community institutions such as families, neighborhood associations, and business firms to establish a nexus of care, supervision, and opportunity around families and children that seem headed for trouble; and third, what these institutions must be able to show to legislatures, political executives, and higher courts to satisfy them that something of value has been created with the use of the public authority and money granted to the institutions. One thing that history has taught us is that these questions cannot and should not be answered in the abstract. Nor should one expect the answer given now to be the proper answer in the future. The only proper answer is one that is rooted in the current realities of the society, but that looks ahead into a dimly perceived future.

Juvenile Crime and Conditions of Child Rearing

As tempting as it is to limit our attention to the problem of juvenile crime, it would be unwise to consider the future of the juvenile court and the juvenile justice system solely in this light. Indeed, viewing the court and the justice system primarily in these terms produces an odd and powerful distorting effect on the entire public deliberation about juvenile crime and public policies toward children. After all, being victimized by children is only the most obvious way in which the society is hostage to its children.

It is also hostage to its children for the simple reason that the society's self-respect is rooted in its ability to care for its children. When a child is beaten or starved, when a child is on the street and vulnerable to adult exploitation, the society often feels diminished, as though it were a less decent and competent society than it should be. That is why the issues of child abuse and neglect are now politically salient. That is why laws are written mandating the reporting of such events. And that is why the public is increasingly interested in criminal prosecutions of such offenses.[1]

It is also true that juvenile crime is only one of the ways the society might pay for failures in the process of socialization. Sometimes juvenile crime becomes the path to persistent adult offending.[2] If no effective intervention occurs, the society will find itself locked in a frightening and frustrating 40-year relationship with a chronic adult offender who will not change and will spend a large fraction of adult life in expensive prisons and jails. At other times, the same conditions that produce juvenile crime will foster other forms of social dependence such as chronic unemployment, mental illness, alcoholism, or drug addiction.[3] Here, too, the society will pay not only financially, but in terms of morale and self-confidence. Indeed, unless the society can guarantee that its children can grow up in conditions that give them a chance to escape a life of crime and social dependence, it must consider the idea that inequalities and misconduct among adults are not the results of a just process in which individuals choose their social position, but instead the consequence of inequitably distributed opportunities.[4] Since, in the end, our self-respect as a democratic society depends on the promise of equal opportunity and the potential for upward mobility for all, and since the only people who will be around in the future are now children, it seems terribly important that the society perform its child-rearing functions well.

Of course, to observe that the society has much at stake in its child rearing is not the same as concluding that public institutions should be involved in this intimate process. It is certainly not obvious that such a specialized institution as the juvenile court should take the problem of socializing children as its dominant concern. Yet, there does seem to be some relationship between this observation and strategic judgments about how the institutions of the juvenile justice system might be deployed to help society with this work.

The argument is simply this: Since society will eventually respond to failures of socialization, the only interesting question is not whether it will respond, but when and how. Moreover, since the society intends to view any inequalities or differences in the status of adults as the fair result of individual choices and the development of individual talents, and since the society understands that children must be helped to develop their talents, there may be a strong social obligation for the society to do as much as it can to ensure that all children have a proper start.[5] Otherwise, some of the potential and promise of a free society will be lost. In this context the question becomes not whether to intervene, but rather which institutions should assume the responsibility.

The Crisis in Leadership

Our society is satiated with agencies and institutions that assume more or less responsibility for helping children, especially children who seem to be at risk or creating risks in publicly visible ways. Each of them might plausibly claim the mantle of overall leadership for the enterprise of moving children toward the status of resourceful and responsible citizenship.

The preeminent institution is the family. Philosophically, legally, and practically, the major responsibility for the supervision and development of children lies with natural families or their legally established substitutes. Indeed, our commitment to natural and adoptive parents as the primary caretakers of children is so strong that only the grossest and most visible signs of failure raise the question whether the legally established private caretakers should retain the rights and responsibilities of guardianship for their children.[6] Even if this question is answered negatively, the change in status is likely to be only temporary. In short, every effort will be made to keep the natural parents or legally established private substitutes in the dominant, responsible role.

In virtually all communities, caretakers and children are wrapped in a nexus of other institutions that also participate in the process of child rearing. Some of these institutions participate by sharing the day-to-day operational tasks of supervising, protecting, and guiding children. Thus, relatives, neighbors, and day-care centers might help a working mother care for preschool children. Public schools assume part of the burden of teaching children to read, write, and think. A local employer might be willing to provide on-the-job training to a teenager. And so on. Some of these are private, some community, and some explicitly public or governmental agencies.

Other agencies and institutions participate not so much by helping with the task of raising children but by commenting on how the task is being performed relative to their ideas about how it should be done. One might think of this as a kind of "oversight" activity that establishes and maintains community norms with respect to child rearing. This function can also be performed by both intimate and impersonal, private and public agencies. A grandmother might complain that a child is being spoiled. A neighbor will complain that a child is unsupervised, or warn that the child has stopped going to school. A teacher may observe that a child comes to school hungry and mention it to the mother. A welfare caseworker may urge a harassed mother to utilize day-care programs or counseling.

To a degree, these observations may have value to the parents. They may contain information about what to do, or how to get help. They may also suggest the standards that are guiding the conduct of other parents in the community, and thereby mobilize parents to meet those standards and to maintain their resolve when their children or other conditions threaten them.

But like all advice and criticism, these observations may have negative consequences. They might lead the parents to reject (explicitly or tacitly) the advice they are offered and to withdraw from the relationship. Or, if there is a larger audience and the complaint is loud enough, the parent may be either tempted or forced to give over some or all of the responsibility for the child to others. In this sense, the institutions that surround the family can sometimes buttress and sometimes undermine the capacity of primary caretakers to take care of their children.

In general, alarms are raised by other institutions when some sign appears that children are not being properly protected or supervised by their parents. The most visible such sign, and the one that most institutions feel most comfortable about reporting, is crimes committed by children. These are obviously matters of public concern. They are also tangible, concrete, and unambiguous. And there is a ubiquitous agency to which they can be easily reported. Only slightly less visible a sign (and almost as appropriate as crime to report to governmental agencies) is unsupervised children in times and places that seem dangerous. The most difficult kind of sign to observe publicly is one in which the child is at risk due to the malevolence or disinterest of the parents. Indeed, only the most extreme of these situations are likely to come to light.

However biased and incomplete these indicators, when a report is made about a crime committed by a child, or a child seems to be at risk because of lax supervision or the brutality of caretakers, a question is raised about the responsibility of the caretakers and the capacity of the arrangements surrounding the child to provide the child adequate care and guidance. If the incident is serious enough or is repetitive, or if the investigation triggered by the event reveals conditions that are obviously very threatening to the security of the society or the welfare of the child, then the society may consider making a deeper, more formal intervention into the life of the family.

In the easiest and most satisfactory case, this intervention will take the form of additional assistance and will be voluntarily accepted by the family. Indeed, many families now avail themselves of many public services such as schooling, day care, and recreational programs without them or the society imagining that the family's diligence or competence has been questioned or their responsibility for their children attenuated. A smaller but still quite large number of families have accepted welfare assistance as a public intervention that allows them to fulfill their responsibilities to their children more effectively than they otherwise could. And while this exposes them to a greater degree of public scrutiny than other families, they are not being directly coerced by the program to raise their children in a particular manner, nor is their responsibility to their children being weakened.

The hardest cases of social intervention involve situations in which the state's coercive powers are invoked and no services are supplied, or in which the parents' responsibilities for the child are (temporarily or permanently) dissolved in the interests of the security of the society or the best interests of the child. This happens when a child is treated as an adult criminal offender, is committed to an institution, or is placed in foster care. If things get to this stage, then the society is facing a disaster, for however good the public intervention is, it will at best only marginally improve an admittedly bad situation.

The task, then, is for the community as a whole to prevent children from reaching this point of no return. This means that each institution and agency—the parents, the relatives, the neighbors, the church, the school, the recreation department, the local businesses, the welfare department, the police, the probation department, the juvenile court, and the youth authority—must see itself as part of a system whose aim is to provide adequate care and supervision to children. Moreover, each must recognize that its job is most importantly to assist the primary caretakers in the enterprise of caring for the child—not to replace them, not to undermine them, but instead to help them do their job as effectively as they can. Finally, each institution also has some responsibility for stating when the effort is insufficient—when the child or the society is at grave risk despite the current arrangements, and when additional help is necessary. Of course, this responsibility conflicts to some degree with the responsibility to support the primary caretakers and the efforts of other institutions. The touchstone in deciding whether the current arrangements should be continued or adjusted must be an assessment of whether the current arrangements are better than any alternative arrangements that could be made to protect the child and the society.

Obviously, this is a large and complicated enterprise. As a result, we should not expect that it will be performed well. Indeed, the enterprise will be quite chaotic. No one will be in charge. No particular decision will ever be quite right. And there will be a great many failures. Given this probable state of affairs, the only interesting question is this: Is there an institution that can provide useful leadership in guiding this complicated mix of institutions in their work, and at the margin, enhance the society's capacities to rear its children to resourceful citizenship? If so, what kind of institution is it?

In principle, any agency could exercise leadership in socializing children. Indeed, in moments of professional hubris, each of the public institutions has claimed this mantle. The social workers have sometimes insisted that their casework holds the key to helping families in trouble. The schools have sometimes accepted broad responsibilities for training in citizenship and tried to substitute for parental negligence. At one stage of their history, the police assumed this role.[7] And we all know that juvenile court judges have sometimes assumed that they can play God and solve the problems of troubled children and disorganized families. But if one were to step back and think seriously about which of these institutions was well positioned to provide leadership to the society in establishing favorable conditions under which children would be raised, it seems that only two are plausible candidates.

The most obvious and appropriate candidate, of course, is the parents or caretakers of children. It is them to whom the society must look to do most of the work, to arrange for assistance when they need it, and to take advice from the rest of the society with relatively good grace when the society raises questions about their performance. For its part, the society owes the parents a rather wide tolerance for their methods, not only to protect the parents' rights and maintain their morale and sense of responsibility, but also to ensure that the society profits from the diversity of its citizens. This means that all community interventions—whether by private or public agencies—must be quite circumspect, that the interventions should be designed to support the parents in their efforts, and that efforts to substitute for or replace the functions of the family should occur only in situations in which the family's capacity to care for their children is virtually nonexistent or actually threatening to the child. Thus, in almost all circumstances, the society should rely on the leadership of parents and caretakers in socializing children.

The question of what other institution might lead the society's efforts to raise children becomes an issue only in particular cases in which the parents' leadership has clearly failed—when the child is at grave risk or is threatening grave risks to the rest of the society, due to the failures of the parents to provide the necessary care or to arrange to get it from the rest of the society. In short, the issue arises only when the parents are absent, terribly negligent and incompetent, or actively threatening. In this situation, it seems that the only institution that can reasonably exercise leadership on behalf of the society and the children is the juvenile court. The reason is simply that no other institution can claim to have an equally broad view of all the interests at stake, to have as wide a range of action, or to be able to make decisions that are designed to reflect the values of the society as expressed in its laws and constitution.

This is not to say that the court is an ideal social institution. Nor will it make perfect decisions. The only argument is that, compared with all the other institutions that might claim this role, the court seems the best bet. This is true primarily because the decisions the court must make about children are generally decisions about who will take what kinds of responsibilities for them and about the purposes the society is trying to achieve. They are decisions about establishing a just and useful structure of responsibilities as well as achieving social purposes such as reduced crime and social dependence.

Nor should one ignore the blemished record of the juvenile court in its efforts to control juvenile delinquency. That blemished record is deserved. But the blemish was created not because the juvenile court dared to define its responsibilities broadly to meet the social challenges of its time, but rather because it was arrogant enough to believe it could achieve its goals all by itself, without the engagement or scrutiny of the community. Indeed, what seems clear now is that if the court is to be successful even with respect to the narrow goals of controlling juvenile delinquency in a moderately inexpensive and humane way, it must find ways of strengthening families and engaging the other institutions in the community in its efforts. Once it has learned how to do this, it might be able to use the same kind of leadership to improve the conditions under which children are being raised more generally.

Finally, in imagining the mechanisms through which the court might provide leadership, the court is not seen as being directly involved in every case. That would clearly defeat many of the purposes for which the court was established. Instead, the court might operate through the kind of remote control that is characteristic of all leadership. The court might have power over child rearing throughout the society simply because it stands as a symbol of the importance of this function. At a slightly more concrete level, the court might exercise influence over the institutions that share responsibilities for caring for children by establishing the rules that define their functions and setting out minimum standards of care. At an even more concrete and particular level, the court might influence the handling of cases that are publicly recognized but handled informally by casting its shadow across the deliberations. This would be true for cases handled in youth authorities following disposition, as well as for cases handled informally in probation departments, police departments, welfare agencies, and schools prior to disposition. Only a tiny fraction of cases in which the influence of the court had been felt would actually be heard by the court. And if juveniles came before the court, they would be held for only a brief time before being turned over to someone else for the care, supervision, and services that had been mandated by the court.

This idea about how the court might operate might seem farfetched. An analogy might make it seem more plausible. Consider how the Internal Revenue Service manages to collect taxes from an independent, freedom-loving citizenry.[8] The IRS is a relatively small, concrete institution. Yet it manages to collect taxes because it stands for a much broader idea—namely, that as citizens of the society we must all do our share to support the larger enterprise. It is the widespread acceptance of the notion that we should all pay taxes that produces most of the revenues that the IRS collects. In addition, the IRS sets out the forms and rules that tell us how to report what we earn and calculate what we owe. Without this kind of guidance, our broad desire to make a contribution would remain unfocused. Finally, the IRS catches some citizens in more or less grave errors and then negotiates an informal settlement. And in an incredibly small number of instances, the IRS prosecutes and convicts people of income tax evasion. The IRS as an organization tends to think of its work primarily in terms of audits and prosecutions, since that is what its members principally do, and this work produces the most dramatic moments in the organization's experience. But an outsider would observe that most of the work of collecting revenues is not done by the IRS directly but by citizens following the general exhortations and specific advice of the agency.

No doubt, this analogy is quite imperfect. It is hard to imagine a body of law that could capture the responsibilities of varied agencies to children and of children to varied caretaking agencies in as simple and concrete a form as the tax code. Even if one could, the text would run to many volumes and become virtually useless as a guide to proper conduct. Similarly, it is possible that the public responsibilities of those who care for children are less salient than the public responsibilities to contribute taxes for public purposes. But the analogy does serve to remind us that visible public institutions, particularly those that have legal powers over others, have effects far broader than decisions on individual cases. This observation may be enough to establish the general idea that a juvenile or family court could exercise this kind of influence.

Establishing the Accountability of Children and Their Caretakers

My principal idea, then, is to establish a court that can hold children, and those who care for children, accountable for their actions in their joint efforts to move children from the status of defenseless barbarians to resourceful citizens. The move from defenseless to resourceful requires investments in skills and capacities. The move from barbarian to citizen involves the internalization of a sense of responsibility to others and to the norms of the large society. Such a court would differ from our current conception of the court in several important ways. Some of the differences would show in the way the court thought about and handled the cases that came before it for formal adjudication. Other differences would appear in how the court managed its relationship to the community.

Perhaps the most important difference in this conception of the court is that the court would not confront only the individual offenders, as the adult court does, but instead would widen the liability to include those responsible for the care, supervision, and guidance of the children as well. These caretakers would be considered parties at interest because they have both interests that might be affected by the court's decisions and responsibilities that might be reinforced or established. The person on trial would not be the child alone, but the child in the context of the private and public agencies that are more or less responsible for the child's current conduct and safety and his or her future development. In this sense, the court would be more like a family court that assumed responsibilities for recognizing and maintaining the institutions and arrangements that could guarantee minimally satisfactory conditions under which children were being raised.

A second important difference between this conception of the court and current images is that it would impose duties on parents, caretakers, and children on behalf of the society as well as vindicate rights and claims to special services. It would begin with the notion that parents, public agencies, and children all had obligations to the society as well as claims on the society. The obligations of parents and other caretakers are to provide minimally satisfactory levels of care for their children so that the children might become resourceful citizens. The obligations of children are to accept this level of supervision and instruction and to commit themselves to preparing for adult citizenship by not committing criminal offenses and by avoiding social dependence. In this context, when children commit crimes or fail to go to school, the parents and caretakers might easily be seen as "codefendants" as well as "partners" with the court in working out an appropriate disposition of the case.

Establishing the liability of caretakers should not diminish the liability of the offending child. Indeed, our image of the court includes the idea that children, as well as their caretakers, should be held accountable for their actions. This means that the court should use punishment as part of the effort to kindle feelings of personal responsibility among juveniles.[9] To be effective in fostering a sense of responsibility, the punishment must come from a source and a process that has a reasonable claim to legitimacy and predictability in the mind of the juvenile offender, be reasonably related to the offense, and be small enough to cause the offender to accept personal guilt and learn rather than to reject the institution that administers the punishment. But punishment must be part of the juvenile court's domain not only to assure the rest of the society that norms against offending are being maintained and that the society's interests in using deterrence and incapacitation to protect itself from crime are respected, but also as part of the process of establishing a proper relationship between the juvenile offender and the rest of the society.

It is also worth noting that the nature of juvenile offenses in this conception differs from the nature of such offenses in either the adult court or the current juvenile court. When a child commits an offense that would be a crime if the child were an adult, but there is some doubt about the maturity and independence of the child, the society's response is different, because the act is not seen as the child's in quite the same way it would be seen if it were committed by an adult. While the child's responsibility is not wholly eliminated (lest the child learn that actions do not have consequences), it is shared with others who have responsibility for him or her. Moreover, the punishment is adjusted to make sure that it produces learning for the child and maintains the relationship with the society rather than severs it. In short, the crime is viewed as a failure of the child (and the parents) to fulfill their obligations to learn (and to teach) social responsibilities. The occasion is regarded as an opportunity to instruct rather than as a criminal act against the society.

A corollary is that the child can be liable for acts that violate special responsibilities of childhood as well as for acts that would be crimes if committed by an adult. Being a child in the society comes with some special privileges, including the right to be treated differently from adults when a criminal offense is committed. But it also comes with special duties, and these include being willing to accept supervision and instruction and making investments in skills that will allow avoidance of social and economic dependence as an adult.

A third important difference in the general orientation of the court is that it should think of itself as operating at some distance from the other institutions that retain day-to-day responsibilities for children. The principal work of raising children lies well outside the jurisdiction of the court. Because that work is important to the society, it is organized by widely accepted norms and specifically established laws. These norms and laws define institutions and set out both general purposes and specific responsibilities. They create particular "offices" with special duties and responsibilities.[10] The office of parent has some social recognition. So does the office of child. And public agencies all have special offices that are created and overseen by both legislatures and the courts. The task of the court as envisioned here is not to assume the public responsibility for raising children. That would never be a proper role for a court. Instead, the task of the court is to oversee the actions of these other public officeholders to make sure that they discharge their duties to one another and to the society. The court becomes involved when the interests of one of the parties (including society as a whole) are being neglected and when these interests will be recognized by the court. When the court becomes involved, its task is to hear the case and decide who must do what for whom on behalf of the involved parties' or the society's interests. It does this in accord with specific statutes, the common law, or the constitution.

Again, an analogy may be helpful. Consider the relationship between a corporation that is going bankrupt and a civil court that is responsible for enforcing contracts. Once a legal structure defines corporations and contracts, private individuals are left free to establish corporations and to enter into contracts. As a result, economic enterprises are established. These enterprises make promises to shareholders, to banks, to employees, and increasingly to the government, to advance public purposes.

Sometimes the company begins to fail with respect to one or more of these responsibilities and is hauled into court by the aggrieved party. In some cases the corporation itself will announce that it can no longer meet its financial and other obligations and is therefore bankrupt. The court is then called upon to sort out the priority of the various claims against the company.

Sometimes the court will simply liquidate the company's assets and distribute them among the claimants. More often, however, the court will try to arrange for a "work-out." Parties with recognized claims are told to wait to make their claims. The hope is that the company will begin performing better, which will increase the value of the company's assets. This would be better than selling the assets in the equivalent of a fire sale. In exchange for this relief, the company is exposed to much more intensive scrutiny from the court. In effect, the company is placed on probation. It is vulnerable to court-ordered liquidation if it fails to perform, and is asked to give frequent, detailed evidence of performance.

The court's role, then, is to hold off claims that would sink the institution and to monitor performance. As a result, the court inevitably finds itself intimately involved in the affairs of the company. Despite this close involvement, no one would ever think that the court now owned or operated the company. It is merely establishing particular relationships between the company and those who have claims against it in a situation in which the broad terms setting out the rights and privileges of a company have not been discharged, but in which there may still be a social interest in keeping the company going. To keep the company going rather than order liquidation, the court must determine that the company has motivated management and some reasonable prospects for economic success.

The analogy to the juvenile court is to think of it as a court for families (or their functional equivalent) that are going bankrupt. The society depends on families to equip children for resourceful citizenship in the same way that it depends on corporations to provide attractive products for consumers, safe jobs for employees, financial returns to equity holders, and payments to those who hold the corporation's notes. The family is beginning to go bankrupt when it can no longer provide the care, supervision, and guidance that keep the children safe, prevent them from committing crimes, and help them toward resourceful citizenship. The court intervenes to make sure that the family can meet its responsibilities to the individuals who have a stake in the family's performance and to the society at large. It decides whether the family is strong enough to go on with a little relief from its creditors and some additional aid, or whether the best thing to do is to liquidate it. Liquidation generally seems the worst option, since everyone knows that when the state assumes the responsibility for child rearing, it will at best be a very poor substitute.

These ideas about the juvenile court have concrete implications for the way the court should handle the cases that come before it. They mean, for example, that parents and other caretakers should be in the courtroom and a party to the deliberations and judgment. They also mean that there might be an important role for victims in the courtroom, not only as witnesses but also as parties to the decision. They also mean that probation officers and caseworkers in youth authorities might be seen as "special masters" for the court in helping to organize and oversee the response of the private and public agencies to the court's decision about who must accept new responsibilities for children.

Casting a Shadow

In this conception of the juvenile court, the court should think of its work not only in terms of what it does in the courtroom, but also in terms of how it affects the orientations and activities of parents, neighbors, schools, welfare agencies, and police departments in dealing with children and caretakers who never appear in the court.

Of course, there is an important relationship between what the court does with individual cases in the courtroom and the shadow it casts over the actions of others. When the court draws caretakers and victims into the court as well as the juvenile offenders, the word spreads about what values the court stands for and what kinds of obligations it is imposing. The court could go further by reporting to the public about the cases it has handled, the decisions it has made, and the reasons. And it could do this in a form that differs from the publications that are now prepared for the legal profession. Just as the IRS must communicate to both the general public and the professional bar about tax matters, the juvenile court may have an obligation to communicate about its cases, decisions, and rulings to the general public as well as to the bar. The court might even urge legislators to open court deliberations to the general public so that those who are interested can see how the court operates and what values it is expressing in its decisions.

Indeed, one might reasonably argue that one of the reasons the basic foundations of the juvenile court are now being questioned is that the court tried to operate too autonomously and too privately. To the extent that it stood for anything, it seemed to stand for a sentimental view that children should be excused from the consequences of their criminal deeds. The fact that it did not reflect this value in its operations, and that it dealt with a much more complicated situation than is captured by this simple stereotype, was not revealed because the court could not give an accurate, aggregate account of its operations. Thus the public was free to hold any view of the court it wanted, because there was no information available to dispute its views. The only way to change these views is to let the public see more clearly what is going on in juvenile courtrooms. Making the court accountable and explaining its actions to the community will have the effect of magnifying its impact, for it will both increase the court's overall stature and allow it to communicate to the community what the community's own laws require of its members.

One common objection to this idea is that it will "politicize" the court. One might argue that in a democracy, politicization is a virtue rather than a vice, since it suggests that the court might become more responsive to and more reflective of community values. One would also add that politicization only seems a vice to those in professions who want to maintain their control over the institutions and impose their own values rather than those of the community.

But this would go too far, for there are real dangers in politicization. It is possible, for example, that the community values are ill-considered or are unfair to minority interests in the community. In this case it would be important that the courts resist adopting an exact expression of the community's interests, lest the society's long-run interests be harmed. But in this situation it is not enough that the court simply makes the decisions it thinks appropriate and tells the rest of the society to "lump" it. That invites the society to overturn the institution. Instead, the court must take the responsibility of reminding the society of its own long-term interests and its previous understandings about what constitutes just relationships in the society.

In the case of juvenile justice, for example, the court may have to remind people about the special status of children, reassure them that their interests in punishment and effective supervision are being discharged, and emphasize the society's interests in ensuring that child rearing is done by parents and the community rather than by public agencies, and that the job is done well lest the society pay for the failure in the form of crime and social dependence for the natural life of the child. The court cannot escape this conversation. Or rather, it cannot escape this responsibility and be free of the consequences of accumulating public suspicions of its actions. To protect the institution, to maintain a proper accountability relationship to the community and to the law, and to strengthen the overall capacity of the community to rear children, the judges of the juvenile court must be prepared to exercise leadership by explaining what the court stands for, why it is making the decisions it is making, and what these decisions imply for the conduct of others. This is how legal values acquire social force and standing.

There is a third way that judges representing the juvenile court might cast a shadow that is wider than their influence on the cases they hear in their courtrooms, and more durable than the brief moments during which they decide individual cases. This way is to make sure that they generally support the private and public community institutions that will exercise the day-to-day responsibilities for supervising children, and that they use these institutions and rely on them in making dispositions. If there is a community group that seems capable of providing valuable services to children who appear before the court, the judge should find it and use it in the disposition. If the welfare department is involved, the judge should ask to see the caseworker whose job it is to provide assistance to the child and the family. This is what it means to draw in the private and public agencies that share responsibility for individual children. But it goes several steps further in that it encourages the court to go beyond public agencies, and even beyond traditional private agencies, to find resources in the community that have not yet been formally acknowledged, and to use them. In addition, judges can help build and maintain these institutions in the aggregate as well as to use them in individual cases.

What all this amounts to is a much broader engagement of the community by the juvenile court. This has been formalized in some states by the creation of community boards, which work in the shadow of the court's authority to make dispositions in minor offense cases.[11] In other jurisdictions, it has arisen informally as some voluntary agency has acquired the capabilities and standing with the court to do much of its work. And in still other jurisdictions, probation offices and youth authorities have acted as intermediaries between the court and the communities in mobilizing both private and public agencies. Clearly, many different institutional structures can create a broader and more intensive engagement of the juvenile court with the community.[12] Consequently, the particular form chosen may not matter very much. What is important is that the court cease thinking of itself and operating as though it were an autonomous organization devoted to nothing more than applying specialized legal knowledge and skills to the cases that come before it, and doing so in private. That makes a mockery of the important function the juvenile courts might perform, and wastes the assets of the institution.

Managing Risks in Juvenile Dispositions

While much attention must be focused on the role of the juvenile court, one must also consider the role of probation departments and youth authorities—the institutions that manage children after they have been (briefly) exposed to the judgment of the courts. Even though these institutions are separate, they cannot really be thought of separately for they are tightly linked in functional terms. Indeed, one of the principal reasons for opposing a broad jurisdiction for the juvenile courts is that there is no disposition the court could make that would make any essential difference in the social development of the child. If this were true, the establishment of any broader right to intervene in the lives of children than that afforded by the society's legitimate interests in controlling crime would be hypocritical. This has been the most powerful criticism leveled at the juvenile court.

Obviously, this is not the fault of the court, but the failure of social service agencies, probation departments, and youth authorities to establish and operate a set of dispositions that could satisfy the society that its interests in both security and the socialization of the child could be reliably advanced. So the key to a just and useful juvenile justice system in the future may not lie with a change in the role and orientation of the court, but with an improvement in the society's abilities to provide appropriate dispositions for children who are at risk or posing risks for others. If these capacities can be created and managed successfully, there will be little objection to the court assuming a larger role. If not, then there is little good and potentially much harm in authorizing a broader role.

In thinking about how to increase the capacities of those who have the day-to-day responsibility for children once the court has declared the parents and whatever help they can muster to be inadequate to the task, all of the themes developed here in the discussion of the juvenile court carry over.

Just as the aim of the court must be broader than the control of crime in the short run, so must the aim of dispositions be broader. Short-run crime control cannot be ignored, of course. But it cannot be the exclusive or even the dominant consideration of dispositions. In addition, one must keep in mind the necessity to prevent crimes and dependence in the future, to provide adequate care and guidance for the child under state supervision, and to economize on the use of the state's limited moral and financial resources as well.

Just as the court must draw the community into a much closer relationship to enhance its legitimacy and operational capabilities, so must probation departments and youth authorities make the same effort. They must be able to report on their operations in terms that have meaning to the broader community.[13] They must explain what values and principles guide their choices. And they must try to use community institutions as part of their efforts to advance the society's interests in security and the socialization of children.

A major difference in the discussion of the juvenile court on the one hand and the probation departments and youth authorities on the other is the issue of risk. To a degree, the issue of risk was absent from the discussion of the juvenile court because the court takes little direct responsibility and therefore faces few risks other than community indignation about the justice or appropriateness of a decision. The court is principally responsible for structuring the tasks of others. In the case of agencies that have day-to-day responsibility for children, however, the risks are those incurred as a result of assigning specific children to programs that differ in terms of closeness of supervision, level and kinds of services provided, and connection to the child's natural community. The youth authorities are responsible in the same way that the parents were before the court intervened and distributed the responsibilities in a different way. Consequently, anything that happens to the child, or anything that the child does, becomes the responsibility of the caretaking agency.

The risks that are most noticeable in youth institutions are the same kinds of risks that brought the child to public attention in the first place—the risks that they will commit crimes or will be harmed by the abuse or neglect of their caretakers. These risks are the most visible because they arise soonest. But there is also the risk that the children will fail to receive the care, guidance, and investment they need to become resourceful citizens. To a degree, there is an overlap in these objectives: If we can keep the children safe, and if their internal drives toward responsibility and resourcefulness are strong enough, then reasonably comfortable custodial care is all that the society needs. Where the problem arises is in the necessity of recognizing and encouraging the independence of children in the context of the community. If an important part of becoming a resourceful citizen is gaining a sense of one's own autonomy, and if part of achieving that goal is learning from mistakes, then the community cannot solve the question of what to do with adolescents who are creating risks by putting them in custodial care. It must give them sufficient freedom so they can reasonably identify the actions they take as their own, a sufficiently alert structure of supervision to provide quick feedback on the consequences of the actions they take, and a sufficiently strong connection with ordinary community life that the lessons they learn are immediately transferable and useful as they make their way in the society. Such actions will reduce the likelihood of long-run failure but increase the likelihood of short-run failure. Children given large degrees of autonomy in the context of the community may well injure themselves and others.

Those who manage dispositions must balance these risks for individual children. Undoubtedly the youth authorities will make mistakes. It is important for them and the rest of the society, however, to remember that there are two kinds of mistakes: One can err by allowing a child sufficient freedom and engagement with the community to put himself or herself and others at risk for exploitation or criminal victimization, or one can err by keeping the child under such tight control and so far removed from the community that he or she never has the opportunity to learn how to become integrated into the community. Our institutions as now set up penalize those who manage youth dispositions for the first kind of error and tolerate the second kind of error. Yet it is the second kind of error that is arguably the most expensive. It is in this sense that the professionals who manage the dispositions of children are asked to manage the risks to the society.

There is a second kind of risk run by those who manage probation departments and youth authorities. That is the risk associated with creating new kinds of dispositions and including them in the portfolio of possible dispositions.[14] One can think of this as the equivalent of technological innovation. There is a great need for such efforts in the field of juvenile dispositions, for our knowledge of what sorts of interventions can be successful in controlling crime and reducing the vulnerability of children in both the short and long run is remarkably limited. Moreover, the range of experimentation with new concepts is quite narrow. From the point of view of those who manage dispositions, however, innovation is a risky business. It is never clear whether a new approach will work. Even if it works, it might be particularly vulnerable to some disastrous mistake. And if the new program does not work, the manager cannot fall back on the time-honored excuse that he or she was following conventional practice. Thus there are lots of reasons to avoid these kinds of risks as well. But unless we try things and examine the results, we are unlikely to know what could work. And since the existing capabilities seem quite weak, it is hard to know how to make progress without running these risks.

In sum, the principal job of those who manage juvenile probation departments and youth authorities must be to manage the level and nature of the risks the society takes in assuming responsibility for the care and guidance of children. It is important to understand that the society as a whole is at risk whatever the managers decide to do. If the society through its juvenile justice system places all children in secure care, it may minimize the short-run risk that the children will commit crimes as juveniles but increase the risk that the children will end up as chronic adult offenders. If it stays with tried and true programs, it may escape blame for operating outside conventional practices but guarantees that its ability to contribute to the socialization of children will be the same a decade from now as it is today. Since the society is already at risk, the real questions are what kinds and degree of risk it prefers to run.

Just as there is an increased and challenging role for juvenile court judges to play, there may be an important leadership role for managers of youth agencies as well. Their challenge is to engage the society in a conversation about their current capabilities and performance, and to propose some alternative approaches.[15] If they worry that the society expects things from their agencies different from what they are supplying, they have to explain why the values the community espouses are wrong or inappropriate. They cannot afford to hide their operations from public view, only to be discussed when a scandal occurs. They, too, must become leaders and innovators who accept their accountability to the communities that give them the money and authority to operate in exchange for the successful performance of their duties.[16] A principal part of this effort must be to explain what success means, and why failures will sometimes occur in a program that is very successful.

Conclusion

The juvenile justice system has before it a unique opportunity—an opportunity to shape and guide the development of the society's most valuable asset, its children. Seizing this opportunity is in its own best interests. It is also in the society's interests to prevent the development of future criminals and social dependents and to define and distribute responsibility among its members for helping children to grow.

Whether the juvenile court will take advantage of this opportunity depends on how urgent the society perceives the need to be for a solution to the current impasse of the juvenile justice system, and how willing critics are, both on the left and the right, to give up comfortable and long-standing notions about juvenile justice to acknowledge the potential of the role laid out for it here, and to make a commitment to experiment.

So far, no other camp has come forward with an overall strategy for juvenile justice that accommodates its diverse aspects. Therefore, the proposal here is unique by virtue not only of being the only one but in the vantage point from which it attempts to position the juvenile justice system for the future. In assuming a leadership role, the juvenile court can act not as society's muscle, but its heart, providing a structure of obligations and management to buttress the collaboration of family, private, and public institutions in raising children to responsible citizenship. Such an opportunity to move toward justice for juveniles should not be dismissed out of hand for ideological motives, but given serious and thoughtful consideration.

Notes

1. Attorney General's Task Force on Family Violence, *Final Report* (Washington, DC: U.S. Department of Justice, 1984).
2. David P. Farrington, "Early precursors of adult offending," in volume 3 of this series.
3. Lee N. Robins, "Sturdy childhood predictors of adult outcomes: Replication from longitudinal studies," in James E. Barrett et al., Eds., *Stress and Mental Disorder* (New York: Raven Press, 1979).
4. James S. Fishkin, *Justice, Equal Opportunity and the Family* (New Haven, CT: Yale University Press, 1983).
5. Ibid.
6. Institute of Judicial Administration–American Bar Association, *Standards Relating to Abuse and Neglect* (Cambridge, MA: Ballinger, 1981).
7. George L. Kelling, "Police and juveniles: The end of the nightstick," in volume 2 of this series.
8. Mark H. Moore, "On the office of taxpayer and the social process of taxpaying," paper prepared for the Invitational Conference on Tax Compliance, Reston, VA, March 16–19, 1983.
9. Richard W. Barnum, "The development of responsibility: Implications for juvenile justice," in volume 2 of this series.
10. Martha Minow, "The public duties of families and children" and Michael Oshima, "Toward a jurisprudence of children and families," both in volume 2 of this series.
11. Mark L. Sidran, "Back to the source: Diversion of juvenile offenders to the community in the State of Washington," in volume 2 of this series.
12. Lloyd Ohlin, "Alternatives to the juvenile court process," in volume 2 of this series.

13. Philip J. Cook, "Notes on an accounting scheme from a juvenile correctional system," and Saul Weingart, "Inventory accounting and production: Problems in juvenile dispositions," both in volume 2 of this series.
14. Edward M. Murphy, "An alternative approach to managing juvenile corrections," in volume 2 of this series.
15. Ellen Schall, "Principles for juvenile detention," in volume 2 of this series.
16. It is significant, we believe, that Ellen Schall gained national recognition for an innovative "case-work" approach to detained juveniles in a program sponsored by the Ford Foundation to recognize important innovations in state and local government.

Index

MIX
Papier aus verantwortungsvollen Quellen
Paper from responsible sources
FSC® C105338

If you have any concerns about our products,
you can contact us on
ProductSafety@springernature.com

In case Publisher is established outside the EU,
the EU authorized representative is:
Springer Nature Customer Service Center GmbH
Europaplatz 3, 69115 Heidelberg, Germany

Printed by Libri Plureos GmbH
in Hamburg, Germany